ROUTLEDGE LIBRARY EDITIONS: ACCOUNTING HISTORY

Volume 32

LEONARD M. SAVOIE

LEONARD M. SAVOIE

Words from the Past, Thoughts for Today

Edited by
DONALD E. TIDRICK

Routledge
Taylor & Francis Group
LONDON AND NEW YORK

First published in 1995 by Garland Publishing, Inc.

This edition first published in 2021
by Routledge
2 Park Square, Milton Park, Abingdon, Oxon OX14 4RN

and by Routledge
52 Vanderbilt Avenue, New York, NY 10017

Routledge is an imprint of the Taylor & Francis Group, an informa business

British Library Cataloguing in Publication Data
A catalogue record for this book is available from the British Library

ISBN: 978-0-367-33564-9 (Set)
ISBN: 978-1-00-304636-3 (Set) (ebk)
ISBN: 978-0-367-50071-9 (Volume 32) (hbk)
ISBN: 978-0-367-50073-3 (Volume 32) (pbk)
ISBN: 978-1-00-304866-4 (Volume 32) (ebk)

Publisher's Note
The publisher has gone to great lengths to ensure the quality of this reprint but
points out that some imperfections in the original copies may be apparent.

Disclaimer
The publisher has made every effort to trace copyright holders and would welcome
correspondence from those they have been unable to trace.

LEONARD M. SAVOIE

Words from the Past, Thoughts for Today

Edited by
Donald E. Tidrick

Garland Publishing, Inc.
New York and London 1995

Introduction copyright © 1995 by Donald E. Tidrick

Library of Congress Cataloging-in-Publication Data

Savoie, Leonard M., 1923–1991.
   Leonard M. Savoie : words from the past, thoughts for today / edited
by Donald E. Tidrick.
   p. cm.— (New works in accounting history)
   Includes bibliographical references.
   ISBN-0-8153-2242-9 (acid-free paper)
   1. Accounting—United States—History. 2. Savoie, Leonard M.,
1923–1991. I. Tidrick, Donald E. II. Title. III. Series.
HF5616.U5S28   1995   95–32849
                                                                 CIP

All volumes printed on acid-free, 250-year-life paper.
Manufactured in the United States of America.

Design by Marisel Tavarez

DEDICATION

In remembrance of Leonard M. Savoie (1923–1991) and Barbara H. Savoie (1923–1994) for their sustained commitment to excellence; for their unswerving loyalty to organizational affiliations, colleagues, friends, and family; and for their integrity and dignity, complemented by a keen sense of humor and genuine enjoyment of life.

And to my father, Ray C. Tidrick, and the memory of my mother, Hazel G. Tidrick (1917–1986), for the same qualities.

TABLE OF CONTENTS

SECTION I: REPORTS TO COUNCIL OF THE AICPA

SECTION II: GENERAL PROFESSIONAL ISSUES

SECTION III: ACCOUNTING STANDARD-SETTING ISSUES

APPENDICES

Leonard M. Savoie
(1923–1991)

REMEMBERING LEONARD M. SAVOIE (1923 - 1991)

Leonard M. Savoie, executive vice-president of the American
Institute of CPAs from 1967 to 1972, died in January of 1991. He was
a man who carved a unique niche in accounting -- as a practitioner, a
professional, and a professor.

Savoie was the first CPA to serve full-time as the chief staff officer
of the AICPA. (In 1974, the office was retitled AICPA president.)
During his term, Savoie was the primary spokesman for the AICPA and
was responsible for coordinating all Institute technical activities. In *The
Rise of the Accounting Profession*, John L. Carey said Savoie's
background resulted in improved relationships between the AICPA and
the financial press: "The press learned to have confidence in his
objectivity and turned to him for explanations of accounting questions
involved in news items or articles."

Before joining the AICPA staff, Savoie was partner in charge of
accounting research and education at Price Waterhouse & Co. He
joined the Chicago office in 1946 after receiving his bachelor's of
science from the University of Illinois. He was admitted to partnership
in the firm in 1960.

Following his service with the AICPA, Savoie served from 1972 to
1979 as controller and vice-president of Clark Equipment Company, a
multinational company with annual sales at that time exceeding $1.5
billion.

In 1980, Savoie joined the accounting faculty at the University of
Notre Dame as a professor. He served as chairman of the Notre Dame
Department of Accountancy from 1983 to 1990. Savoie's time at Notre
Dame blended his administrative, technical, and human resource skills.
He taught graduate courses, counseled undergraduate and graduate
students, worked with accounting practitioners and professors through-
out the United States, and was involved in a variety of academic and
professional activities at the local, regional, and national levels.

Commenting on a common thread in all phases of his career,
Savoie once said, "Throughout my career I have had a strong and

enduring interest in accounting education." For example, at Price Waterhouse, his responsibilities included serving as the partner in charge of the firm's continuing education activities. He received a leave of absence from the firm during the 1962-63 academic year to serve as a Dickenson Fellow on the faculty of Harvard University, where he taught financial accounting. Savoie served on the advisory councils or boards for the accounting departments of Northwestern University, the University of Michigan, the University of Illinois, and the University of Lancaster (England).

Savoie delivered more than 160 speeches, published more than four dozen articles (many of which were reprinted in other publications), and contributed chapters to several books. In a 1974 speech to the California CPAs Accounting Education Conference, Savoie expressed enthusiasm for the variety of career paths available to an accountant. He quipped, "My only regret is that I cannot at the same time be a practicing professional accountant, an industrial professional accountant, and an educator of professional accountants."

Savoie's marriage to Barbara H. Savoie spanned nearly 40 years. Barbara passed away in February of 1994. They are survived by ten children: Mary, Joan, Carol, Leonard, Bob, Paul, Don, James, John, and William.

Editor's Note: This career summary is based upon the January 1992 Journal of Accountancy tribute to Len Savoie written by Donald Tidrick and Ken Milani. Tidrick and Milani were colleagues and friends of Len and Barbara Savoie at the University of Notre Dame, where Tidrick was an assistant professor and Milani was (and continues to be) a full professor in the Department of Accountancy.

EDITOR'S FOREWORD

I was privileged to be on faculty in the Department of Accountancy at the University of Notre Dame during Leonard M. Savoie's chairmanship. I was impressed early on by Len's constant professionalism, his sincere commitment to the development of his junior faculty, and by the warm collegiality Len projected.

After he was diagnosed as having terminal cancer, Len bequeathed the materials in his Notre Dame office to three of the assistant professors with whom he was close (Larry Davis, Greg Trompeter, and myself). Along with a few books, I received Len's extensive collection of speeches that he had given -- all neatly organized chronologically in several large binders. I believed that this impressive body of work had historical significance, and that "something" should be done to recognize Len's extraordinary career and life.

This book is an attempt to honor Len's memory, while contributing to the accounting literature a sampling of his wisdom and personal convictions for strengthening the accounting profession to which he was dedicated. I selected these 26 speeches (which have not been published elsewhere) based on their apparent historical importance and their contemporary relevance to the accounting profession. Section I consists of reports to council of the AICPA; Section II deals with general professional and educational issues; and Section III focuses on more specific accounting and auditing standard-setting issues.

The reader should remember that most of these speeches were given in the 1960s and 1970s to predominantly male audiences. In the interest of historical accuracy, I have tried to remain true to the original speeches, even where some references might appear somewhat dated. For example, the male gender pronoun attributed to the accountant or auditor is conspicuous by today's standards. I hope that readers will view such characteristics within the historical context.

I am grateful to Father "Monk" Malloy, Mr. Ralph Kent, Mr. Tom Buck, and Professor Charles Horngren for writing letters to be included in this book. I hope this volume will be pleasing to Len and Barbara's family and to their many friends across the country, while offering useful insights about the profession to students of accounting.

Donald E. Tidrick   Austin, Texas

PHONE 219/631-6755
FAX 219 631-7428

UNIVERSITY OF NOTRE DAME
NOTRE DAME, INDIANA 46556

February 16, 1995

Professor Donald Tidrick
College of Business Administration
University of Texas
Austin, Texas   78712-1172

Dear Don,

I relish this opportunity to say a few words regarding Leonard Savoie. At Notre Dame, Len was able to bring his life experience as a partner in a major accounting firm, as a leader in the principal association of CPAs and as controller of a major corporation to bear in the classroom. His teaching enriched the lives of many of our students. His leadership helped shape our Department of Accountancy, and his friendship touched many members of our faculty. Finally, Len was an inspiration to all of us in the way he dealt with his illness.

Len Savoie's contributions to the field of accounting and to the University of Notre Dame are worthy of our collective recognition and praise. This volume is a fitting tribute to the man and his words.

Cordially,

(Rev.) Edward A. Malloy, C.S.C.
President

xiv

February 8, 1995

Mr. Donald E. Tidrick
Department of Accounting
University of Texas
Austin, Texas 78712

Dear Don:

Leonard Savoie brought a high level of accounting and auditing professionalism to the top staff officer position at the AICPA, when he succeeded the legendary Jack Carey in 1969. While no one could match Jack's public relations skills, Len brought his own impressive areas of expertise to the Institute.

Len was greatly interested in the technical work of the Accounting Principles Board and the auditing standards groups within the Institute. His interest and knowledge had been honed by the years he spent in research and quality control responsibilities in a major accounting firm. Understandably, these were his major areas of attention while at the Institute.

In the many speeches and articles Len addressed to accounting and business audiences across the country, he emphasized the need for concentrated attention to quality performance by accounting and auditing practitioners. With hindsight, his message was particularly germane. It came at a time when litigation directed at independent auditors was changing from a rare occurrence to one of the most difficult and seemingly endless problems facing the profession.

All students of accounting are fortunate to have this insider's perspective on a period of dramatic change in a rapidly growing profession.

Cordially,

Ralph E. Kent

Editor's note: Mr. Kent was the Senior Partner of Arthur Young from 1965 to 1977, and served as AICPA president in 1968-69. He received the AICPA's "Gold Medal Award for Distinguished Service to the Profession" in 1973.

202 South Michigan Street, South Bend, Indiana 46601

February 3, 1995

Professor Don Tidrick
Department of Accounting
University of Texas
Austin, Texas 78712

Dear Don:

This is in response to your request for a letter concerning Len Savoie.

Len and I first became acquainted in late 1951 or early 1952. Len was a senior accountant on the Chicago Price Waterhouse staff when I joined that staff. I was assigned to many of his jobs, and he was a tough guy to work for. He was extremely aggressive, intolerant of incompetence, a perfectionist, and expected others to work as hard as he did.

In 1957, Price Waterhouse sent me to Denver, and, at about the same time, transferred Len to New York where he headed up the staff training program and the research department. When I came back to Chicago in 1960, I was assigned to the staff training function, and once again worked with Len.

I was sent to South Bend, Indiana, in 1963. Several years later, Len left Price Waterhouse to head up the AICPA. For several years, I had little contact with him.

In 1972, Clark Equipment Company was looking for a new Vice President and Controller, and at about the same time Len decided to leave the AICPA. John Darling, a PW partner in Chicago, and I discussed the possibility of Len filling that position. John arranged for me to meet Len for dinner the following week, and I then arranged for him to meet with the Clark people. They hired him, and he moved from New York to Buchanan, Michigan.

As the engagement partner for Clark Equipment, I worked closely with Len again. He had changed very little. I think he found the transition to industry a

xvi

bit difficult, but he soon realized that practical application of accounting was more important than abstract concepts. Under Len's guidance, Clark adopted LIFO, and saved a lot of money in taxes. Len's career at Clark was enhanced by the high integrity that he brought to the job, and he insisted that things be done right.

When he departed Clark, Notre Dame made a brilliant move in hiring Len for the accounting faculty and in later selecting him as chairman. I kept in touch with him during those years, and tried to help him in any way I could -- although his fairness in dealing with other major accounting firms irritated me sometimes.

After I retired from Price Waterhouse in 1988, he called me one day and asked if I would teach an intermediate accounting course for a semester. I did so, and again worked with Len.

I visited him in the hospital the day before he died, and thought to myself as I drove away, "That guy did everything you could possibly do in accounting. He was a Big Eight partner, head of the leading professional organization, the chief financial officer of a Fortune 500 company, and the head of the accounting department of a major university." I doubt that anyone will ever again have such a career in accounting.

Sincerely,

Tom Buck

Tom Buck
Retired partner, Price Waterhouse

GRADUATE SCHOOL OF BUSINESS
STANFORD UNIVERSITY, STANFORD, CALIFORNIA 94305-5015

CHARLES T. HORNGREN   TELEPHONE: (415) 723-2764
EDMUND W. LITTLEFIELD PROFESSOR   FAX: (415) 725-7979
OF ACCOUNTING

December 23, 1994

Professor Donald E. Tidrick
College of Business Administration
University of Texas
Austin, TX   78712-1172

Dear Don,

Leonard Savoie had a distinguished career in a variety of key professional roles:

- chief executive officer of AICPA

- partner in Price Waterhouse

- educator at Notre Dame and Harvard

- vice president and controller of Clark Equipment

Few individuals could match Len's wide-ranging contributions throughout the accounting field in its broadest sense.

My closest, continuous interactions with Len occurred throughout my 5.5 years on the Accounting Principles Board. My respect for Len grew steadily as I observed his leadership and dedication to the profession during some stormy years. Given his perceptions of the interests of the profession as a whole, Len worked energetically and effectively toward advancing the profession's image and contributions to society.

My fellow educators and I found Len's speeches and articles to have the following laudable characteristics:

- show uniformly high quality

- demonstrate significant effort

- deserve the respect of thoughtful scholars and practitioners

- command the attention of professors and students

Len's work showed an ability to deal with important, difficult topics in scholarly fashion.

In summary, Leonard Savoie always had my highest respect as a professional and as a friend. He was a notable leader in many aspects of accounting. He was the epitome of balanced excellence.

Sincerely,

Charles T. Horngren

SECTION I:

REPORTS TO COUNCIL OF THE AICPA

REPORT OF THE EXECUTIVE VICE PRESIDENT
Before Members of Council
of the American Institute of Certified Public Accountants
September 23, 1967

I would like to give you my view of the state of technical affairs of the Institute based upon what I have seen and learned in my short term in office -- dating from July 1. During this period, I have not been able to probe in depth all of the technical affairs of the Institute, but I do have observations on some important accounting and auditing matters that I wish to pass on to you.

As all of you know, in the area of accounting principles some observers have claimed that a "credibility gap" exists in financial reporting. The Accounting Principles Board is currently working hard to close this gap, with many important subjects on the docket. As Jack Carey has pointed out to you, the comments about the profession and especially the activities of the Board are becoming increasingly favorable. Nevertheless, we must face the fact that as the Board extends its area of influence, it will continue to encounter complaints from those who cling to their desire for latitude of choice or who are being obliged to comply with provisions which may adversely affect their long-term or short-term goals. Now that business is aroused to the problems and results of setting accounting principles, the Board will for some time need a lot of courage to continue to take firm positions.

The need for narrowing areas of difference in accounting practice has been so amply demonstrated that the remaining controversy centers largely around how it is done and what effect this will have on business. The accounting profession has quite rightly taken the position that financial statements are representations of business management and that the independent accountant assumes a separate responsibility in expressing an opinion as to whether these statements are in conformity with generally accepted accounting principles. The Board is seeking to establish, amplify, and clarify these principles in order to provide more substance and meaning behind the opinion of the accountant. In doing so, the Board has tried to involve business management to a greater extent. There are several reasons.

First, there is a real need for management to recognize clearly that the statements are theirs and they should be concerned over the accounting that is followed and the credibility with which the statements

3

are received. Second, corporate financial management contains a vast pool of knowledge on accounting and financial reporting matters which must be made available to the Board if it is to establish principles wisely. Third, management must be involved in determining accounting principles to provide assurance to all that the Board is not acting arbitrarily without regard to real practical problems.

It is plain that management is becoming very much interested in the work of the Board. Just this week, in addition to the mailing to our 60,000 members, more than 7,000 copies of an exposure draft of the proposed Opinion on income tax accounting were sent to corporation presidents, university professors, bankers, financial analysts, and other business leaders. Hundreds of comments are expected, representing the collective views of thousands. But even before this formal exposure process was started, between July 10 and September 12, the Board received 100 letters from interested persons commenting on the subject of income taxes.

These comments have been stimulated in part by nineteen meetings held in late July by a subcommittee of the APB with business and government groups for the purpose of exchanging views on key issues, even before arriving at the exposure draft. However, the letters indicate clearly that most of them stemmed from three strong campaigns to oppose the Board's proposed action. Respondents were without benefit of knowledge of the Board's reasoning or its specific recommendations.

On July 10, a major airline circulated to a large number of companies a letter suggesting they request an appearance before the APB to object to any change in *APB Opinion No. 4*, Accounting for the Investment Credit. A reversion to the principle of *Opinion No. 2*, the letter said, "... would have an extremely adverse effect upon the net earnings of industry in general."

On July 21, an accounting firm held a press conference and issued a pamphlet entitled, "Is Generally Accepted Accounting for Income Taxes Possibly Misleading Investors?" This firm urged financial executives, accounting professors, and others to protest to the APB and the Financial Executives Institute against providing for deferred income taxes, a practice which has for many years been well established.

On August 1, the Financial Executives Institute issued a brief, but biased, questionnaire to its members and also asked them to communicate their views on the investment credit and deferred tax accounting directly to the APB and the Chairman of the SEC.

All three of these campaigns were kicked off well in advance of the APB's first public exposure of the proposed Opinion, which took place just this week with a press conference on September 19. Through the end of last week, these three efforts had brought to the Board a total of 100 letters, of which 90 opposed the single method of spreading for handling the investment credit and 69 opposed comprehensive tax allocation. Only five favored spreading the investment credit and only two favored comprehensive tax allocation. What weight can and should the Board give to these views from industry and universities? Quite obviously, many of the views are sincerely-held beliefs based upon reasoning that has some merit. But just as obviously, many respondents have an eye on earnings per share, a fear for the loss of an advantage now held, and inadequate understanding of what the Board's proposed Opinion really says.

For example, there were 36 complaints about unnecessarily detailed work to provide deferred taxes on all book-tax differences, regardless of size. But the Opinion, like all Board Opinions, is intended to apply only to material items. Several objections were from public utility executives. But the exposure draft clearly makes an exception for rate-regulated utilities. Some letters protested the commingling of "real" taxes and "hypothetical" taxes. But the draft Opinion calls for a separate disclosure of taxes currently payable and deferred taxes. These and many other negative reactions will, I think, be eliminated by the terms of the Opinion itself.

There is a strong temptation to ignore completely the comments evoked through efforts which are outside the scope of the Board's own careful, studied procedures. The Board is a deliberative body which strives hard to elicit fairly all pertinent facts relating to a subject. The issues in the exposure draft have been studied carefully by the Board over a period of years. Each Board member has had ample opportunity to convince the other Board members of the merits of his position.

The Board is not tallying votes in a popularity contest. To do so would cast this current experience in the same mold as the 1956 All-Star Baseball Game election by the fans, when a get-out-the-vote campaign in Cincinnati was so effective that seven of the eight starting positions went to Cincinnati Reds baseball players. The Commissioner of Baseball felt compelled to redress this patently unfair situation by overruling the so-called popular vote and appointing other players to the starting team. A vote count of that kind is clearly not a democratic process and certainly has no place in the far more serious setting of the determination of accounting principles.

Nevertheless, the many comments received (and to be received) must be studied carefully and weighed by the Board as to their merit. In particular, those which offer new problem situations or new slants to an old issue must be considered as to possible changes that may be appropriate to accommodate them. On the other hand, the Board must reject the comments which simply repeat old arguments that have been thoroughly explored, researched, debated, and rejected. It is not easy for individual Board members to determine which of a myriad of suggestions require changes in a Board position and which suggestions must be rejected in the interest of fairness and consistency, and usefulness to investors.

The Board has exerted strenuous efforts in tackling the controversial subject of accounting for income taxes, and Board members have advanced spirited arguments for various positions. Nevertheless, a two-thirds majority approved positions taken in the exposure draft. This does not close debate, but simply opens it to a broader public. However, whether or not the commentators like the positions taken, there is a growing feeling that the Board is confronted with a test of whether it can deal effectively with a controversial issue -- whether the public can be adequately served by a private professional group. I believe the Board has the tenacity to pursue this subject with due deliberation in accordance with its usual operating procedures and come up with a final Opinion in December, as scheduled. A reminder may be in order that in unity there is strength. The profession will be able to withstand pressures if we all remain united in supporting the authorized group which has faced up to a cold, hard choice.

Occasionally, the Board arrives at a position which, for some reason, may need clarification or interpretation. Two such instances have arisen from Opinions issued just last December, and the points involved are being further studied and additional consultation with affected groups is now going on. *APB Opinion No. 9*, paragraph 33, has created considerable difficulty in determining what constitutes a "residual security" for the purpose of determining earnings per share. This issue is back for re-study with the original drafting subcommittee of the Board, and they are working very closely with the SEC and investment bankers in trying to decide what clarification, if any, is needed. Admittedly, there are many computational problems left unanswered in *Opinion No. 9*. And very likely some additional guidance will be provided, but not necessarily in another APB Opinion. The Board does not attempt to write a detailed rule book to cover every conceivable situation. Quite significantly, the protests are coming largely from companies which have capital structures with significant potential dilution, whereas some financial analysts and financial writers have praised the Board for leading in a healthy reform in reporting practices by their requirement for disclosure of the effect of potential dilution.

APB Opinion No. 10, paragraphs 8 and 9, have similarly given rise to a number of problems. Last month, Board members each received a telegram requesting a study of these paragraphs. The telegram was signed by twelve of the country's largest investment banking firms and five of the largest law firms; and it stated that the Investment Bankers Association wished to discuss these paragraphs with the Board. Although the usual extensive exposure process had been followed in finalizing this Opinion, and the Investment Bankers Association had received the exposure draft and had ample opportunity to comment, they remained silent. The information now being presented to the Board was not made available before. Later this week, a subcommittee of the Board is meeting with representatives of the investment bankers and their lawyers and other groups to reconsider these two paragraphs.

The questions being raised relate mainly to practical difficulties in arriving at a value to place on the conversion feature of convertible debentures through the process of relating the convertible debenture price to the price of a straight debt security without the conversion feature. This issue, too, has overtones of earnings per share. Allocation of a portion of proceeds of a convertible debt issue to the conversion feature results in a debt discount which must be amortized against future earnings. Thus, convertible debt is less appealing than it would be without this requirement. Of course, the Board is not anxious to amend an Opinion immediately after it becomes effective; but, on the other hand, the Board must be willing to reconsider its position in the face of new evidence. It is safe to assume that in the future at least one important group, the investment bankers, will give more serious consideration to proposed APB Opinions.

The APB has just taken another courageous step by issuing a statement favoring further research and experimentation in the presentation of financial information by industry-lines for conglomerates and diversified companies. Here again, there is a strong industry opposition to this kind of reporting. The Board's pronouncement is simply an interim statement and not a definitive pronouncement and, therefore, does not require compliance in the same manner as APB Opinions do. Nevertheless, this is an area where the Board should exercise leadership, and it can be expected to take a stronger position in the future.

The Institute is also making progress in providing guidelines for better accounting and auditing through the channel of special industry audit guides, which deal with both accounting principles and auditing procedures. While these guides do not have the authority of APB Opinions, they nevertheless have proven to be extremely helpful in those industries where they have been prepared. Furthermore, a guide is likely to have a considerable impact on the specific industry, and ordinarily it can be prepared and issued more expeditiously than an APB Opinion, which customarily affects all of industry. Two such guides, in print for some time, are now being reviewed and revised. They are on savings and loan associations, and brokers or dealers in securities.

An audit guide for banks has been more than nine years in the making. In a few days, a ballot draft will be sent to committee members to obtain approval for final issuance. Here, the Institute's Bank Accounting and Auditing Committee, after settling its own differences, took a strong position with industry. Bank financial statements traditionally have been designed to emphasize the soundness of financial position. Now that bank stocks are traded widely, more attention is being directed to the income statement. Careful study has led the Committee to the conclusions that the income statement of a bank should present a net income figure in compliance with APB *Opinion No. 9*; that securities gains and losses are ordinary income of banks; and that an adequate, but not excessive, provision for loan losses is an ordinary charge against operations. These and many other issues have been contested by the banking industry and to some extent by the three federal regulatory agencies. After many hearings with these protesting groups, the Committee finally saw that it could compromise no further; so now, after one more hurdle is overcome, the guide will be finalized in spite of industry and regulatory disapproval of parts of it. The end result is one of which we can be proud, for this guide is bound to be a major force in improving accounting and financial reporting for banks.

An audit guide is being prepared for the life insurance industry. This effort, too, is encountering some very difficult accounting problems, and industry objections are anticipated. Audit guides are also being prepared for defense contractors, finance companies, medicare audits, hospital audits, and personal financial statements. The latter is proving to be an interesting experiment in meeting a public need on a timely basis. While the main purpose for issuing guides is to help members of the Institute in carrying out their professional engagements, the matter of personal financial statements will undoubtedly assume wide-spread public attention during the political campaigns of 1968. The practice of disclosing finances of candidates having been set in the 1964 presidential campaign, it is almost certain to be increased in 1968 with many more political candidates voluntarily presenting audited financial statements to the public. A guide on this subject will provide solid technical support for members of the Institute in performing examinations like this. Work commenced on this guide in June, and a first-draft was delivered on September 9.

The Committee on Auditing Procedure has just approved final Statements on Auditing Procedure on unaudited financial statements and on auditor's working papers. These Statements are expected to be issued within a week or two. A subject currently before the Committee relates to the correction of financial statements and revision of the independent auditor's opinion in cases where the auditor discovers, after issuance of his opinion, facts, existing prior to such issuance, which lead him to believe the financial statements may have been substantially misstated.

The Committee on Auditing Procedure is also working assiduously an the revision of the auditor's short-form opinion. Often, we hear that our standard language is not really informative to the reader -- that it fails to convey the degree of responsibility the auditor takes, and that it gives the implication there is greater accuracy attached to financial statements than we know really exists. It is relatively easy for anyone of us to state in his own words what an audit report means. But those close to this project can attest that it is difficult indeed to develop standard audit language that another person would be willing to use, that accomplishes all of the public service objectives we have, and, at the same time, does not jeopardize our position as to legal liability. Nevertheless, this project shows good promise and before long it should be ready for exposure to the membership and others.

If there is a common experience running through the problems of raising technical standards of the profession, it is that, in the face of an irreversible trend toward tighter accounting standards, there persists in some quarters a reluctance to move ahead from the *status quo*. It seems to me that business should be willing to accept principles thoughtfully and painstakingly worked out by the accounting profession as a part of our private enterprise system in preference to regulation that might well otherwise be imposed by government. Regardless of how businessmen may react to the profession's attempt to narrow differences in accounting practices, the only danger to the profession (and to business as well) lies in inactivity. As illustration, one has but to recall the APB's 1965 withdrawal of a proposed pronouncement on classification of deferred taxes on installment sales and the resolution of this issue in the SEC's *Accounting Series Release No. 102.*

I have made no attempt to give you a rundown of all the technical accounting and auditing activities of the Institute -- you will hear reports from the Accounting Principles Board and the Committee on Auditing Procedure which will cover their affairs more specifically. I have tried to convey to you in a few words the seriousness of purpose of the technical projects of the Institute, the increasing involvement in these matters of the business community, and the great need for independence, objectivity, and integrity in dealing with these problems.

In carrying out its responsibilities, the accounting profession might well take heed of these words addressed to Wall Street last week by Robert W. Haack, new president of the New York Stock Exchange:

> When public interest and private interest do not coincide, I submit that the public interest, properly defined, must prevail. The public may be willing to forgive us for mistakes in judgment, but it will not forgive us for mistakes in motive.

PUBLIC RESPONSIBILITIES OF THE PRIVATE SECTOR
Before Members of Council
of the American Institute of Certified Public Accountants
April 29, 1968

A basic feature of the professional practice of accounting is the CPA's involvement with the public. Indeed, "public" has been the CPA's middle name since the term was invented late in the last century. The word "public" was used to emphasize responsibilities that went beyond reporting to owners and managers who engaged an accountant's services.

It was because of the public necessity for auditing and financial reporting that accountancy legislation was adopted in each state. In almost every case, legislation entailed education, experience, and examination requirements to assure that an accountant holding forth his professional ability to serve the public would have to comply with at least minimum standards of competence and could be held responsible for his professional actions.

Throughout this century, there have been growing and shifting demands for accounting services. As a result, the CPA has greatly expanded the scope of his activities to include many services beyond the function which gave rise to the regulatory legislation. But this does not mean that the CPA's public responsibilities have diminished. On the contrary, they have expanded. No phase of the professional practice of accounting is more involved with public interest than the area of financial reporting and the accounting principles on which financial statements are based.

As the very nature of our private enterprise system has undergone change, with government regulation becoming more and more pervasive, the development and application of accounting principles for business remain uniquely -- and I hope solidly -- in the private sector. The accounting profession has earned the right to set accounting principles by giving constant and careful attention to the maintenance and elevation of its standards. But if the profession is to continue to enjoy this privilege, it will have to redouble its efforts to meet the rising expectations of a better-informed public. In a widely publicized speech about two years ago, J. Howard Laeri said:

> Bankers, investors, and the general public view the auditors'
> responsibilities in a far broader context than does the
> accounting profession.... Some auditors seem to see
> themselves as non-questioning reporters, working within the
> confines of "generally accepted principles." The fact is, of
> course, that the auditor is actually working for the investor....

The SEC in its 1966 annual report said that, in the large area of
financial reporting not covered by its rules,

> the Commission's principal means of protecting investors from
> inadequate financial reporting, fraudulent practices, and
> overreaching by management is by requiring a certificate of an
> independent public accountant, ... which expresses an opinion
> as to whether the financial statements are presented fairly in
> conformity with accounting principles and practices ... which
> have attained general acceptance.

Others, too, have added their voices to those asking for a more
acute awareness by CPAs of their responsibility to the public. In the
seven months since I last addressed Council, I have spoken before
groups of financial writers, financial executives, security analysts,
women investors, accounting students, graduate business school
students, business school alumni, management accountants, bankers,
company presidents, and federal government accountants. In each case,
there was an opportunity to learn what representatives of the group
think about the role of CPAs in reporting to the public. The
predominant view of all but the management groups is that the
accounting profession should accelerate its efforts to improve financial
accounting principles, and to narrow areas of differences in accounting
practices.

Management attitudes are mixed. At a Young Presidents
Organization meeting, one company president complained bitterly about
the accounting profession's actions that deny him the right to report
earnings in any manner he chooses. The more he talked about his right
to cover up a bad year by manipulating reported earnings, the more
apparent became the need for tighter accounting standards. He received
no support from his fellow presidents and, in fact, made *my* point very

effectively.

In response to these attitudes and expectations on the part of important segments of the public, the Accounting Principles Board has taken on the very large task of improving standards of corporate financial reporting. Along with the increased intensity of activity of the Board has come strengthened authority for its pronouncements. This Council added significantly to that authority through its 1964 action calling for disclosure of departures from APB Opinions. Still to be considered by Council, in this year or next, is a proposal for a rule of ethics requiring disclosure of departures from APB Opinions.

The spotlight of the financial press has also been influential in adding strength to Board pronouncements, through stories on the issuance of APB Opinions and on the way CPAs apply those Opinions in practice. *Fortune Magazine* is right now preparing a feature article on accounting for inclusion in its annual "500" issue to be published in June. I do not know what it will say, but their writers seem inclined to write about the concentration of auditing in eight firms, the work of the APB, specific cases which they believe are not in accord with APB Opinions, auditing fees and client pressures, and accountants' legal liabilities.

The accomplishments of the Board in the last two years are impressive, and they are full of public interest implications well beyond the limits of technical matters, which for so many years characterized the professional pursuits of the Institute. For example, the Board has taken charge of earnings per share calculations -- a move which plainly serves the public interest. In a very forthright manner, the Board broadened responsibilities of CPAs by calling for earnings per share figures on income statements. Until recently, the profession had largely ignored the public's need for refined earnings per share standards. Many in the profession took the position that this was not our concern, but belonged more properly in the area of financial analysis. Greatly increased emphasis on earnings per share, and related times-earnings ratios, focused attention on the lack of standardization in computations and occasional abuses in presentation.

The APB was also in the right place at the right time in defining "residual securities," and in calling for supplementary disclosure of pro forma earnings per share that would result from dilution arising through conversion of convertible securities and exercise of options and warrants. Not everyone likes the APB position. One listed company having convertible notes, convertible preferred, stock options, and warrants has taken three full pages in its 1967 report to denounce the Board. But they do agree that per share earnings figures will hereafter be reported on the APB-basis.

A professor friend, who is an accomplished needler, tells me we should give up trying to specify how to compute earnings per share, as the aggressive and imaginative promoter will always be ahead of us in devising new securities that enable him to show a rising earnings trend. Convertible preference stock with an accumulating conversion rate was just a start. The latest is a class AA stock offered to common stockholders on a one-to-one basis, which is convertible back into common at increasing rates beginning at .75-to-one and rising to 1.50-to-one in 1980, and with no cash dividend, but a 3% annual accumulating stock dividend. The professor is right in saying that the promoters are ahead of us, but at least we have them thinking harder.

But setting standards is not the only major area of public responsibility of the profession. It is just as vital to have the independent CPA support and carry out these standards. Unless APB pronouncements are adhered to by the Institute's members, the Board has achieved a hollow victory.

Compliance with Institute pronouncements has, with few exceptions, been generally good over the years. More recently, with greater status accorded to APB pronouncements, adherence to them by members has appeared to be nearly unanimous. This is borne out by the almost total lack of cases where auditors have pointed out departures from APB Opinions. It is gratifying to observe that a high level technical body is carrying out its public responsibilities conscientiously and that practitioners are responding faithfully to the requirement to adhere to its pronouncements.

But each forward step serves to reveal remaining inadequacies, both in the establishment of standards and in carrying them out. For example, in dealing with the subject of earnings per share, the APB strongly recommended the disclosure of earnings per share figures on the face of income statements. Large numbers of companies, presumably at the urging of their auditors, adopted this presentation in 1967 annual reports. Unfortunately, there are also large numbers of companies which did not respond to the recommendation. We have no indication as to whether the resistance came from the companies or from their auditors. Whatever the source, outside observers interpret this situation as widespread violation of an APB Opinion, and they are asking what we are going to do about it.

It is plain that the Board will have to rely less on "suggestions" and "recommendations," if it is to fulfill its public responsibilities. On the specific matter of disclosure of earnings per share, I am hopeful that the Board in 1968 will change the words "strongly recommends" to "should."

In addition to deviations from the spirit of Board pronouncements in the case of earnings per share, there is occasional evidence of the use of loopholes to evade the intent of the Board. Let me cite some specifics and, in so doing, draw your attention to the significance of the segment of the public which is criticizing the performance of CPAs; and it is criticism from informed sources.

Here is one brought to my attention by a Harvard Business School professor of finance: The annual report of a large company contains a footnote describing a change in vacation pay policy which caused a charge for vacation expense, in addition to the normal cost of vacations paid, in excess of 10% of 1967 income. The expense is included in income before extraordinary items. Although disclosure in the footnote is made, the same footnote describes an offsetting credit of nearly the same amount arising from reversal of reserves for incentive compensation and adjustment of deferred income taxes. The professor who brought this to my attention considers this to be a glaring example of profit manipulation -- and substandard reporting even though disclosure reveals enough of what happened to permit telling this story. Whether or not there is a loophole that permits this kind of reporting, there is no doubt that the public -- the informed public -- believes it is poor reporting.

The partner in charge of research at a leading investment banking house thinks that another annual report violates *APB Opinion No. 9*. In it, earnings per share figures are not given on the income statement; but they are presented in the highlights section, in the historical summary, and in the text of the president's letter. But none of these figures relates to the net income shown on the income statement! To compound the confusion, three figures appearing in the income statement above net income start out with "net earnings" -- these are labeled: "net earnings from operations," "net earnings before provision

for income taxes, and "net earnings before extraordinary items." Total
and per share amounts for this last caption, redesignated simply as "net
earnings," are all that appear in highlights and the president's letter. Is
there a violation here of *APB Opinion No. 9*, especially for a company
which has had extraordinary charges in each of the last four years? A
well-informed security analyst thinks there is. This is the very kind of
reporting the Opinion is intended to prevent.

In another case, a highly respected investment advisory service
noted that the reported 1967 earnings of a company indicated it had just
completed its most successful year, but that this conclusion may be
superficial. It went on to note that dividends from unconsolidated
subsidiaries declined, so that consolidated earnings, if reported, would
have shown a decline from 1966 of some 22%. This example was
picked up by a financial columnist in a leading daily newspaper, who
questioned whether the company's approach to its earnings statement
fitted *APB Opinion No. 10*, which calls for equity accounting for
unconsolidated subsidiaries. The writer also questioned a change in the
company's auditors in 1967. This case reveals the strong light of public
opinion which is shining on financial reporting. It also suggests some
highly competitive relationships among CPA firms.

Another case of competition driving a firm to a borderline decision
was brought to my attention by a member of this Council. He says that
a brokerage client has a subsidiary that leases a computer to the parent,
yet does not capitalize the lease or consolidate the subsidiary in its
financial reporting. The client's resistance is particularly strong because
"net capital" requirements of the SEC and stock exchanges make it
advantageous for brokerage firms to exclude fixed assets and related
debt from the balance sheet. Before taking a stand, the member
checked with other accounting firms as to their position; and found none
that would require capitalization or consolidation. That left him in the
unenviable position of going along with a reporting treatment which he
believed violated an APB Opinion.

His decision, he says, was arrived at very reluctantly and only after
recalling painfully how he lost a major client recently on another matter
of interpretation. The issue of accounting for computer leasing
subsidiaries of brokerage companies has been referred to the AICPA
committee on stock brokerage accounting and auditing and the
committee on relations with the SEC and stock exchanges. Eventually,

it will probably be referred to the APB, as it seems there is no substitute for more specific rules to close loopholes.

Not many years ago, the public would probably not have questioned the kind of accounting that is demonstrated in these examples. But it does not take many of them to drive home the point that the public is now interested in accounting, and the public will demand establishment of higher standards and adherence to them. A profession in which members ignore professional pronouncements is, I submit, in real trouble. If standards are being violated for competitive reasons, a question may very well be asked whether accounting is a *profession* or a *business.*

I am convinced that the profession must not let up in its efforts to improve accounting and reporting standards. Furthermore, it must not equivocate, but must spell out flatly what is required. Experience shows that suggestions and recommendations will not do the job.

Beyond that, there appears to be need for a reporting surveillance carried out by the profession itself. Financial analysts, business writers, and bankers can be counted on to step up their actions in bringing to light deficiencies in financial reporting. But it is surely unbecoming to a profession to rely on others for the policing of its standards. The practice review concept is still a good one and it should be continued. But new ways should be devised to make it more effective. Members of Council could help in the self-discipline of the profession by referring cases to the practice review committee. The committee and its staff cannot do the job alone.

You may wonder what kinds of firms are involved in these cases. Of the four cases I have cited, two auditing firms are national and two are local. I have heard people from national firms say that they adhere to high standards, but they know that some local firms do not. And I have heard smaller practitioners say that APB Opinions are largely for the big firms, who can pick and choose which ones they wish to follow, that they are too complicated for the small firms to bother with, and besides, their reports are really not distributed to the public. Neither of these attitudes is admirable. There is only one set of standards for members of the AICPA, and it is entirely reasonable to expect all members to live up to them. The more specific APB Opinions are, the easier it will be for any firm, large or small, to insist upon good accounting and to prevail over the occasional client who may wish to deviate.

Recently Andrew Barr, Chief Accountant of the SEC, pointed out that last year in statements filed with the SEC there were opinions from more than 500 accounting firms. Many of them were quite small. Because of the expanded corporate merger movement in this country and the continuing activity of initial offerings of small, but rapidly growing companies, there are increasing prospects that a small accounting firm will sooner or later be involved in a filing with the SEC.

In carrying out our public responsibilities, we have been fortunate in enjoying excellent working relations with the SEC. This has added real strength to the work of the profession. Without the cooperation and support of the SEC, we could not begin to discharge our public duties. As we proceed more vigorously to take on added public responsibilities, this congenial working relationship must be further nurtured and developed. My observation of organized Institute relations with the SEC leads me to believe that the relationship is soundly based on mutual respect.

Nevertheless, two changes may be in order: One lies in the Institute's position on technical matters where we lack assurance of SEC enforcement. It would be unwise to issue an APB Opinion that the SEC actively opposes, but it may well be advisable for the Board to take a stand where the SEC says it favors our position, but will give no advance assurance that it will either confirm its own rules or enforce the Board's Opinion.

A second change which may be in order in our relations with the SEC is at the practice-level. Relations between practicing CPAs and the SEC are generally very good, I am told. But there is evidence that CPAs sometimes argue on behalf of a client for an accounting treatment that appears to be prohibited by an APB Opinion. This kind of loophole-looking does not attract as much attention as the other cases I have cited -- usually because the SEC closes the loophole before it can be seen. But a professional posture seeking to evade professional pronouncements can only detract from the stature of the profession.

The public aspects of the professional practice of accounting have never been of greater importance than they are today. We have our work cut out for us at the professional organization-level and at the practicing-level, if we are to retain the public trust in our professional services and keep the accounting function in the private sector.

MARKETING MYOPIA
Before Members of Council
of the American Institute of Certified Public Accountants
October 12, 1968

The title of this talk is taken from Professor Theodore Levitt's classic article of that name which appeared in the *Harvard Business Review* a few years ago. His theme was that short-sighted managements have often failed to define their industries in a way to assure their companies' continued growth. Some industries were product-oriented rather than consumer-oriented. For example, railroads stopped growing because they were *railroad-oriented* and not *transportation-oriented*. Hollywood barely escaped oblivion when TV took over because the film companies saw their business as movies instead of entertainment. The oil industry, although still strong, was in danger of retrogressing because of defining its business as oil instead of energy. In a very similar sense, I think that the accounting profession is in serious danger of suffering from marketing myopia.

Too many CPAs think of their practices as serving the managements of their clients by performing audits and preparing tax returns. This attitude, in the present environment, is almost certain to impair the growth of the profession -- and possibly even to lead to its early demise as a true profession. (Accountants might still make a living from a service business without assuming professional responsibility.) For it is becoming increasingly apparent that the CPA is expected to provide to the public a full range of accounting services based on high professional standards. The public interest has become the dominant factor in the professional practice of accounting. An accountant who thinks merely in terms of providing a company's management the same old audit based on the same old loosely defined practices is product-oriented. Unfortunately, his product is obsolete. The old product and old rules are not good enough to satisfy the rising expectations of the public.

Without question, the accounting profession has been led by men of vision who have brought it to a position of great stature and prestige. But this position cannot be sustained unless the profession is responsive to the winds of change which are blowing strongly and steadily throughout the land.

19

The public interest is inherent in almost all the CPA does. It is most widely observed in the field of auditing, where third party reliance has long been recognized as involving special responsibilities. Nevertheless, too often auditors have not really thought of third parties as their clients, but have considered the client to be corporate management. Many cling to this view in the face of a wave of publicity demonstrating demand for a broader concept of public responsibility and despite court decisions which hold auditors to ever higher standards.

Myopia in the accounting profession can occur at two levels -- at the practice level and the professional organization level. While it is important for individual CPAs and accounting firms to become consumer-oriented, it is even more essential that the professional organization respond to the public expectations. An organization that is not willing to raise professional standards in response to demonstrated needs must then defend the *status quo*. It thus becomes a kind of pressure group striving for the continuation of inadequate practices. But this can accomplish no more than a delaying action. The American Medical Association opposition to medicare is a case in point.

The public also has a real interest in CPA services other than auditing, but this has not often been identified. More often than not, the position is taken that, except in the auditing area, the CPA practicing public accounting should be concerned only with the needs of client management, and should be a strong advocate of management's interests.

For example, it is widely taken for granted that the CPA is an advocate in his tax practice. Yet, the public interest in the tax services CPAs provide is becoming more and more apparent. In order to justify our claim to professional status, overall standards, applicable across the board, are necessary. The public is skeptical of double standards, one proclaiming independence, the other encouraging advocacy. It is not good for the CPA to be known only as an expert who will minimize his client's taxes. It is important for him to become known as a professional, living up to standards which command the respect of the government and the public, as well as the taxpayer.

In the area of management services, the CPA can hold himself out as an expert technician who can install a money-saving system, or he can take a broader view and become known for the professional quality of his objective advice. It has become popular to suggest a conflict of interest in performing management services and expressing an opinion on financial statements for the same client. The independence of the auditor is sometimes questioned if he has done management service work. An investigation by a high-level Institute committee failed to disclose evidence of such a conflict, but that does not mean that public opinion will be assuaged by our assertions that no conflict exists. I believe it is preferable for the CPA to be aggressive in demonstrating independence and objectivity by the manner in which he performs *all* of his services. If this is impossible, perhaps the proper scope and role of the CPA in the several areas of practice should be reappraised.

A large part of audit work is no different from tax and management services work, in that it is designed to save money for clients -- not only managements, but the stockholders and third parties, also. Certainly, services which are designed to improve efficiency and economy in the operations of a business are in the interest of stockholders, investors, credit grantors, and all concerned. Efforts to help in this regard are not, *per se*, incompatible with independence and objectivity in reporting on financial representations.

The record of the accounting profession up to now has been good on the whole, but it is not all that it should be. In the area of accounting and auditing, tremendous effort has been devoted to the development of standards. APB Opinions and Statements on Auditing Procedure have gone a long way toward elevating professional practices. Yet, these efforts are not as extensive or as expeditious as they must be, if the profession is to become consumer-oriented and fulfill the role that is expected of it. The financial press keeps telling us where our deficiencies lie, and courts are establishing rules by hindsight where professional standards have not been enunciated. If we are to overcome myopia in this area, we will have to face the facts squarely. This will spur us to improve standards at an accelerated pace.

A strong element of our professional standards is the Code of Professional Ethics. Self-discipline is vital to the survival of any profession. No group can aspire to professional status without having ethical rules and means of enforcing them.

Our professional standards have mainly been directed to accounting and auditing. But we have made a start also in taxes and management services. This start is none too early -- standards in all areas will have to be raised if we want to maintain and extend the scope of the profession's practice. The Committee on Federal Taxation has made an excellent beginning with its series of Statements on Responsibilities in Tax Practice. This is a very commendable program which, I believe, is essential to the continued development of tax service as a part of professional accounting practice. If tax work cannot be done under professional standards, a serious question arises as to whether it is an appropriate part of a true professional practice.

Last week the tax committee's program received a severe jolt when a proposed tax practice Statement on knowledge of error failed to receive the two-thirds vote of tax committee members required for adoption. A majority favored it, but not a two-thirds majority.

As proposed standards impose increasing responsibilities on our members, it is likely that there will be difficulty in getting the necessary votes for enactment. Thus, we are beginning to see symptoms of myopia in the form of opposition to elevation of standards. Similar obstacles have become widely publicized in the development of accounting principles. Yet, if we don't discipline ourselves, someone else will do it, or we shall lose professional status.

Tax practice is not immune from legal supervision. A recent court decision went against an accounting firm that failed to detect or disclose an embezzlement of funds by the managing agent of a cooperative apartment building. No audit was made, and the firm's main assignment was to issue a tax letter to shareholders setting forth state and federal income tax deductions. Nevertheless, the accountants lost the case.

In the management services area, we are still farther away from development of professional standards. Here it has taken years to gain agreement on Statements on management services practice, even for exposure. Soon though, there will be exposed the first two Statements: one on the broad general nature of management services practice, and the other on competence. These are only first steps and they are sorely needed; but it has been exceedingly difficult to make even this much progress.

Management services practice has also appeared in a recent court case. I have been told that an accounting firm engaged to install back office procedures for a brokerage concern has been sued for not advising that the company was losing money and was in violation of net capital rules of the SEC.

Professional standards should be enacted only after careful consideration by responsible representatives of all segments of the profession.   But there should be a greater facility in coming to agreement on what standards are needed, and how existing standards can be improved. Minority views are expected, and indeed they are needed, if for no other reason than to test the merit of majority positions.

But James Reston's recent *New York Times* column entitled, "The Tyranny of Minorities," demonstrates the adverse effects of control by minorities. He cited a small minority which closed the public schools of New York; a militant minority which halted registration at Columbia University; a third making shambles of a Brooklyn Welfare agency; a fourth howling down Vice President Humphrey and Senator Edward M. Kennedy in Boston; and still another blocking the confirmation of Associate Justice Fortas as Chief Justice of the Supreme Court. He went on to cite the danger "that this tyranny of the minority will in turn lead to a tyranny of the majority and to extreme repressive measures, which will not lead to either order or reconciliation, but to more disorder and division."

Unless the accounting profession can escape the tyranny of its minorities and move ahead faster in the development of professional standards, it stands in great danger of suffering decline from a severe case of myopia.

THE ROAD TO PROGRESS IN ACCOUNTING
Before Members of Council
of the American Institute of Certified Public Accountants
May 6, 1969

The road to progress in accounting leads across flood-swollen rivers, through boulder-strewn plains, and into snow-blocked mountain passes. And the accounting profession appears to be traveling this road on foot.

Occasionally, accounting is aided by an unexpected airlift such as occurred two weeks ago when President Nixon urged dropping the investment credit. If this proposal is enacted, with the aid of Wilbur Mills, it will swiftly and effectively remove a major problem which the Accounting Principles Board was able to solve, but unable to make effective.

But, unexpected help from above is a rare exception. The profession is committed to surface travel and this leads inevitably to various road blocks. The APB is trying hard to remove them. Three Opinions have come out this year including the one which was adopted only last Friday.

I believe this is significant progress, although critics have observed that each of these Opinions was anywhere from five months to two years or more late -- and that each merely modified or reversed another recent pronouncement of the Board.

What have been the major obstacles to progress? The foremost obstacle is the complexity of the problems the Board is facing. There is no doubt that business itself is becoming more complex, that financing schemes are more diverse, and that in spite of these complications, there is increasing demand from the public for greater simplicity in financial reporting.

For example, earnings per share has assumed a tremendously prominent position in the securities markets at a time when securities are becoming more intricate. While this subject has been largely ignored by CPAs for years, the Accounting Principles Board has devoted a great deal of attention to it recently. The Board has attempted to refine calculations of earnings per share and rule out misleading practices.

This action has not gone unnoticed. Although many financiers and business conglomerates complain about what the Board is doing, many more thoughtful and objective observers are commenting favorably about this kind of activity. One syndicated columnist in a recent piece about the APB entitled, "They act as Management's Conscience-- Men of Principles," had this to say:

> Accountants are getting bolder .... They've brought the controversial "earnings per share" into the back-of-the-book figures covered by the opinion. They are trying to draft rules to cope with the problems raised by conglomerates and other new developments, and to win acceptance of those rules.... It's remarkable that in this era of big government, so much of this regulation has been left up to the accountants.

While we appreciate this favorable notice, the writer might well have gone on to observe that big government is having a major impact on the so-called regulation that is being carried out by the accountants.

The Securities and Exchange Commission had prodded us for some time to issue a clarifying Opinion on earnings per share. It has been even more outspoken in its demands for APB action on the pooling of interests, purchase accounting and goodwill problems. Unless a definitive APB position is reached by the end of 1969, the SEC might well establish its own accounting rules in this area. A report on the current thinking of the SEC staff already has been filed with a congressional committee and made known to the accounting profession.

In other ways, too, the SEC is taking a more aggressive position on accounting matters. Its proposals for product-line disclosures by diversified companies in their registration statements are almost sure to be put in final form soon. Because these disclosures would be required elsewhere than in the financial statements, the APB has the opportunity to spell out product-line reporting requirements for fair presentation of financial statements. This opportunity may not last long. It is extremely unlikely that a Board pronouncement on this subject would not call for some disclosure of profit by line of business.

Other significant SEC proposals have been made so recently that I doubt if many of us have found time to study them and assess their impact. These are contained in the voluminous report on SEC Commissioner Francis M. Wheat's study entitled "Disclosure to Investors -- A Reappraisal of Administrative Policies Under the '33 and '34 Acts." Although it covers some problems of the securities markets that are not of direct concern to the accounting profession, it also deals with many financial reporting disclosures. The following are a few of the study's recommendations:

o   The proposals for reporting sales and income by separate lines of business in the registration statements would be carried over to annual reports filed with the SEC.

o   Form 10-K would be revised to include a five-year summary of earnings and a statement of source and application of funds.

o   Advertising expense and research and development costs would be reported in the financial schedules, if significant.

o   A quarterly financial report would be filed with the SEC.

These and the many other proposals presumably will be subjected to further study by the SEC and then introduced through the Commission's usual procedure for exposure and comment. The potential impact on financial reporting is great indeed. The American Institute should consider each proposal carefully and determine what professional standards are needed in these areas before the SEC takes final action.

Big government consists of far more than the SEC. The General Accounting Office has been directed by law to study the feasibility of uniform cost accounting standards to be applied to all defense procurement contracts in excess of $100,000 and to report to Congress by December 31, 1969. It is warming to the task and my prediction is that such standards will be found to be both feasible and necessary. It now appears that the suggested standards may become so entwined with generally accepted accounting principles as to create many additional problems for a large segment of industry and the accounting profession.

The American Institute has engaged a team of professors from Stanford University to carry out a research study on "A Statement of Basic Cost Concepts and Implementation Criteria." This research is bound to be highly useful even though only preliminary papers can be presented before the GAO feasibility study is completed.

Big government includes three bank regulatory agencies, which now have authority over bank financial reporting to investors. Their required form of income statement is grossly inadequate and deviates in major respects from the income statement format presented in the Institute's bank audit guide. For several months now the Institute has been working with the regulatory agencies and the American Bankers' Association in an effort to reach a position that can be accepted by all parties. To me, prospects for agreement seem to be diminishing. I have a very dim view of "negotiation" as a way of arriving at accounting principles.

In the field of auditing, the need for change is very evident and major road-blocks lie in the path of progress. For about three years now, the Committee on Auditing Procedures has been giving serious consideration to a revised form of opinion. There seems to be little love for our old form, but hardly anyone wants to accept a change suggested by another person.

The concern of some members over legal liability poses a serious obstacle to the work of the Committee on Auditing Procedures. These members believe that the issuance of further Statements on Auditing Procedure will increase the liability of auditors in some way.

This can hardly draw an argument. To the extent that new standards impose additional obligations, liability may well be increased. But the very existence of standards may serve to limit liability in those cases where auditors adhere to the new standards.

The Institute's Division of Federal Taxation, too, is encountering an occasional obstacle. Its series of "Statements on Responsibilities in Tax Practice" is an admirable effort to raise professional standards. The setback received by the proposed Statement on knowledge of error appears to be only temporary. The series should be moving ahead again soon. The Division's committee on tax policy is a notable venture into areas of public service, with which the profession should be concerned.

The Division of Federal Taxation has long advocated amortization of goodwill over a ten-year period. As the APB considers accounting for goodwill, it will be interesting to see whether they will take the same position and, if not, whether the Institute can justify different positions for accounting and income tax purposes. The APB is yet to be heard from.

An excellent start on developing professional standards in another area has been made by the Committee on Management Services, with its new series of Statements. The Institute is well on the road to accounting progress in all technical areas, but it is far nearer the beginning of the road than the end.

The newly formed research committee should be particularly helpful in its role of coordinating all of our research efforts. It will aid in identifying research needs and in allocating scarce resources to specific projects.

Progress will be hastened if we obtain more Institute staff to perform the bulk of the work. We need to attract more CPAs to the staff -- not just ordinary CPAs, but CPAs of high potential. We are filling a number of new positions which will aid in these efforts.

One is in the area of unofficial accounting interpretations. This service should be very helpful to members in providing additional guidance on technical accounting matters and should relieve the APB of the burden of putting excessive details in its Opinions. The woefully inadequate numbers of staff supporting the Committee on Auditing Procedures will be augmented in a few weeks by a manager of auditing research -- another new position. An additional technical writer has been added to the APB administrative staff. These and other new staff positions to be established should greatly aid the Institute in its journey down the road to accounting progress.

More staff will not solve all the problems. We need a sense of urgency on the part of all concerned with our efforts to raise professional standards. We need also a willingness to listen to all views and to accept majority positions when our own views do not prevail. We need to consider the desires of industry, government agencies, and users of financial information. But in making final judgments, we need to avoid negotiation with others and come to our own conclusions -- and to observe our own standards in practice -- even if they are unpopular with others. Only in this way can real progress be made.

LIVING WITH A HIGH PROFILE
Before Members of Council
of the American Institute of Certified Public Accountants
May 5, 1970

Never before has accounting been the subject of such widespread public attention. We have, in the jargon of today, a high profile. We must learn to live with it.

Newspapers and magazines publish pieces about accounting with increasing frequency. Inadequacies in financial reporting and proposed changes in reporting requirements are always controversial and, therefore, newsworthy.

There can be no doubt about the implications of this press attention. The public is learning of the importance of the accounting function. It is expecting a better performance by the accounting profession, collectively and individually. The public expects the organized profession to raise the level of technical standards. It expects individual CPAs to report financial conditions fairly and objectively in accordance with the higher standards.

The American Institute embarked on a campaign to reform accounting principles and financial reporting before a good many of its members were ready for it. The time for reform had come, and there was no avoiding it. With reform inevitable, the only question remaining is, "Who will do it -- the profession or the government?"

While the need for improvement is obvious, and the dedication of the accounting profession to accomplishing it is earnest, the pressures resisting reform are strong indeed. Let me cite a few specific instances.

The Accounting Principles Board achieved high visibility with its announced intention to tighten accounting rules for business combinations. The issue is complex and controversial, but not insoluble. The APB arrived at a tentative position which would clarify merger accounting and eliminate the choice of alternatives. Predictably, the Board's proposal has not received universal support. In fact, some opponents have organized campaigns to try to defeat it.

For example, the Financial Executives Institute has urged its members to write to the APB to register strong opposition to the proposal. And the FEI has very belatedly authorized a research study of accounting for business combinations which were effected in 1967. The research prospectus implies that its purpose is to demonstrate the

31

incorrectness of the APB's exposure draft. FEI representatives have admitted, upon questioning, that their position is to continue present practices of accounting for business combinations.

At least one accounting firm has advised its clients of the firm's opposition to the APB proposal and has suggested to clients that they express their views to the APB. Other accounting firms also have made known their opposition to the APB stand.

Corporate managements have opposed it, too -- some darkly suggesting drastic actions to thwart the APB's efforts. In a way, this is reminiscent of the income tax Opinion of two-and-a-half years ago when the FEI, some accounting firms, and business managements were trying to block its issuance. The Opinion was issued, but treatment of the investment credit was withdrawn from it.

One might speculate on whether opposition to the APB on business combinations will keep it from issuing a final Opinion. If this happens, I believe the abuses of merger accounting will be curbed surely and swiftly by the Securities and Exchange Commission. The opponents then will not only have failed to preserve the advantages they now see in today's loose practices, but they will have dealt a body blow to the accounting profession. And they will have forced the transfer of an important business function from self-regulation to government regulation.

I believe, however, that the APB will issue an Opinion on business combinations that will greatly restrict use of the pooling-of-interests method and will require amortization of goodwill that arises by using the purchase method. *Business Week* has predicted that, "In the pooling-of-interest squabble, the accountants are expected to prevail, despite their many critics."

For one thing, the APB has a powerful ally in the Securities and Exchange Commission, whose chairman has supported the APB position in a statement before the Senate Antitrust and Monopoly Subcommittee. Many other organizations, including the Financial Analysts Federation and the National Association of Accountants, have indicated their substantial agreement with the Board's proposal. Members of Council could help by offering their support and encouragement.

On another issue -- bank accounting -- a final pronouncement was released some time ago, but opponents of reform have managed to keep the controversy alive. In January, 1968, after nearly ten years of trying, the Institute's Committee on Bank Accounting and Auditing issued its guide, *Audits of Banks*, even though the banking industry and the bank regulatory authorities did not agree with the format of the income statement. A year ago, the APB removed the bank exemption from *Opinion No. 9*, thus requiring banks audited by CPAs to report a net income figure which includes securities gains and losses and a provision for loan losses.

Meanwhile, the SEC was becoming increasingly involved because of filings with it by bank holding companies. Last July, the Chief Accountant of the SEC called together representatives of the three bank regulatory agencies, the American Bankers Association, and the American Institute. This meeting resulted in agreement on an income statement substantially as called for in our audit guide, but with some minor modifications. The bank regulatory agencies issued new regulations to the banks and the American Institute put out a short supplement to the audit guide. The 1969 financial statements of banks were presented in accordance with the new format which we all agreed to.

One might think that would end the matter. Not so. Last month, just after the first quarter financial statements were published, bank security analysts and bankers began a campaign to get the news media to drop the reporting of net income and revert to reporting net operating earnings, which would exclude securities gains and losses. The analysts talked to the *Wall Street Journal*, after which an article was published quoting their criticism of the new format. We asked for equal time and got it, but so far we have not had equal coverage of our views in the *Journal*.

The same group of analysts asked for a meeting with the *New York Times*, and a luncheon with them was set for Friday, April 24. We were invited by the *Times* to attend. After the meeting was scheduled, but before the date arrived, the *New York Times* of Sunday, April 19, carried an article headlined "Banker Scores New Accounting." It carried the byline and a picture of Walter B. Wriston, president of the First National City Bank of New York.

Now we asked for equal coverage of our views in the *Times*. They agreed, so we quickly prepared a piece for the Sunday, April 26, issue. When the five bank security analysts showed up for the April 24 luncheon at the *Times*, they were surprised to be handed my bylined

article and to see Al Mentzel, Chairman of our Committee on Bank
Accounting and Auditing, and me. Three reporters were present, with
a tape recorder. There followed a two-hour recorded debate during
which the analysts did not convince us they were right, nor did we
convince them. We may not know for some time whose views the
Times found persuasive. We do know that it has plenty of controversial
material to publish as it chooses. The paper did publish our article on
April 26.

An ironic twist to this episode occurred the day before the meeting
with the reporters and analysts. I received an unsolicited letter
enclosing the Wriston piece, deploring it, and strongly supporting our
net income requirement for banks. The letter was from David Norr,
chairman of the Financial Accounting Policy Committee of the Financial
Analysts Federation, and he was speaking in that capacity on behalf of
the entire Committee. The *Times* men were delighted to learn that the
security analysts could not agree among themselves. This episode
brings to mind some words of Niccolo Machiavelli who said nearly 500
years ago:

> There is nothing more difficult to carry out, nor more doubtful
> of success, nor more dangerous to handle, than to initiate a
> new order of things. For the reformer has enemies in all those
> who profit by the old order, and only lukewarm defenders in
> all those who would profit by the new order.

Our high profile has been showing in many other ways. A couple
of weeks ago, the *Wall Street Journal* discovered the prospectus of
Donaldson, Lufkin and Jenrette, the first stockbrokerage firm to go
public. An editor had noticed three figures for earnings per share,
called the company for an explanation, learned that they were unhappy
about it, and that he had a story.

The firm carried its marketable securities at market values with the
unrealized appreciation and depreciation taken through income.
Securities not readily marketable were included in the statements at
cost; but in the summary of earnings, earnings per share figures were
presented on three lines -- one for net income, one for changes in fair
values of non-marketable securities, and the sum of the other two. We
can only guess as to whether the company's unhappiness was

conceptual or practical. The *Journal* noted that fair values increased greatly in 1968, but decreased in 1969.

This new presentation is an example of the quick decisions we often face. Brokerage firms were going public before our Committee on Stockbrokerage Accounting and Auditing could issue its revised audit guide. The Committee did meet and decided that marketable securities of a broker should be carried at market values and non-marketable securities should be carried at fair values, with unrealized appreciation and depreciation included in income. Some reservations were expressed about the practical difficulties of determining fair values of securities which are not readily marketable.

The tentative solution was that used in the Donaldson, Lufkin and Jenrette prospectus. It was agreed to at a meeting of the SEC, New York Stock Exchange, Investment Bankers Association, National Association of Securities Dealers, and the AICPA. Our Committee, subject to approval of the Chairman of the Accounting Principles Board, will be arriving at a final solution soon.

The accounting profession has high visibility in government circles, too. Relations between our Federal Tax Division and the Treasury Department are close. More than a dozen regulatory agencies have asked for liaison committees with the American Institute. Congress is showing an increased interest in the accounting profession. We have filed statements at Senate hearings on franchise companies and on conglomerate mergers, and we have testified at Senate hearings on uniform cost accounting standards.

Nearly two years ago, uniform cost accounting standards were proposed for use by defense contractors. Congress called for the Comptroller General to make a feasibility study of the application of such standards. In January of this year, he issued his report which concluded that uniform cost accounting standards are feasible and desirable. Bills were introduced calling for the Comptroller General to set uniform cost accounting standards for use by defense contractors.

The hearings on these bills considered this proposal as well as an alternative one which would place the function in a new board created within the executive branch of government. We and the Comptroller General favored the latter proposal. Whichever position prevails, the accounting profession is sure to have a greater involvement in this area.

Having a high profile, as we do, means that more people in more places are watching us. They are increasingly aware not only of deficiencies in our underlying standards, but also of deficiencies in carrying them out. Financial writers, security analysts, and other informed observers recognize marginal or substandard reporting, even though it may be condoned because of some loophole in our rules. They are alert to changes in our pronouncements on accounting principles, changes in accounting methods, and changes in auditors.

We face an important challenge to see that our standards are enforced in *spirit*, as well as in technical compliance. In short, we must learn to live with a high profile.

THE ACCOUNTING PROFESSION'S ROLE
IN FEDERAL GOVERNMENT MATTERS
Before Members of Council
of the American Institute of Certified Public Accountants
May 10, 1971

In the April issue of its house publication, the Morgan Guaranty bank in New York carried a tongue-in-cheek article which reached the conclusion that by the year 2049 everyone working for wages or salaries in the United States will be employed by the government. To arrive at this prediction, the publication used a calculation worked out by that whimsical Englishman, Professor C. Northcote Parkinson, and applied to his own country.

The bank noted that in 1960 the U.S. civilian labor force numbered 69.6 million. In 1970 the labor force had reached 82.7 million -- thus showing an increase of 1.75 percent annually. Meanwhile, during the same decade, government employment in the U.S., counting all levels of government (but not including the armed services), grew from 8.4 million to 12.6 million -- a rise of 4.2 percent annually. Extrapolating these rates of increase on a chart, one finds that the two lines of growth cross in the year 2049, thereby demonstrating that, by that point in time, every member of the civilian labor force will be absorbed by government!

Needless to say, the bank concedes that this is a bit of "statistical drollery." But it does serve to highlight the basic condition underlying my remarks today -- namely, the immense growth of government.

That growth has been accompanied by a great increase in the demands of government itself for accounting services. Each year hundreds of bills introduced in Congress call for accountability on the objectives of the proposed legislation. Many of the bills call for new measurement methods. Some specifically provide for reports from firms of independent public accountants.

The accounting profession already participates heavily in federally-stimulated independent audits. More than 50,000 such audits are performed each year, and the rate of growth in this activity is high.

The profession is interested in expanding its role in these areas. And federal agencies, some of which disburse sums running into billions of dollars, want to engage independent public accounting firms to help them discharge their responsibility for accounting. For example, the Department of Labor is right now requesting proposals for audits of manpower training project contracts of three-quarters of a billion dollars. Occasionally, however, obstacles are encountered to the use of independent accountants. I submit that this fact raises questions about basic assumptions of the profession and should cause us to reappraise our policies. Let me cite just three problem areas:

First, the profession seems often to take the attitude that our staple product is the standard short-form audit report, even though the government may have a need for something different. The department or agency involved may want a report on internal control, or on compliance with a particular law, or on performance evaluation of a program.

These are new and intriguing areas of auditing which provide great challenges, and in turn should arouse professional interest and provide professional satisfaction. Performance evaluation may even require participation with people from other disciplines.

Government auditors are already performing audits of this kind, to a much greater extent than are independent auditors. Yet there are not enough of them to meet the need, so administrators must turn to the accounting profession for help. In this circumstance, should not the profession find some way to provide the prospective client what he needs, rather than to insist that the client accept the auditor's traditional product?

Second, some federal agencies which use independent CPAs want information on the cost of an auditing service before engaging a firm. This has caused problems in states where Boards of Accountancy and CPA Societies hold that giving an indication of estimated cost is a violation of the competitive bidding rules.

I believe the profession should reexamine this posture. One reason, as you know, is that legal counsel advised the Institute five years ago that its rule on competitive bidding subjected it to risks under the antitrust laws. Another reason is that federal administrators understandably want some idea as to costs of services before they contract for them. Actually, this is not much different from the private businessman who insists on a fee estimate before engaging an auditor, and who obtains estimates from several firms -- except that the businessman's quest for this information does not attract the public attention that is directed to a published federal request for proposals.

A third area where the profession encounters problems with federal administrators is in client-auditor relations. When an audit of a business or non-profit organization is called for under a federal program, who is the client -- the entity audited or the government? If the profession maintains that the entity being audited is the principal client, is it any wonder that a government administrator may question the auditor's independence for the purpose of the administrator's own accountability?

These three problem areas are of major importance to the profession. Even though federal agencies want to use independent accountants, the continued existence of such obstacles may force the building of large staffs of government auditors to perform needed work.

The problems cannot be solved by individual CPAs or their firms, but only by the organized profession. And if the profession does not take the initiative, the issues will probably be resolved unilaterally by government agencies, one at a time, and perhaps to our detriment.

In the three cited problem areas, I suggest that the Institute take these specific actions:

1. Intensify efforts to establish professional standards for examining and reporting on internal control, compliance with laws, and performance under federal programs. Some good work has been done in these areas, but much more remains to be done.

2. Assume leadership in recommending a policy to State Boards and State Societies which will help them avoid confrontation with federal antitrust laws, will give independent auditors reasonable opportunity to submit fee estimates in response to requests from governments at all levels which is in the public interest, and still will guard against unscrupulous competitive bidding which is not in the public interest.

3. Clarify client-auditor relations to assure that audit reports to federal agencies and to owners and other interested parties are equal in independence and objectivity.

I realize that these three recommendations are not solutions, but actions which, with a lot of hard work, should lead to solutions.

Turning to another aspect of government-profession relations, there are at present more than 25 Institute committees which maintain liaison with various federal departments and agencies. No doubt more could be used effectively to help communicate with this vitally important sector. For the Institute has the opportunity to assume a more positive role in setting policies for the profession in its relations with the government.

Some individual CPAs and firms are now conspicuous in federal matters primarily because of work related to federal agencies. Occasionally, the attention they receive is unfavorable. For seldom is solid professional performance in an ordinary business-setting likely to attract attention. Only the problem cases get attention, and often auditors must share in criticism when things go wrong.

So far, I have been talking mainly about federal matters that affect the practice of public accounting directly. But a citizen should view his government also from the standpoint of its objectives in meeting the needs of the people. A citizen who is a professional man has a special obligation to consider how his knowledge could help the government in the accomplishment of its objectives. To do this in an organized way means that the Institute should take the lead.

There are federal issues of broad concern on which the Institute has taken a position, many more where it should take a position, and still others where it has an opportunity to take a position if it wishes to broaden its horizons and become known as a profession concerned with the great issues of the day. Let me give you some specifics.

For years the Institute has advocated accrual accounting for the federal government. The Executive Committee of the Institute issued a statement recommending the reporting of budget expenditures and receipts on an accrual-basis. The Budget and Accounting Procedures Act calls for accrual accounting and cost-based budgets. The concept of accrual accounting has generally been agreed to throughout the government, and good progress in adopting it has been made by many departments and agencies. Yet, the Department of Commerce is the only executive department to secure approval by the Comptroller General of the accounting systems of all of the department's major agencies with appropriate ADP documentation. This would indicate that the Institute could be more active in urging accrual accounting and budgeting for federal departments and agencies.

Government auditing standards are being developed by an Audit Standards Work Group composed of representatives from several government agencies including the General Accounting Office. The

Institute is keenly interested in these standards and has set up a task force to work with the government's study group. With this kind of close cooperation, it is likely that the Institute will want to support the standards which are ultimately adopted.

Clearly, accrual accounting and auditing standards are issues on which the accounting profession should have a position. But let me turn now to some issues which are not so directly identified as relating to our field of competence, but which nevertheless involve subject matter about which accountants have as much knowledge as other groups in the private sector.

One such issue is the proposals for reorganization of the executive branch of government. These proposals were recommended by the President's Advisory Council on Executive Reorganization and outlined by the President in his State of the Union message of January 22, 1971. Inasmuch as professional accountants have particular interest in and knowledge about concepts of organization, it is only fitting that the Institute take a position on this subject.

The proposals would consolidate seven existing cabinet departments into four new ones, with related functions grouped in the same departments. Admittedly, these recommendations are controversial, with opposition coming from some congressmen, affected departments, and special interest groups.

However, if the Institute wants to have a voice in national affairs, it must have the courage to speak up on issues. It does not take courage to support a non-controversial item -- and it follows that such support brings little credit.

If we really want to show courage, we should take a position on a separate recommendation of the Advisory Council which calls for a single administrator to replace multiple commissioners in certain regulatory agencies, including the SEC.

Many other issues should attract the scrutiny of the accounting profession. Take revenue sharing as an example. When the President proposed general revenue sharing, accountability became the most controversial feature. Critics contend the plan is devoid of accountability for the billions of dollars which would be handed over to state and local governments, and proponents claim accountability would be enhanced. Professional accountants are highly qualified to speak out on accountability.

The profession has an opportunity to take advantage of the current emphasis being placed on accountability. But to do so requires a reexamination of some basic attitudes, as well as allocation of more resources to studying major issues confronting our government.

I have touched on only a few matters which should be of concern to the accounting profession. And I have not even mentioned the federal income tax and securities laws, which are the federal areas best known to most CPAs. I hope I have conveyed, however, the idea that the federal government is of great and growing importance to us. I strongly believe that we should take budgetary and organizational steps to deal more broadly and more creatively than we now do with our relations in this area.

I am pleased to say that this general subject was discussed in some depth at the Board of Directors meeting on May 10. The Board expressed support for the idea that we develop additional capability to study the big issues of government, to determine appropriate Institute policies concerning them, and to make the positions known to the government and public. I look forward to an increasing effort by the accounting profession in federal government matters.

REPORT OF THE EXECUTIVE VICE PRESIDENT
Before Members of Council
of the American Institute of Certified Public Accountants
October 9, 1971

Today I want to talk about a few matters which I believe will be of interest to you. Some relate to happy circumstances, some not so happy; but they are things members of Council should know about.

Some of the matters are so highly sensitive that no constructive purpose would be served by circulating a written report about them. Therefore, I am asking that these remarks be off the record. I want to report to you in much the same frank and unrestrained manner in which I report to the Board of Directors on a more frequent-basis. It may be ominous that all of the matters I will discuss are directly related to actions of the federal government.

Wage and Price Controls

Late Wednesday afternoon, Secretary of Commerce Maurice Stans called to ask the Institute to furnish five or six highly qualified CPAs to spend one to two weeks full-time, beginning at 10 a.m. Tuesday, October 12, to assist in formulating guidelines for continuing wage and price controls. I am proud to say that, less than 48 hours later, the profession responded by submitting the names of eleven outstanding CPAs who are willing and able to aid the administration in this highly critical assignment. The profession has an excellent opportunity to perform a constructive public service, and to attain high visibility in doing so. Also, I understand that a CPA will serve on either the price commission or pay board that is being formed.

Competitive Bidding

On June 22, 1971, the Antitrust Division of the United States Justice Department issued a Civil Investigative Demand requiring the Institute to produce for their inspection all documents and correspondence in our files since January 1, 1967, pertaining to restraints against competitive bidding. We are uncertain as to what precipitated this action at this time. Probably the Justice Department is investigating anti-competitive rules and activities of various professional

43

organizations. But it is also possible that the action may have been instigated by a federal agency having difficulty in obtaining proposals for auditing services or by some other organization.

A Justice Department lawyer appeared at the Institute office on July 23 and took with him copies of dozens of items from among the hundreds made available to him. Shortly after that, the investigator resigned from the Justice Department, leaving further action to others in the Department. We do not know whether the investigation will be dropped or the Department will bring suit against the Institute for violation of antitrust laws.

Although the Institute has built a clear record of non-enforcement and attempted removal of the anti-competitive bidding rule in our Code of Professional Ethics, a Justice Department suit may be based on charges that the Institute has encouraged state societies of CPAs and state boards of accountancy to enforce comparable rules. We believe chances are good that the matter will be dropped. If not, the Justice Department will probably seek to enjoin the Institute from future acts which could be considered to be in violation of antitrust laws. Such an action should provide little cause for concern by the Institute.

In my view, a more likely outcome than a suit against the Institute would be an action against a state society of CPAs or a state board of accountancy that has vigorously enforced an anti-competitive bidding rule. Our legal counsel advises us that in any such confrontation the federal government would be in a very strong position, as rules prohibiting competitive bidding are in violation of federal antitrust laws. The government's case would be even stronger where the organization seeking bids is a government agency. The government has adopted the position that competitive bidding is in the public interest and rules against it are not.

The sooner that all segments of the profession recognize this fact, the better off we all will be. This does not mean that the profession should take a 180-degree turn and now encourage competitive bidding. It should be possible to adopt a rule prohibiting the quoting of an estimated fee which is so low as to virtually insure an inadequate performance of work.

I have some concern as to present practices. It is a common, and probably predominant, practice for a businessman to get some idea as to what professional services will cost before contracting for them. Often he will get an estimate of the cost of accounting services from one or more firms, whether or not there is an anti-competitive bidding rule in the state. Now is the time for all organizations within the accounting profession to drop their anti-competitive bidding rules, and get on with more constructive activities.

Equal Employment Opportunity

On September 15, 1971, we received a call from the Technical Assistance Division of the Equal Employment Opportunity Commission. The caller stressed that his office provided assistance and not enforcement of the act.

On September 24, he visited our office, spending some time with John Lawler, John Ashworth, Tom McRae, and myself. The representative pointed out that EEOC statistics on minority group representation among professional staff of accounting firms is only about 2%, which is low compared with minority group representation in the general population. I believe he was impressed with the Institute's program for integrating the profession. Nevertheless, his mission is to help us accomplish the job faster.

After doing what he can through the Institute, he plans to contact larger accounting firms to help them increase the percentage of minority group people on their professional staffs. One example of his help is to note that the head office of a firm encourages employment of minorities, but a branch office manager lacks the authority to spend money on a special training program for minorities. He spoke of holding public hearings to obtain more information about employment practices.

Our visitor also said his statistics show that women are being discriminated against in the accounting "industry," as he called it, particularly at the partner-level. Our effort to dissuade him from helping us along this line was to no avail, and he reminded us ominously that 51% of the population of the United States is female. So, unless 51% of your partners are women, brace yourself for a lot of technical "assistance" from EEOC.

Investment Credit

Few issues have caused the accounting profession so much grief and turmoil as the issue of accounting for the investment credit.

Although laid to rest by the Tax Reform Act of 1969, it is about to be reborn as the "job development credit," which will be part of the tax law to be enacted later this month.

Once more the Accounting Principles Board has an opportunity to set forth the proper method of accounting to be followed. And once more the APB seems to favor deferral of the credit and amortization of it over the life of the property as a reduction of cost. Yet, there is an understandable reluctance on the part of the APB to issue an Opinion, unless there is some assurance that the Securities and Exchange Commission will support it in practice.

We are now seeking that assurance, but we must recognize that the SEC is under no obligation to provide it, even if it should share the Board's preference for the deferral method. We have explored this subject with appropriate people in the SEC and the Treasury Department. I am optimistic that the APB will get the support it needs; but, to be fair, I must confess that some others are not optimistic.

Ideally, the APB should issue its Opinion based upon sound accounting principles, which will result in the fair measurement of income; and they should do this regardless of promised support or lack of it. The profession should follow that Opinion in practice, thus presenting a strong united front. If, in these circumstances, others take action to thwart the effect of the Opinion, they will clearly be responsible for any consequences, and the accounting profession will have performed responsibly. I confess, also, that many others do not share my view on this matter.

Change in Auditor

A recent encouraging development is the new SEC requirement for reporting a change in auditor. The Institute worked closely with the SEC in arriving at the Form 8-K reporting requirement.

In a dialogue continuing over several months, the SEC and the Institute became increasingly concerned over "shopping for accounting principles." The concern went beyond the relatively few instances where a change in auditor appeared to involve a dispute between auditor and client over accounting principles. The concern went to the pressure that might be applied by a client, even though a change in auditor is not made.

Proposed amendments on this and other matters were issued by the SEC for comment on May 6, 1971, and the final amendments were adopted on September 27. Now, if a new auditor has been engaged, the registrant must report on Form 8-K the date of engagement and furnish the Commission a separate letter stating whether in the preceding 18 months there were any disagreements with the former auditor about accounting principles which, if not resolved to the satisfaction of the former auditor, would have caused him to refer in his opinion to the subject matter of the disagreement. Furthermore, the registrant has to furnish the Commission a letter from the former auditor addressed to the Commission stating whether he agrees with the statements in the registrant's letter.

This reporting requirement goes a long way toward strengthening the hand of the auditor in dealing with his client. The public will benefit from improved accounting principles.

Stockbrokerage Accounting and Auditing

Troubles on Wall Street have focused attention on accounting and auditing problems of stockbrokers and dealers. Whenever an industry or even an individual company is in trouble, accounting and auditing are sure to be viewed critically.

Investigations are currently under way in both the House of Representatives and the Senate. Congressman John Moss' Subcommittee on Commerce and Finance has already held several hearings on the securities industry -- including sessions on the net capital ratio, use of customers' funds, surprise audits, information furnished customers, accounting procedures, and selection of auditors. Lee Dill and Ed Fisher, Chairman and a member, respectively, of the Institute's Committee on Stockbrokerage Accounting and Auditing, performed very well in testifying at the Moss hearings. But securities industry investigations are far from completed.

Senator Harrison Williams has announced his Senate Finance Subcommittee will be looking into the same area. Much of the attention on accounting arose from some spectacular failures on Wall Street. This criticism included a highly publicized investigative report by Louis Lefkowitz, Attorney General for the State of New York. His report wrongly heaped blame for the collapse of securities firms on the auditors, and ignored the fact that regulatory authorities are responsible for acting on weaknesses revealed by auditors' reports. The Institute has tried to set the record straight, and will continue to do so as occasions require; but this problem area may remain troublesome for some time.

Certified Pesticide Applicator

The federal government seems to be fascinated by initials, with many agencies and programs being readily recognized by them. Current fascination centers around our initials -- CPA. The latest "CPA" to come to our attention is the Certified Pesticide Applicator. The Institute has protested to the sponsor of the bill that he is taking our name in vain. But congressmen seem little concerned about our concern for protecting the dignity and sanctity of our professional designation.

We had earlier protested the use of CPA for the Consumer Protection Agency, which is contained in another House bill. But we were unsuccessful in getting that title changed.

If the Certified Pesticide Applicator bill becomes law, brace yourself for ads like this: "Troubled by rats, termites, cockroaches, vermin? Call your friendly neighborhood CPA." We are still trying to defeat this one, but if we can't beat them, maybe we should join them. Perhaps it would be satisfying and rewarding to extend professional services to include stamping out pests.

Summary

I have given you a brief review of just a few matters which are currently receiving the attention of the Institute. As I said earlier, they all relate to the federal government. And I believe that is the pattern of the future. If the profession wishes to control its own destiny, it must recognize this situation and organize in a way to deal with it effectively. Failure to do so will assure that the government will put us in a place where we don't want to be.

TAKING TIMELY ACTION
Before Members of Council
of the American Institute of Certified Public Accountants
May 1, 1972

This spring meeting of Council has an unusually heavy agenda, so I shall make my remarks relatively short. An advantage of this, besides saving time for discussion of the important matters on the rest of the program, is that at the conclusion of my comments you may applaud my brevity, if not my wit.

As you know, this is my last appearance before Council as the Institute's executive vice president. And I should like to take the occasion, not to present a formal report, but rather to offer a few observations of a somewhat philosophical nature.

Let me begin by simply reminding you of something you already know -- namely, that in the period during which all of us in this room have been in the practice of accountancy, our profession has grown immensely in scope, in prominence, and in importance. I believe it is no exaggeration to say that the vital role of CPAs in the nation's society and economy are more widely recognized today than ever before.

The increased awareness of our function and its significance has led to increased scrutiny of our activities, and also to increased expectations of our performance. The profession has responded to enlarged demands upon it in a fashion which I think any impartial observer would have to judge laudable. Tremendous effort and study have been devoted to serving the business community and the investing public in better and better ways.

But in today's world of instant communication, rapid technological development, and high social mobility, expectations rarely stand still. And it follows that our profession cannot stand still either. If it is to remain a vital, respected, and effective calling, it must -- through its organized bodies, particularly the American Institute -- respond promptly and appropriately to changes taking place around us.

And this brings me to the thought I want to leave with you as I stand at the edge of a big personal change -- a change from the public practice of accountancy, in which I was engaged for twenty years, and from work with the Institute, where I have been for five years, into corporate life as vice president and controller. My thought is this: Why do we so frequently see organization after organization, and group after group, delay in taking plainly necessary action until after the psychological moment has passed?

Perhaps the reason is a certain timidity. A person or group perceiving the first small signs of a need for some change or innovation, may think, "Why should we stick our necks out? Let's wait and see if somebody else tries it, and watch what happens to him." Or the reason may be just inertia, the natural reluctance to disturb behavior-patterns that have become comfortable: "Why rock the boat? The pressures aren't great as yet; maybe they'll evaporate." Whatever the reason, the result is procrastination.

Now, I do not know whether procrastination can rightly be called a vice, but its consequences can often be as damaging. The 19th-century English writer, De Quincey, gave this matter a reverse-twist in a humorous essay. "If once a man indulges himself in murder," he said, "very soon he comes to think little of robbing; and from robbing he comes next to drinking and Sabbath-breaking, and from that to incivility and procrastination."

One of the disadvantages of procrastination in the business and professional world is that of missed opportunity for building a good reputation. One gets scant credit for a desirable action if it is taken only after one's arm has been twisted.

Another disadvantage is that pressures may mount to the point where action is taken by some outside power -- probably government. In such cases, the action may be overdone instead of being fitted nicely to the circumstances; and the excess produces ills of its own. Or the remedy may be unnecessarily constrictive, because it was devised by people unfamiliar with the industry or business to which it was applied.

The sad thing about such over-reactions or ill-formed remedies is that they could so often be easily avoided. Those who are successfully engaged in a given field of endeavor are in position to perceive needs for improvement sooner than anyone outside the field.

Professional advertising people, for example, probably spot a misleading advertisement sooner than the Federal Trade Commission. An auto manufacturer can detect a weakness in a new model car before Ralph Nader. Wall Streeters are likely to know about derelictions in certain brokerage houses before the faults force themselves upon the attention of the SEC. Labor leaders are no doubt aware of undesirable union practices before they grow to a stage that can sully the whole labor movement. Auditors can discern accounting practices that flout the profession's standards before a company falls into disaster.

All these groups -- the advertising profession, the auto makers, the Wall Streeters, the labor leaders, the CPAs -- all of them, I'm sure, want to have as much freedom as possible to run their own affairs and to set the standards for their work. And it is right that they should, for they are the people who are most knowledgeable about how to conduct the work intelligently and efficiently. They also know how to conduct it decently and with full regard for the public interest, whether they do so or not. The way to keep such activities in the private sector, and not to have more and more of them gravitate into an all-pervasive, cumbrous political bureaucracy, is to take alert, timely, and responsive action.

In our own profession, if we are to preserve the right to run our own affairs, we must make better use of the fact that we know more about accounting problems than anyone else. In all the comments in the public press these days, have you seen much written about accountancy that you didn't hear some thoughtful accountant enunciate five or ten years ago? What criticism has there been that wasn't expressed first within the profession?

Peter Drucker, the economist and author, has pointed out that whenever a group has been the first to suggest the need for controlling its activities, it has invariably been granted a large hand in whatever legislation had to be written. This has been illustrated by the experiences of our own profession. Largely through the state societies, for example, the profession has taken the lead in getting state legislation to assure that those practicing public accounting have sufficient education and competence to protect the public. The Institute has developed the uniform CPA examination and advisory grading service, which have become the national standard for measuring the competence of all who seek to enter the profession.

More recently, the profession became the first to recognize the need for continuing education, with the drive being led by the profession in Iowa and later being endorsed by this Council. The Institute has also acted to guide the profession in the area of technical standards. The Institute has steadily and successfully led the way toward higher auditing standards over a period of more than half a century. In the area of accounting principles the profession has similarly been the spearhead.

In addition, we can identify several specific opportunities to participate in the shaping of standards or legislation where, in doing so, the profession did have or could have a great deal to say about the rules it must live by. The positions on accounting taken in the Securities Acts and in their administration were conceived in large measure from the findings of the joint study by the Institute and the stock exchanges. The study pointed up the need for the reform of financial reporting practices and, because we helped to determine the need, we had a good deal to say about how reform was to be effected.

Several years later the Committee on Accounting Procedure was formed, and over the next twenty years its 51 Bulletins clarified existing practice. Progress was made, but dissatisfaction persisted because of the wide variety of principles that were still acceptable. We responded with the creation of the Accounting Principles Board, backed by a highly competent staff. It has tackled many tough assignments, and has been subject to many pressures. But it cannot be claimed, after thirteen years and 21 Opinions, that progress was not made.

We are now entering a new era, with the examination of a new concept in establishing financial accounting standards -- a full-time Board, independent of professional and business organizations; yet, hopefully, attuned to their needs and to the public interest. Thus, another opportunity is presented for continuing to determine financial reporting standards in the private sector.

The accounting profession owes no apology for the fact that progress has not been made as fast as many people (myself included) would have liked. But it should face up to the fact that, in our past efforts, we have tended to the failing of procrastination.

The changes now proposed are wide-ranging, and modifications may be needed to achieve the results we all desire. But, irrespective of the final form of structure and methods, the accounting profession bears an ultimate responsibility to itself and to the public. It can and will meet this responsibility as long as it heeds the ringing declaration (slightly paraphrased) of the philosopher Comte: "Integrity is our principle, order is our foundation, progress is our goal."

Integrity has always been fundamental to the profession, and must be preserved at all costs. Our foundation of order has not been so firmly established, perhaps, as some other aspects of the profession; but when Bob Trueblood's group completes its work, I am sure that the conceptual foundation will be greatly reinforced. Then, with the support of all groups concerned with financial reporting, substantial progress can become a continuing reality.

Finally, I must tell you that I leave my position at the Institute with deep regret. But I assure you that I shall continue to take an active interest in its affairs and those of the profession. I might even speak out from time to time, a habit I have developed over the last five years and may find difficult to give up.

I wish to thank my colleagues on the staff who daily make so many positive contributions to the well-being of the profession. They constitute an impressive array of talent, including more CPAs than in most CPA firms and more Ph.D.'s (or the equivalent) than in most university accounting faculties. Not only do the non-technical and technical staff members present a wide diversity of abilities and interests, they consistently display a united dedication to the profession.

I am continually amazed at the extent to which our members give unstintingly of their time to the Board of Directors, to Council, and to the many boards and committees which keep our Institute functioning. To all these people we owe a debt of gratitude.

As we enter a new era for the profession, I would like to conclude with the words of the late John Kennedy who said, "It is time for a new generation of leadership to cope with new problems and new opportunities. For there is a new world to be won." If the Institute continues to recognize problems as they arise, and if it leads in taking action to solve them, the accounting profession will become even more respected -- and more essential than it is today. I am confident that this new world of accounting can and will be won.

SECTION II:
GENERAL PROFESSIONAL ISSUES

A VIEW OF THE ACCOUNTING PROFESSION AND ACCOUNTING EDUCATION FROM A PROFESSIONAL ACCOUNTANT IN INDUSTRY
Before California CPAs 1974 Accounting Education Conference
California State University -- Hayward
February 22, 1974

I am pleased to have this opportunity to express my personal views about the accounting profession and accounting education.

Accountants in Industry Are Part of the Accounting Profession

Your conference organizers asked me to present "a view from outside the profession." However, they gladly agreed to my request to change the title to "a view from a professional accountant in industry."

To me, this is an important distinction, for I believe I am still in the accounting profession. When I entered industry, I did not change appreciably. My background of 25 years of professional experience in public practice and with the American Institute of CPAs was not suddenly forgotten. My respect for professional and ethical standards remains.

I still feel like a professional accountant, and I believe that other accountants in industry do, too. By "professional accountant" I mean an accountant with a sound knowledge of accounting who approaches his work with objectivity and integrity, and adheres to professional and ethical standards.

I have consistently taken the position over a period of several years that accountants in industry are part of the profession broadly construed, and that they should adhere to standards of the profession. If all accountants, in industry as well as public practice, were united in a common dedication to professional standards, the role of accounting would be greatly strengthened. There would be fewer accounting-related scandals, and there would be greater public confidence in business as a whole and the private enterprise system.

Let me refer to one bit of evidence of my longstanding dedication to professionalism for accountants in industry. Nearly a decade ago, I suggested to a National Association of Accountants audience that their organization develop a code of ethics for management accountants. This stirred up some interest and my comments were published in

57

Management Accounting and other journals, although the suggestion still has not been adopted. I acknowledged that a code of ethics is only one hallmark of a profession and that enforcement of it would be difficult, but concluded that an attempt should be made to set up and enforce a code of ethics to demonstrate that accountants in industry are part of the accounting profession.

Now, as the chief accounting officer of a large multinational company, I have tried to instill a professional attitude in all of the people throughout the accounting organization. We expect our division and subsidiary controllers and other accountants to be professional accountants. We expect them to maintain the integrity of our accounts and our financial statements. Our policy is to adhere to professional standards. This policy has caused an occasional confrontation with other members of the company's management team, who, for reasons justifiable to them, believed deviations from these standards best served the company's interests. For example, a manager wished to report operations for a 33-day month, but our policy prohibited this. In such cases, our professional standards have prevailed, and in so doing, have earned respect for the accountants.

I hope that in this brief introduction I have made a case for the proposition that accountants in industry are part of the accounting profession. So, if you will pardon my personal prejudices on that subject, I will proceed to give some views on the professional practice of public accounting.

My Views of Public Accounting Have Changed Somewhat

Public accounting is a field with which I have been closely associated for all of my adult life. It has been very good to me. It has provided enormous professional satisfaction and reasonable financial rewards. I still admire and respect public practice as much as I always have. But now public accounting doesn't look quite the same to me as it did when I was in public practice and when I served as chief spokesman for the American Institute of CPAs. I do not disavow positions I have taken in those previous capacities and I do not wish anything I say to be construed as derogatory or representing an attack on public accounting. Yet, some of my views have changed.

Practicing Accountants Display Mixed Attitudes Toward Industrial Accountants

For example, the thing I resent the most about CPAs in public accounting is that they are all younger than I am! Beyond that, it seems to me that public accountants practice in an environment which leads to a strange mixture of attitudes toward accountants in industry. Occasionally, I have noted a touch of arrogance and condescension -- which may be aggravated by an "I gotcha" approach when mistakes are found -- but which is never noted when the fee is submitted.

In fact, some deference is absolutely necessary, if the public accountant wants to retain the client. Those who are skilled at the care and feeding of a client have an annuity for life. My company has had the same auditing firm for 57 years.

When they are not collecting fees, superiority feelings of practicing public accountants may be ill-concealed. Public accountants seem to view themselves as having superior knowledge of accounting. Frequently they take the position that Mr. X won't make it with us, but he would be a good employee for you. Also, our method is right and your method is wrong, even in cases where official literature is silent on the subject and other authorities are divided. A superior attitude is only a natural consequence of being an outside expert. And in fairness to all, I might add that occasionally accountants in industry feel superior to those in public accounting. But such an unwarranted posture is seldom displayed at a level below vice president and controller.

Auditing is by its nature a process of looking for mistakes and it leads often to an "I-gotcha" approach. Auditors must get satisfaction from finding errors. A profession devoted to reviewing the work of others would be dull indeed if it were impossible to find something that needed to be changed. Yet, the smoothest public accountants are those who hide this bit of satisfaction.

Which is More Broadening, Public Accounting or Industrial Accounting?

An argument is often made that public accounting is a broadening experience because the practitioner is exposed to so many different clients. It is true that the auditor does enjoy a broad view of many businesses, but he covers only a narrow range of accounting and financial information -- only enough to give a professional opinion on the fairness of the financial statements. Furthermore, his knowledge of each client is superficial compared to that of the client's own accountants. Tax and management services specialists in public practice experience a similar breadth of clientele and narrowness of professional expertise.

Thus, accountants in public practice, while broadly exposed to many businesses are narrowly confined to their special function within the overall field of accounting. On the other hand, accountants in industry, while narrowly confined to one company, are broadly exposed to all facets of accounting.

Even public reporting of financial information, with which public accountants are associated, is the direct responsibility of accountants in industry. But public reporting is a small part of their function. In addition, they provide the information needed to manage the business. They keep the books, prepare management reports, prepare budgets, analyze profit plans, prepare tax returns, audit operations, maintain accounting and financial controls, and participate in a wide range of management decisions.

Public Accountants Perform a Useful Function

Even though their range of professional interests is limited, public accountants are nice people to have around. Their opinion is essential for adding credibility to our financial statements, thereby increasing investor confidence in our company. It is comforting to know that public accountants are checking our records, for we sometimes do make mistakes. It is also good to have a review of our judgment in applying professional standards, for certainly we are not infallible.

Public accountants are noted for their integrity, competence, and independence. This is important to us, for association with auditors having these qualities reflects well on us.

The auditing function is helpful in assuring that financial statements are presented in a manner that is not false and misleading, for management bears the direct legal liability if they are not so presented. I am well aware of the legal liability under the Securities Acts for the presentation of financial information that is false and misleading. My office is next door to our vice president and general counsel and we are in almost daily contact. We try hard to follow the letter and the spirit of the laws; and, consequently, I sleep well at night, and so does he, he says.

Accountants in Industry are Future-Oriented

Industrial accountants are concerned not only with operating results of the month just ended, but also with forecasts for the current month, the current quarter, the current year, and the next five years. Public accountants seldom get involved in these things. It is rewarding to be part of a management team that is operating a business in a competitive environment and to know that the accounting function is an absolute necessity for planning and attaining goals.

Earlier this month our auditors were working long hours ticking and checking accounts which entered into 1973 results of operations. Earnings had been published weeks earlier and nothing short of discovery of a major error would change them. Meanwhile, we closed the books for January and issued and analyzed the operating results.

We were also analyzing profit forecasts for February and having fun preparing revised 1974 profit plans for nearly all operating units. This was necessary due to a host of current developments, such as the collapse of the economy in England, floating foreign exchange rates, and world-wide shortages of energy, materials, and components.

Public accountants do not get involved in all that fun. Some would like to, but most of them seem shocked at the thought of being associated with a forecast. They have good reason for their concern, for forecasts are difficult to meet and circumstances on which they are based are constantly shifting. Yet, I believe that demand by investors and pressure from government regulators will some day force the public accountants to provide opinions on the reliability of forecasts.

Some Disclosures Are Influenced More by the SEC than the Accounting Profession

Several interesting dialogues with our auditors took place recently concerning information to be disclosed in our 1973 annual report, which is being mailed to stockholders today. We encountered only minor differences of opinion on determination of income, and these were easily resolved. On matters of disclosure, however, we were far apart.

Everyone in the accounting profession seems to have some vague and different standard of materiality for disclosure of financial information.   Only the Securities and Exchange Commission is consistently coming up with specific standards of materiality. For example, *Accounting Series Release No. 149*, issued in November 1973, calls for improved disclosure of income tax expense, and sets forth percentage materiality tests for disclosing components of total tax expense, tax effects of timing differences, and reasons for the tax expense being different from amounts computed by applying the U.S. federal income tax rate to income before tax.

Our auditors quite correctly pointed out that the Release states that these detailed disclosures will be primarily of interest to professional analysts and may not be required in financial disclosure designed for the average investor. Nevertheless, we insisted that all disclosures required by *Release No. 149* be made in our annual report to stockholders.

We believe stockholders should have ready access to the same information used by analysts, and we have noted the trend to make annual reports more like the Form 10-K report filed with the SEC. SEC Commissioners for years have been urging companies to present more of the 10-K information in the annual report to stockholders. In the case of the income tax disclosures, I am happy to include them in the annual report, for security analysts ask for this information routinely, and I feel better about disclosing it to them now that all stockholders will have it, too. In fact, I am grateful to the SEC for providing a standard form for presenting the income tax information. Investors will become accustomed to the format and will find it easier to make comparative analyses of different companies.

Accounting Series Release No. 148, also issued in November 1973, called for disclosure of compensating balances and short-term borrowing arrangements. Again, our auditors noted the comment in the Release that the disclosures are of primary interest to analysts and may not be required in financial disclosure to the average investor. As there was no guidance as to what may or may not be required, we decided to put all of the disclosures in the annual report.

Thus, we are acknowledging and contributing to the trend to make the annual report look more like the 10-K. For years we have incorporated the annual report financial statements in the Form 10-K, but we have had to file several additional pages of information in compliance with SEC regulations. In this year's annual report we stated we would furnish stockholders a Form 10-K upon written request. Our board of directors is pleased that our management is insisting on fuller disclosure than that recommended by our auditors.

The SEC Will Continue to be the Dominant Force in Determining Accounting Standards

In preparing our 1973 financial statements, the only new official pronouncements which had an important impact were those of the SEC. Terminal production of the Accounting Principles Board in 1973 concerned interim financial statements, non-monetary transactions of which we had none, unusual transactions of which we had none material in amount, and disclosure of lease commitments which was completely overwhelmed and superseded by SEC *Release No. 147*. The new Financial Accounting Standards Board issued a modest Statement calling for disclosure of foreign currency translation gains and losses. We could have ignored it on grounds of immateriality, but chose to make the disclosures anyway.

In *Release No. 150*, issued in December 1973, the SEC said it would look to the FASB for leadership in establishing and improving accounting principles. Yet, by its actions in other Releases, the SEC has shown it will not wait for the FASB when it sees a problem that needs resolving.

Even *Release No. 150* promised the SEC would be active in this area. The FASB has clearly moved into the same subordinate position to the SEC which was vacated by the APB. And the American Institute of CPAs, for which I retain a deep affection and loyalty, has joined the swelling ranks of organizations which comment, usually negatively, on proposals of rule-making bodies like the FASB and the SEC.

No longer do the large accounting firms have a representative on the rule-making body. They will have no personal involvement to provide a degree of respect and responsibility for the pronouncements of the FASB. Some may point out that these qualities did not apply to APB Opinions either, as some firms can claim with considerable justification that their partner on the APB dissented to nearly every Opinion the APB issued.

In abandoning its rule-making function the AICPA has lost its most conspicuous source of prestige and good public relations potential. At the same time, it has extricated itself from the center of dissent and turmoil caused by recalcitrant accounting firms that were more interested in pushing their own views than in working within the institutional structure and reaching a consensus. These firms may merely redirect their efforts to the FASB, in which case professional disarray will continue to be displayed. Thus, the loss of the APB leaves the public image of the accounting profession more at the mercy of the accounting firms -- by the actions and positions they take, and by any scandals they become involved in.

Perhaps it is of passing interest now to note that the event which, for all practical purposes committed the AICPA to ultimate abandonment of responsibility for accounting principles, took place on January 7 and 8, 1971, at the Watergate -- at a meeting of managing partners of 21 firms, clandestinely arranged, but later publicized as a major advancement in determination of accounting standards in the private sector. From this meeting emerged the studies of the objectives of financial statements and of the organizational structure for setting accounting principles.

Meanwhile, the success of the FASB will depend on the willingness of the SEC to support it on controversial issues. Beyond that, the survival of the FASB will depend on the combined ability of the SEC and the FASB to counteract congressional lobbying, which will inevitably arise over issues such as capitalizing leases and pooling of interests.

Another interesting development to watch will be the attitudes of modestly paid (but powerful) SEC Commissioners and staff toward highly paid (but powerless) FASB members and staff. Although I am no expert in human behavior, I will not be surprised if the SEC gets some quiet satisfaction out of "zinging" the FASB on occasion.

Accounting Educators Do an Excellent Job in Preparing Students to Enter the Profession

I have already talked too much about my views on the accounting profession and I would like to take a few moments to talk about accounting education. I continue to be impressed by the excellent job accounting educators are doing in preparing young men and women for entry into the profession. The body of knowledge of accounting has expanded considerably; yet, educators have found ways to impart the expanded knowledge to accounting students successfully. Let me comment on just two specific educational issues.

Education for Public and Industrial Accountants Should be Essentially the Same

I have come to question the need and desirability for having two separate tracks for educating accountants for public practice and industry. I believe that the fundamental knowledge needed for either field is basically the same. There are greater differences within public and private practice than there are between them. In both public and private practice, there are specialists in taxes, auditing, systems, and operations research.

College education should be designed only to prepare a person for entry into a profession, not to teach him a specific job. He must learn how to perform the job when he is assigned to it. On the other hand, once the common body of knowledge is covered, I see no reason why, if hours are available for electives, a student should not be permitted to elect additional managerial accounting courses or public accounting courses according to his desires.

The Accounting Profession Needs Professional Schools of Accounting

Another matter of accounting education I have advocated for some time is the professional school of accounting. Of the several attributes of a profession -- a body of specialized knowledge, a professional school, a qualifying entry examination, professional standards, a code of ethics, a public interest in the work performed -- public accounting lacks only the professional school. I believe that a professional school of accounting can be a viable institution if the approach is broadened to include education for industrial accounting as well as public accounting, and if the school is not severed from its natural business environment. A professional school of accounting within a college of business administration would add greatly to the prestige of the profession and enhance public recognition of accounting as a real profession. It should also attract more bright students who could then clearly see accounting as a professional field and not merely a difficult and probably dull adjunct of business. I am aware of the controversial nature of this suggestion, but I believe the advantages of a professional school of accounting outweigh the disadvantages.

Finally, I cannot resist passing along some advice. I do not know how much SEC rules are taught in college, but I urge you to give this subject a great deal of attention. There is a wealth of material which could constitute a separate course.

Conclusion

From my remarks, I think you can tell that I enjoy being a professional accountant in industry. This is a privilege I never planned or expected, or even considered to be a privilege when I was in public accounting practice, for I was one of the most zealous extollers of public accounting's virtues of the time. I still have the highest respect for this part of the profession and those who practice in it.

My only regret is that I cannot at the same time be a practicing professional accountant, an industrial professional accountant and an educator of professional accountants. Thank you for your kind attention, and for letting me express my personal views on the accounting profession and accounting education.

PERSONAL VIEWS OF ACCOUNTING EDUCATION
Before the 23rd Annual Illinois Accounting Educators Conference
Northern Illinois University
November 12, 1982

Ladies and gentlemen. I now live in Michigan and teach in Indiana, but I am always glad to come home to Illinois. The last time I was here in DeKalb was May 5, 1965, when I spoke on the subject, "Don't Be a Continuing Education Drop-Out," at the Northern Illinois University's College of Business Administration Annual Awards Dinner. Many important events in my life have occurred since then, not the least of which is that Professor Ray McClary's CPA-son, Tom, married my CPA-daughter, Joan. I am very happy to be with you here in DeKalb tonight.

As you know, I am now on the faculty at the University of Notre Dame, which has long been known for its excellence in teaching theology, ethics, and accountancy. After last year's football season, we added a course in humility.

This evening I would like to talk about the future of higher education, in general, and then speculate how the expected developments might impact upon our field of interest, accountancy. Finally, I would like to make some observations about relationships between the educational needs of the accounting profession, both public and private, and the academic institutions providing the accountancy education.

Some wag has said, "It is always difficult to make predictions, especially about the future." For higher education, however, we are fortunate in having a comprehensive report on the next twenty years, until the millennium -- that is, the year 2000.

I refer to the final report of The Carnegie Council on Policy Studies in Higher Education, under the chairmanship of Clark Kerr of Berkeley. The report, entitled "Three Thousand Futures," was issued in 1980 after seven years of study. The president of Notre Dame, Reverend Theodore Hesburgh, used this report as the theme of his entire address to the faculty last month. I shall refer to the report only to set the stage for reviewing the future of accountancy education.

The report lists thirteen reasons for gloom and doom, followed by fifteen reasons for hope. Thus, hope wins out, numerically at least, but the council seems to have strained to tip the balance. We are told that

67

there is no compelling reason for either panic or euphoria, that what is most certain is that the next twenty years (eighteen now) are full of uncertainty, that higher education's recent problem of managing growth has suddenly become a much more troublesome and difficult problem of managing retrenchment, and finally, that the last three decades of full steam ahead through clear seas to wide open horizons now are to be followed by two decades of avoiding shipwreck and planning survival. I will refer to several salient points in the report:

1.   There is not one future, but three thousand futures for higher education -- that being roughly the number of individual institutions and the title of the report. Each institution must study itself and prepare for its own future.

2.   Although the future is mostly uncertain, we do know some facts. The students who will attend our institutions in the year 2000 are already born, and there are 23.3% fewer of them than the number now attending our institutions. With fewer students available, competition for them will become intense. Students are the lifeblood of colleges and universities, public ones because they are generally funded on a per capita basis and private ones because they operate mainly on tuition income. Although it is depressing to think of this, dozens, perhaps hundreds, of institutions will not be around in the year 2000.

3.   Another fact is that more than half of the current faculties in higher education were appointed in the 1960's and 1970's. About three-quarters of them are on tenure and thus will be holding most of the available faculty positions until the millennium. This suggests slim hopes for junior faculty competing for tenure and for those who are seeking Ph.D.s for teaching posts that do not exist. Think of what it will mean to have an aging and aged faculty not being stretched by younger colleagues.

4.   Now for the uncertainties: Which institutions will get the fewer available students? What happens to new programs and new facilities in the face of diminishing financial

support, from the federal and state governments or from donors who now have their own new financial problems? What happens to "research" when funds run out?

5.   When financing shrinks and inflation grows, a whole series of things happen with a high degree of certainty: Positions are vacated without replacement. Salaries presently paid get frozen or reduced. Maintenance is deferred, which means you pay ten times more later to replace the whole roof for not having fixed the leak. Laboratory equipment becomes not one, but two, or three generations obsolete. Library resources are cut, books are not bought, and periodical subscriptions are cancelled. Computer facilities shrink or become outdated, or both. Programs without sufficient students or strength are cancelled and with them, attending faculty, even though tenured. New promising programs are simply shelved for a better day, new opportunities lost for decades. Faculty development, books and travel, sabbaticals, conferences, secretarial help, fringe benefits all look relatively unimportant in the face of survival. This is not a complete list of the adverse consequences that will be felt in higher education as we approach the millennium, but it is enough for the Council's report to forecast that many institutions will die. But enough of the bad news.

The good news can be put in more of a capsule form, and it is both a wish and a possibility. At Notre Dame, we throw in a prayer as well. The good news goes: The strong institutions might just get stronger, not by growing externally, but by pursuing frugality, integrity, and quality internally. It will require a good deal of analysis by all parts of the university to be sure of the facts and to predict, as far as possible, the general uncertainties as they will or will not apply. This will call for leadership and understanding on all levels of the university, cooperation of all in applying stringent solutions instead of competing for scarce turf. Fundamentally, all must believe that in a time of potential disaster, their institution can and will not only survive, but prevail.

I will not go into details of what a college or university should do to achieve this lofty goal, because the diversity of institutions will undoubtedly lead to different strategies for different institutions. However, a few items in the report seem to me to be worth universal consideration. Quality is central to the whole endeavor and should be the focal point to be emphasized and not compromised in any and all academic adjustments in a time of crisis. In the face of financial adversity, it is better to do fewer things and do them well, than it is to spread the effect of a cutback evenly across all segments of the university. The institution must also seek ways to make more effective use of resources.

With that broad overall view of higher education until the millennium, let us consider how higher education in accounting might fare.   The accounting profession has been a growth profession throughout this century, and in the 1960s and 1970s growth has been phenomenal.   Students have been attracted to accounting in large numbers as they became aware of increased salaries and attractive professional work.

There are signs, however, that the days of rapid growth are over. The latest study by the American Institute of CPAs notes that there is a somewhat stabilized demand for accounting graduates. The study notes that while the demand for public accounting recruits in 1972-73 was up 28 percent over the previous year, the 1980-81 demand rose only 1 percent over the previous year. The AICPA figures show that CPA firms will have about 17,700 positions this year and about 20,200 positions in 1984. The pool of graduates will be about 60,000 and 65,000 in the respective years. Many of these graduates will take positions in industry and government.

The AICPA projections are for a very short period, only three years, because of the difficulty of predicting farther in advance. Nevertheless, the AICPA study shows growth in the number of accounting students through 1984, whereas the Carnegie report charts a high point for the number of students in the years 1979-1983, followed by a decline to a low point in 1997, then rising again to the 1983 level in the year 2010.

I am certain that the general decline in student population will have some impact on the number of students majoring in accounting. Yet, I believe accounting will fare better than most fields of study. The recent slowing of growth in demand for accounting graduates probably results from the prolonged recession that has produced a slowing of growth across the entire economy. When the economy regains vitality, as I am sure it will, the factors which have made accountancy a growth industry will still be in place. These include increasing complexities in accounting standards, securities laws, and tax laws. Also, the public has been demanding increasing accountability from virtually all institutions in our society. As growth in demand for accountants increases, the number of accounting students should increase as a percentage of total students.

I would like to quote from Father Hesburgh's address to the faculty two years ago. He said:

> The most popular course on the American college campus is not literature, not history, but accounting. I do not say this to denigrate accounting -- it is important to know how to do it and to do it well. However, I think the single fact that a how-to-do course is more popular than the traditional liberal arts courses is indicative of many modern currents of educational thought regarding the purposes of higher education, what education might be expected to produce, what the country most needs at this particular time from its educated citizens, and, especially, how all this relates to the position of our country, America, in a wider world context.

Although Father Hesburgh did not denigrate accounting, he was plainly not pleased at its popularity compared with liberal arts. How will this popularity and this attitude toward it, which surely must be shared by other administrators, affect the future of accounting education? I believe that institutions of higher learning as a whole will provide the accounting education that students want. Competition for dwindling resources within a particular university may result in a decline in course offerings in accounting in that university. Nevertheless, in the system of higher education as a whole, I believe accounting departments will enjoy relative prosperity.

How can an administrator overlook the department which continues to grow in numbers of students or, at least, declines in numbers at a slower rate than other departments. In many universities, the business school, in general, and the accounting department, in particular, provide revenues which support the essential, but less popular, liberal arts departments. In a declining student population, this phenomenon is likely to be accentuated.

Altogether, in competing for scarce resources and for survival, accounting should fare very well in most circumstances. I am not suggesting that accounting should push out the liberal arts. Far from it. The accountant should first be broadly educated and then educated in business and the accounting profession.

Some forty years ago when I was in college, an undergraduate accounting major was required to take about half his courses in liberal arts and sciences, a quarter in accounting and a quarter in other business subjects. I see little change in that mix today. Even the five-year programs which are appearing provide no diminution of the liberal arts and sciences.

Perhaps we should concentrate on merchandising the liberal education issues in accounting, which are not widely understood outside the profession, and perhaps not widely recognized inside the profession. Father Hesburgh lists a number of human questions liberally educated students should consider, among them the conflicting roles of truth and error, certainty and doubt, integrity and perverseness. All of these issues are encountered in the accounting profession. The whole basis of the attest function is fairness. I believe a case can be made for making accounting a required course within the College of Letters and Arts. It has at least as much usefulness and relevance for a well-rounded educated person in our business-oriented society as college algebra.

The accountant plays a central role in the management of business and in the allocation of resources throughout our society. His decisions determine how financial results of operations will be reported, and these decisions are made within a framework of high professional and ethical standards. From my background in public accounting, as an executive in industry, and as chairman of the audit committee of several boards of directors, I think of the accountant as the conscience of business.

The accountant is in a position to determine truth or error in situations where the dichotomy is clear. The accountant has the independence to make the morally and ethically correct decision when certainty and doubt are in conflict. The accountant is in a better position than most others involved in business to distinguish between integrity and perverseness. Thus, the questions Father Hesburgh says liberally educated students should learn are being answered daily by accountants.

Although I acknowledge that there inevitably are "how-to-do" aspects to accounting education, I believe deeply that there are important human questions which can and should be introduced into accounting education. Now that I am an educator, of sorts, I try to do just that, and I encourage others to do likewise.

Accounting courses will be perceived to contribute to a liberal education only if the public is made aware that fundamental human issues are involved. Throughout my career, I cannot remember a time when accountants, businessmen, and educators were not telling each other about the rapid changes that were taking place in accounting issues, data processing, business practices, industrial technology, educational methods, and almost anything else one could mention. This observation has usually been followed by a plea for closer relations and better understanding between the academic community and business and the accounting profession. I agree that good relations and understanding are very desirable, but I think this condition has existed for a long time and continues to exist. The accounting profession has always been highly supportive of education, through grants, faculty internships, furnishing speakers at academic classes and conferences, and in many other ways.

I continue to be impressed by the excellent job accounting educators are doing in preparing young men and women for entry into the profession. The body of knowledge of accounting has expanded considerably; yet, educators have found ways to impart the expanded knowledge to accounting students successfully. Let me comment on just two specific educational issues.

I have come to question the need and desirability for having two separate tracks for educating accountants for public practice and industry. I believe that the fundamental knowledge needed for either field is basically the same. There are greater differences within public and private practice than there are between them. In both public and private practice, there are specialists in taxes, auditing, systems, and operations research.

College education should be designed only to prepare a person for entry into a profession, not to teach him a specific job. He must learn how to perform the job when he is assigned to it. On the other hand, once the common body of knowledge is covered, I see no reason why, if hours are available for electives, a student should not be permitted to elect additional managerial accounting courses or public accounting courses according to his desires.

Another matter of accounting education I have advocated for some time is the professional school of accounting. Of the several attributes of a profession (a body of specialized knowledge, a professional school, a qualifying entry examination, professional standards, a code of ethics, and a public interest in the work performed) public accounting lacks only the professional school. I believe that a professional school of accounting can be a viable institution if the approach is broadened to include education for industrial accounting as well as public accounting, and if the school is not severed from its natural business environment. A professional school of accounting within a college of business administration would add greatly to the prestige of the profession, and enhance public recognition of accounting as a real profession. It should also attract more bright students who could then clearly see accounting as a professional field and not merely a difficult and probably dull adjunct of business. I am aware of the controversial nature of this suggestion, but I believe the advantages of a professional school of accounting outweigh the disadvantages.

Let me assure you that I do not advocate, nor do I foresee, the early demise of four-year programs in accountancy. The market for their graduates will not permit it. At Notre Dame, for example, we do not have a five-year accountancy program, nor do we have a concentration in accounting within our MBA program. Yet, recruiters descend upon our campus in droves to hire our four-year program graduates.

A five-year program is a logical evolution, but, in my opinion, we are at least several decades away from having this the only way to enter the profession. Also, the professional school faces many obstacles. Political considerations within universities are difficult to overcome. What business school dean wants to give up control over entrance requirements, curriculum, granting of degrees, and budgetary matters of his largest and most prestigious department? Of the professional schools now in existence, many of them appear to be marketing strategies, wherein titles of "School of Professional Accountancy" and "Dean" are substituted for "Department of Accountancy" and "Department Chairman," with little or no autonomy.

In closing, thank you for your kind attention, and for letting me express my personal views on the accounting profession and accounting education.

SHOULD THE PRACTICE OF PUBLIC ACCOUNTING BE LIMITED TO THE GRADUATES OF PROFESSIONAL SCHOOLS OF ACCOUNTING?
Before the Symposium on Professional Schools of Accounting
Sponsored by the Ohio Society of CPAs
Columbus, Ohio
April 23, 1976

Good afternoon, ladies and gentlemen. I am pleased to participate in this Symposium on Professional Schools of Accounting -- and to share the platform with an old friend, Joe DeMaris.

I must confess some puzzlement as to my role in these proceedings. In his letter about the Symposium, Charles Mecimore stated that a practitioner has been paired with an educator in an attempt to present views with potentially different self-interest. This pleased me for I felt that he was considering me, an industrial accountant, to be a "practitioner" of professional accounting, because Joe certainly is the educator. Then I looked at the agenda and saw that my specific topic is: "Should the practice of public accounting be limited to the graduates of professional schools of accounting?" This question seems to brush aside the educational needs of industrial and governmental accountants, but I intend to touch on that subject anyway.

I could answer the question "yes" or "no" and sit down. Or I could answer it "no for the present, but yes for the long term, several decades into the future." In the interest of full disclosure, I must confess my bias in favor of professional schools of accounting, and I have written and spoken on this subject before.

The Ad Hoc Committee coordinating this Symposium developed a brief outline of the area to be discussed, and I will try to be responsive to its wishes. The Committee starts off with the proposition that "the public interest needs to be recognized in arguing for the establishment of professional schools of accounting."

I think we can all agree that the public has shown a great need for the services of public accountants, for public accounting has been among the fastest growing professions. Public accounting was unheard of when this nation was founded. In this Bicentennial Year, there are more than 150,000 CPAs in the United States, of whom more than 100,000 are members of the American Institute of Certified Public Accountants. The number of AICPA members has doubled in the last ten years. Many CPAs are not in public practice: but, on the other hand, many accountants in public practice are not CPAs. These figures indicate that the profession of public accounting is important and growing rapidly.

It is obvious that this growth has been sustained by the existing educational institutions, so that the real issue is whether professional schools of accounting can *better* educate professional accountants. In recent visits to campuses, I have been impressed by the large numbers of students enrolled in accounting programs, and also by the quality of the students.

The Ad Hoc Committee has suggested that in considering professional schools of accounting, the public expects competent professional assistance at a cost commensurate with the benefit to be received. In spite of the public's increased demands for public accounting services, the public is probably not concerned as to whether public accounting is a profession, and has little awareness of its professional education needs.

The growth and prosperity of the public accounting profession has demonstrated that the benefits of public accounting services have justified the costs in the past. I have no doubt that this would be true of the added costs of a graduate degree from a professional school of accounting. Throughout the growth of the profession, there has been a trend toward more and more accounting education. A bachelor's degree is the minimum entry requirement for public accounting now, although an increasing percentage of entrants have graduate degrees.

While the advanced education leads to higher costs, the public has been willing to pay for it. And the accounting firms have become prosperous indeed. At least one large public accounting firm publishes an annual report that discloses a very high average compensation of its partners.

Some resistance to the higher costs of a professional degree may be provided by undergraduate students who are anxious to graduate and find a job. As a person who was raised during the depression and was about to get a bachelor's degree thirty years ago, I can sympathize with those who want to end educational costs and begin earning an income.

Nevertheless, public accounting entrants with graduate degrees apparently believe that the benefits of obtaining that higher degree are worth more than the costs of obtaining it. So do accounting firms apparently believe that job applicants with advanced degrees are worth the higher salaries they must be paid. I believe this cost-benefit relationship would be even more favorably regarded for a professional school of accounting.

The growth of public accounting obviously has been supplied from existing institutions. In fact, the growth and prosperity of public accounting are outstanding tributes to the existing schools and colleges which have educated the entrants to the profession. My advocacy of professional schools should not be interpreted as criticism of our fine existing institutions.

Nevertheless, for professional schools of accounting to flourish and ultimately become the only source of entrants into public accounting practice, they will have to compete successfully with these existing institutions. Their ability to compete successfully will depend on whether the competitive advantages outweigh the competitive disadvantages. The Ad Hoc Committee has revealed its bias by listing several competitive advantages of professional schools and barely hinting at competitive disadvantages.

Looking at the advantages, a highly visible professional school would counteract some of the negative influences prevailing in some business schools today. There is a tendency for business schools to consider themselves solely schools of management or administration, with a virtual elimination of functional specialization. In some cases the catalogs of graduate business schools make no mention of accounting. In other cases, the number of hours a student can devote to accounting is limited to as little as 12 semester hours. In these circumstances, where is a student to prepare for a career as a professional accountant?

The autonomy of a professional school faculty would permit effective control over the curriculum which could be designed for the specialized needs of the person entering the accounting profession. Accounting is the only recognized profession within the field of business and it has the only identified body of knowledge. For this reason alone, a professional school would have a solid curriculum on which to stand.

One objective of the educational program of a professional school should be to equip students with the knowledge necessary for successful CPA examination performance. Yet, within business schools and even among some accounting professors, we hear continuing criticism of accounting review courses designed to help students pass the CPA examination. On the other hand the accounting profession has shown a great interest in retaining these courses, and in hiring graduates who have taken review courses and passed the CPA examination.

Law schools are expected to prepare students to pass the bar examination, and nearly all law graduates do take and pass the bar upon completion of law school. Among graduates of accounting programs, the nationwide percentage of those passing the CPA examination upon completion of the program is very low by comparison, with fewer than 30% of those taking the examination passing it the first time.

Medical schools are not referred to as "doctor mills." Law schools are not referred to as "lawyer mills." With the advent of professional schools of accounting, perhaps we could end forever derogatory references to strong accounting programs as "CPA mills."

The CPA examination itself is now academically oriented and each examination coincides more closely with the recommended content of the Common Body of Knowledge. I think it is significant that this body of knowledge extends well beyond the confines of business. The professional accountant is concerned with social measurement and governmental and other nonprofit accounting subjects, such as program budgeting and program review and evaluation.

A visible professional school would benefit entrants to the profession in an intangible, but important, way by providing career identification. Career identification is a normal urge on the part of many students at some point in their college years. Identification as an "accounting major" does not adequately satisfy this desire. Attendance at a visible professional school would serve to identify people who are headed for a career in professional accountancy.

This professional identification should make it easier to attract capable people -- both students and faculty. Outstanding faculty would be drawn to these programs because of the opportunity to work with graduate students in their specialized fields of interest. The program should also attract a desirable class of students having three or four years of liberal arts or engineering undergraduate backgrounds. Some of the best young people do not make their career decision until after three or four years of college and it is important to have a school to accommodate them.

A visible professional school of accounting would also enhance two important functions which professional schools typically contribute to their professions -- development of professional consciousness and creation of new and better professional knowledge of practical import. These functions suffer in the absence of the strong sense of professional identification that a visible professional school provides.

A professional school of accounting offers the opportunity to develop professional attitudes and consciousness among its students. It can emphasize development of a strong sense of public and social responsibilities so important to the work of all accountants, whether in public practice, industry, or the public sector. At a time when the ethical standards of the profession are challenged by charges of insufficient independence and objectivity, a professional school of accounting could perform an important role. By bringing together students with similar career interests, a professional school can engender a cohesiveness and ethical attitude which carries over to their later professional life.

Social responsibility is a popular subject these days and sometimes its injection into a discussion is too glib. But social responsibility is not a fad in the accounting profession. Our concern with responsibility to the public goes back several decades. Now that public attention is focused on the social responsibilities of business, the accounting profession has an opportunity and is strategically placed to act as the social conscience of the business community. We cannot, however, fulfill this function adequately unless appropriate attitudes are instilled at an early point in future accountants.

A visible professional school of accounting is also in a strategic position to identify pressing professional problems and to work in cooperation with practitioners in seeking solutions through research. A university professional school is well-equipped for the task of applied research. Its academic environment makes it possible for all members of the staff to be part-time scholars and researchers, and for some to carry on these activities full-time, borrowing the resources of knowledge from other university departments.

Scholars of the sociology of professions have noted that medical professors enjoy a higher status vis-a-vis practitioners than is found in other professions. They believe this is due, in part, to the fact that medical research has produced more dramatic results than research in most other professional specialties. Consequently, medical schools have probably played a larger part in medical history than other professional schools have in the development of their disciplines.

In contrast, accounting research performed for the Accounting Principles Board was noted in the Wheat Committee Report as being ineffective in assisting the APB to establish accounting principles. Also, many accountants would probably agree with me that much of the accounting research reported in the *Accounting Review* seems to have little relevance in developing professional standards and disciplines. A professional school should provide a favorable setting for more productive research. There is ample potential in the field of accounting for beneficial change through research, and I am sure there would be commensurate recognition for such accomplishment.

Notwithstanding the many advantages of professional schools of accounting, there are some practical problems in establishing them. Not the least of these problems is the existing structure of an accounting department within a business school and the practical politics of change within a university administration. Deans are not likely to look with favor upon spinning off an area as important as accounting, and university presidents are not likely to welcome another administrative unit to deal with.

Furthermore, university presidents usually come from disciplines other than accounting and they may not appreciate the significance of a professional education for accountants. For example, a few years ago while on an airplane, I sat next to the president of another Big Ten university -- one not so well known for its football team as Ohio State, but with a highly regarded accounting department. I tried to interest him in the attractions of a professional school of accounting. He summarily dismissed the idea by saying if he let the accountants have their own school, the advertising people, insurance people, marketing people, and other specialists would want their own schools and then there would be no remaining business school.

I respectfully disagreed with this proposition, but I do not underestimate the practical political problems of establishing new professional schools of accounting within existing administrative structures. Universities seem to be less willing to change organizational structures than the accounting profession.

In the continuing saga of setting accounting standards, the accounting profession every few years comes to an impasse on principles, but instead of solving its problems by reference to basic objectives, postulates, principles, and standards, it destroys an old structure and starts a new one which continues its work in the same fashion as the old.

Another benefit a professional school can expect is the generous support of the practicing members of the profession -- in both monetary contributions and in time and effort. A professional school would be able to draw upon the experience of the most capable members of the profession, as well as the material advantages of financial support. Strong financial support may help in convincing university administrators of the merits of the professional school.

A frequently raised objection is that a professional school would lead to excessive specialization (too many accounting courses) and a narrow education, with undue emphasis on education for public accounting over other fields of accounting. This objection reflects too narrow a view of accounting in general and the practice of public accounting in particular. Public accounting is moving toward (and in many cases has achieved) a scope of practice that encompasses all elements of the information system, even though some members of the academic community may still retain a view of accounting that does not encompass this variety of skills and knowledge.

The same body of knowledge should be suitable for the education of all professional accountants, whether or not they expect to enter public practice. There are greater differences within public and private practice than between them. In both public and private practice, there are specialists in taxes, auditing, systems, and operations research. The professional school I favor would not be limited to a school of public accounting. It would be called a "school of professional accounting" and would attract students planning accounting careers in industry and government as well as in public accounting.

Recognition is growing that the public interest is involved in everything the CPA does. He carries his professional status and obligations with him into industry and government. Thus, a professional accounting program at the graduate-level could have a broadening influence. Students would have an opportunity to become acquainted with many new concepts, both in accounting and other business subjects, which the crowded undergraduate curriculum cannot accommodate.

A related set of objections concerns the role of non-accounting subjects. According to this argument, accounting programs could not be operated in a "vacuum," apart from a college of business which provides the administrative structure for faculty and course work in areas such as quantitative methods, computer science, business law, organization theory, and other subjects important to and related to academic preparation for accounting. If the professional school remains within the administrative structure of the college of business administration or is separate but closely related to business administration, the problems of attracting outstanding faculty in non-accounting areas and developing non-accounting courses of desirable quality do not arise.

In the final analysis, the desirability of professional schools of accounting is not the sort of question that can be answered by rational argument alone. Many value judgments are involved and so are emotions. The several advantages and disadvantages being discussed here today are typically raised in discussions of professional schools of accounting to forecast the consequences of such schools and, thereby, to determine the most desirable course of action. This is a common and a sound approach to resolving questions of value judgment.

I believe the advantages far outweigh the disadvantages. However, the only real answer is to actually implement a professional school of the type suggested. I believe we should encourage these actions and get on with the establishment of professional schools of accounting.

Back to the original question of "should the practice of public accounting be limited to the graduates of professional schools of accounting? My answer is "yes." But, it is a long road to travel from no professional schools to a network of professional schools sufficient to meet the growing demand for professional accountants. However, there is no better time to start in this direction than now.

Some of our best professional advances have occurred when we reached outside the profession to have other professionals help provide us with insight more objective than we ourselves can have. The Common Body of Knowledge Study was headed by Dr. Robert Roy, an engineer. The Study on Establishing Accounting Principles was headed by Francis Wheat, a lawyer. I suggest that the AICPA and the American Accounting Association collaborate in sponsoring a study headed by a non-accountant to examine as objectively as possible the merits of professional schools of accounting, and (if found meritorious) to explore practical means of changing the institutional structure of education to accommodate these schools.

A study like this could examine all facets of a professional school and identify specific problems to be overcome. Such a study should provide guidelines for those who wish to establish professional schools of accounting. I would be interested in your reactions to this suggestion, and I thank you for letting me share my thoughts with you today.

THE PURPOSES OF EDUCATION
Before Alpha Eta Chapter of Beta Alpha Psi
University of Michigan
April 2, 1975

Fellow members of Beta Alpha Psi and ladies and gentlemen. I appreciate the opportunity your Chapter has provided for me to participate in your initiation program. I had the good fortune of being initiated into Alpha Chapter of Beta Alpha Psi a long time ago. It was a stimulating experience, and I remain grateful for having had this extracurricular exposure to faculty members and fellow students who were dedicated to professional accounting education.

Partly because of this experience, I have become thoroughly committed to the virtues of education as a lifelong pursuit. Since leaving public accounting and entering industry, I have come to think more in terms of a broad business education than just accounting education, but I assure you I consider accounting to be a most important aspect of business.

Over the years, education for business has advanced greatly within higher educational circles in terms of quality, credibility, and respectability. Business education has become accepted as a major avenue for entry into business management, and business management is increasingly recognized as playing a leading role in developing and maintaining our economic well-being.

History has shown that a solid economic base facilitates cultural development. Therefore, it is not surprising that we find commerce and culture to be entirely compatible in business and in education for business.

This proposition is consistent with the educational approach taken at the Graduate School of Business Administration of the University of Michigan and at other leading business schools. Specialized education in business is provided to those who have already been exposed to broad areas of liberal arts and sciences.

This concept of specialized and general education is not new, however, for it has long been accepted as the appropriate route for education in law, medicine, and other professions. Philosopher, mathematician, and educator, Alfred North Whitehead, said in his 1916 essay, *The Aims of Education*:

Culture is activity of thought, and receptiveness to beauty and humane feeling. Scraps of information have nothing to do with it. A merely well-informed man is the most useless bore on God's earth. What we should aim at producing is men who possess both culture and expert knowledge in some special direction. Their expert knowledge will give them the ground to start from, and their culture will lead them as deep as philosophy and as high as art. We have to remember that the valuable intellectual development is self-development.... As to training, the most important part is given by mothers before the age of twelve.

Whitehead's thoughts on the aims of education remain as valid in 1975 as they were in 1916. I believe that the best business schools are aiming at producing men and women who possess both culture and expert knowledge in business.

Bear in mind that I say "aiming at," for no university by itself can produce educated people. Knowledge cannot be assimilated without exerting the effort for learning. I know of no way for a person to learn without exerting effort. Learning is a matter of attitude -- with a properly eager, inquisitive approach, not only formal courses but virtually all everyday activities become learning experiences.

All education is really self-education. Educators can only make available educational opportunities and inspire individuals to devote the necessary time and effort to educating themselves. John W. Gardner in his book, *Self-Renewal*, said:

The ultimate goal of the educational system is to shift to the individual the burden of pursuing his own education. This will not be a widely shared pursuit until we get over our odd conviction that education is what goes on in school buildings and nowhere else. Not only does education continue when schooling ends, but it is not confined to what may be studied in adult education courses. The world is an incomparable classroom, and life is a memorable teacher for those who aren't afraid of her.

I believe, as does Gardner, that education should be a lifelong process. Let me discuss briefly three reasons why continuing education is a vital necessity today.

First, continuing education is a traditional means of getting ahead. The young person willing to work hard, to study, to improve skills and knowledge has always been the one who has progressed. This has not changed. A reminder of this route to success is particularly appropriate for business students, as they are being educated for leadership in business. The ones who fulfill the promise of leadership are those with the vitality and interest to continue their education, those who are ever alert to opportunities to learn and to put this learning to use. *The New York Times* reported more than a decade ago that, "Education rather than a wealthy father is the new American key to managerial success." And they went on to back this up with hard statistics taken from a research study.

Second, in today's rapidly changing world, a great deal of education is required just to stay even. To meet this challenge of change, new skills and new techniques are being developed daily. This is just as true of business management (and the many functional components of it) as it is of engineering and scientific fields. In the field of accounting, for example, a strong movement is sweeping the states toward a requirement for formal continuing education as a condition for renewing the state license to practice public accounting.

In addition to being needed for getting ahead and for staying even, there is a third need for continuing education -- and it is on a higher plane, totally apart from job considerations. This need relates to individual self-fulfillment and to cultivating interests which increase enthusiasm and add flavor to life. Today there is a great emphasis placed on making a useful contribution to society. The person who does this at the same time makes a useful contribution to his or her own development and satisfaction. An individual must use the abilities he or she has and devote them to worthwhile endeavors. Psychological research has proven that the need for self-fulfillment can be a powerful motivator.

As viewed from the world of business, what was studied in college is yesterday's knowledge. What is being studied today is today's knowledge. But what will be needed for a future business career, is tomorrow's knowledge. No one wants to learn outdated skills or to teach them. Yet, there is no established body of knowledge which will survive and suffice for a career in business. Techniques of production are rapidly changing. Marketing methods are undergoing constant research and experimentation. Accounting practices are evolving steadily.

The real education that we are seeking is more a way of thinking which will enable us to solve problems, to learn new techniques and practices, and to approach future problems with creativity and imagination. This kind of education will bring confidence in one's own ability so that changes in business practices, in industrial technology, and in social behavior will not erect a wall of fear. This kind of education is for the good of the individual, for the good of business, and for the good of society. It will never go out of date.

We have learned that there are no diminishing returns to education. Those with the highest education are those most likely to be continuing their education. They feel a need for still more knowledge, and there is no saturation point for this need. They are not satisfied to learn superficial techniques, but they establish interests on a deeper basis; they seek understanding. They have a positive attitude toward learning and toward life.

No matter how much education one has, it is not enough. It will not last a lifetime; it will soon be obsolete.

Students joining the Alpha Eta Chapter of Beta Alpha Psi at Michigan are doubly fortunate. First, you are attending one of the world's greatest universities; and, second, you are becoming members of a fine professional fraternity devoted to improving professional business and accounting education.

You are off to a great start. I hope you will be inspired to continue learning for the rest of your lives.

BUSINESS ETHICS AND GOVERNMENT REGULATION
Cardinal O'Hara Memorial Lecture
The University of Notre Dame
March 29, 1976

Thank you very much. Ladies and gentlemen, I am honored to be invited to deliver a Cardinal O'Hara Memorial Lecture. This is a great tradition you have in honoring his Eminence, Cardinal O'Hara, and I will try to live up to that tradition.

As a businessman and an accountant, I am particularly pleased to have the opportunity to talk to future business and accounting leaders. There are two subjects I wish to discuss with you: business ethics and government regulation; and I believe there is a strong relationship between the two.

For several months we have been reading almost daily of new disclosures of bribes and illegal payments made by some companies. These actions have been widely reported in the press and the result has been serious damage to the reputation of American business at home and throughout the world. I have no doubt that many students have become disillusioned with business and would like an explanation of this behavior.

The great majority of business people and business organizations join you in demanding explanations, for all of business has been tarnished unjustly by the actions of a guilty minority. I am carefully calling for explanations, not excuses, for there can be no excuses for illegal behavior. We must always obey the laws, no matter how much we disagree with them. If laws are onerous, we may seek to change them through proper legislative channels, but we must not disobey them.

Those found guilty of making improper payments have been punished severely -- by damage to their reputations and in some cases termination of careers -- and some still face legal actions. These sins will not soon be forgotten.

But here is where I see a bright spot in an otherwise dismal picture. The public has shown that it will not tolerate improper behavior, and this situation demands that we take a new and hard look at ethical standards. We have an opportunity to extend the high level of ethical behavior practiced by the innocent majority to embrace the entire business community, and thus restore public confidence. But this is easier said than done. The problem is *how* to do it.

One simple positive step to help restore public confidence is for business leaders to speak out in favor of honesty and fair dealings in the conduct of business. If they do not make these views known, silence may be interpreted as condoning illegal and unethical behavior and thus may more firmly entrench in the public mind the notion that everyone is doing it and only the unlucky have been exposed. Should this view prevail, our entire free enterprise system would be in jeopardy.

Recently, suggestions have been made that the business community should prepare a code of ethics and police itself according to its own ethical standards. In an article on business ethics published in several accounting journals in 1965, I recommended that business establish a code of ethics. The idea attracted some attention in accounting circles, but I felt that I was a voice in the wilderness and the idea did not get very far. Now that it has become stylish to recommend a code of ethics, the idea has much less appeal to me.

The reason for the lessened appeal of a code of ethics for business is that such a code would be unenforceable and possibly illegal itself in some respects. In fact, the National Association of Manufacturers has had a Code of Business Practices for several years; however, it unfortunately has not been very effective, perhaps because enforcement is so difficult.

"Business" includes thousands of operating units, and there is no organizational structure for administering an ethical code. Also, business is highly competitive and attempts by one competitor to police or censure another would arouse the suspicion of self-interest. If companies in one industry were to try to censure one of its group, this would surely raise serious anti-trust questions.

Even bar associations, medical associations, and accounting associations have seen their highly respected codes of ethics come under anti-trust attack. The lawyers are being attacked for their ban on advertising, and the accountants have been forced to drop their rules against competitive bidding.

I question the effectiveness of ethics codes in providing public protection. Most ethics codes are designed, first, to protect members from outsiders; second, to protect members from each other; and, third, to protect the public from unethical members.

The Code of Professional Ethics of the American Institute of Certified Public Accountants, for example, is enforced quite effectively in matters dealing with protection of members, but disciplinary machinery works very slowly in matters affecting the public. In nearly every case of alleged violation of technical accounting and auditing standards affecting the public, legal action is pending or threatened. Ethics enforcement is thwarted until the defendant's last right of appeal in the courts has been exhausted, and this may be eight or ten years after the alleged violation of technical standards.

Enforcement of the Code of Professional Ethics at this point is anticlimactic, ineffective, and trivial. The worst sanction under the Code is expulsion from the Institute, which is seldom imposed. When expulsion does occur, it usually is a mild punishment compared with that already meted out by the court. Thus, in matters of major importance, laws and the courts provide the public with protection as to competence and technical standards of accountants. Self-regulation through the Code of Professional Ethics cannot do this.

I can find no reason to believe that business, which lacks the single national organizational structure of accountants, could do even as well in enforcement of a code of business ethics. Although a censuring agency in the business community is unworkable, the publication and widespread distribution of a code of business ethics may have a salutary effect on the behavior of business people.

Many, perhaps most, companies have written or unwritten policies stating that their employees are expected to refrain from illegal and unethical behavior. Surely companies that do not have such policies (and even many that do) would benefit from having a national code of conduct for adoption or for guidance in setting their own standards.

The board of directors of the National Association of Manufacturers stated earlier this month that adoption of individual codes of good business conduct by member companies represents a more practical and viable approach to business ethics than any attempt by NAM to write, monitor, and enforce a code of ethics for American business generally. NAM President E. Douglas Kenna went on to say, "The individual company management is in the best position to define derelictions and to apply censure to those who may violate standards of ethical conduct."

Top management of a company can set an example of ethical behavior and can establish enforcement procedures for adherence to ethical policies. Even this is not easy to do in a company with far-flung operations and decentralized decision-making. Many companies today are drafting more formal codes of conduct concentrating on two areas of current controversy: political contributions and overseas payments to increase sales.

Political contributions by corporations are not inherently immoral, but they are illegal in the United States. In contrast, they are legal in certain other countries. In a speech in Ann Arbor last month, Thomas A. Murphy, Chairman of General Motors Corporation, said, "In neighboring Canada, for example, General Motors has contributed equally to the support of both major political parties -- and our action was not only legal, it was expected, both looked for and looked upon as a responsible act by a responsible corporate citizen."

We must learn that we cannot impose our laws and our ethical standards on the rest of the world. In other countries, their laws and ethical standards prevail. In hearings before the House Subcommittee on International Economic Policy, Mark Feldman, Deputy Legal Adviser of the Department of State, said: "It would be not only presumptuous but counterproductive to seek to impose our specific standards in countries with differing histories and cultures." Moreover, enforcement of such legislation -- and I think this is the most important point -- would involve surveillance of the activities of foreign officials as well as U.S. businessmen and would be widely resented abroad.

Extraterritorial application of U.S. law, which is what such legislation would entail, has often been viewed by other governments as a sign of U.S. arrogance or even as interference in their internal affairs. We must obey the laws of every nation in which we do business, but we ourselves may follow higher ethical standards if we find local practices objectionable.

We often hear that payments to government officials are customary in a particular country, even though these payments are clearly illegal bribes. In our company, we believe that we should not make payments like that; and, if competitors are willing to make these payments, we are prepared to lose that business. Our goal is to distribute our products in every nation in the world where we are permitted by law to do so. And this is without regard to whether we approve of the country's form of government or policies. We believe free trade and fair business practices can be a constructive force in any nation.

Often business people are confronted with hard choices in countries with political and economic structures widely different from our own.

Paul McCracken said the following in a speech last month:

> Those nations where government manages extensively the
> details of economic life tend also to be corrupt societies.
> Where favorable government decision is the route to success,
> rather than performance in open and competitive markets, it
> should surprise no one that increasingly the price for favorable
> decisions will be paid and received.

What makes business decisions so difficult is that often there is no
clear-cut standard to follow. In some countries business is done through
commission agents, who perform a service in completing a sale to
government agencies. Where those commissions are legal in the
country, is the American company obligated to find out what the
commission agent did with his commission?

Some decisions involve the dilemma of choosing the lesser of two
evils. Killing in self-defense is a classic example. Medical and legal
dilemmas are found in currently debated issues of abortion or an
unwanted child, and prolonging life by extraordinary means or peaceful
death.

In business hard choices can also exist. I am told that one
company resorted to bribing only when it learned that its very survival
was at stake. Of course, this does not mean that we should condone the
illegal act. I understand that another company resorted to bribery when
it was threatened by the government with confiscation of its entire
business. When faced with this kind of extortion, there is no easy
choice.

These companies apparently acted in what they thought was good
faith in carrying out their stewardship function on behalf of
stockholders. But there are times when moral behavior should be
placed higher than stewardship responsibility.

The Wall Street Journal recently quoted a "simple" test proposed
by Arjay Miller, dean of Stanford University's Graduate School of
Business: "Do that which you would feel comfortable explaining on
television." I do not contest the wisdom of that statement, but I submit
that there is a more complex, more profound, and more satisfying test:
"Do that which you would feel comfortable explaining to your
conscience." A well-defined *personal* code of conduct should be

helpful in making conscientious business decisions.

I have difficulty envisioning separate levels or degrees of morality between business life and private life. A good place to start is to be honest, tell the truth, and obey the laws. To do otherwise will not support a long successful career in business, but will almost inevitably lead to ultimate failure and disgrace. Having a solid *personal* code of conduct should help greatly in facing ethical decisions. But it will not entirely eliminate hard decisions.

I believe that, in the long run, *ethically right* decisions are also *economically right* decisions. I don't believe that a company can enjoy a long period of success as a result of illegal and unethical practices.

Not surprisingly, the illegal and unethical payments have brought forth demands for aggressive governmental action. This leads me to the second subject I wish to discuss: business regulation. Regulation is a phenomenon that has happened over and over again, not only to business but also to other groups. When the public becomes dissatisfied with the performance of any sector of society, it pushes government into action because private efforts were too little and too late.

Why do we so frequently see organization after organization, and group after group, delay in taking plainly necessary action until after the psychological moment has passed? Perhaps the reason is a certain timidity.

A person or group perceiving the first small signs of need for some change or innovation may think, "Why should we stick our necks out? Let's wait and see if somebody else tries it, and watch what happens to him." Or the reason may be just inertia -- the natural reluctance to disturb behavior patterns that have become comfortable: "Why rock the boat? The pressures aren't great as yet; maybe they'll evaporate."

Whatever the reason, the result is procrastination. Now, I do not know whether procrastination can rightly be called a vice, but its consequences can often be damaging. The 19th century English writer, Thomas De Quincey gave this matter a reverse twist in a humorous essay: "If once a man indulges himself in murder," he said, "very soon he comes to think little of robbing; and from robbing he comes next to drinking and Sabbath-breaking, and from that to incivility and procrastination."

One of the disadvantages of procrastination in the business and professional world is the missed opportunity for building a good reputation. One gets scant credit for a desirable action taken only after one's arm has been twisted.

Another disadvantage is that pressures may mount to the point where action is taken by some outside power -- probably government. In such cases, the action may be overdone instead of being fitted nicely to the circumstances; and the excess produces ills of its own. Or the remedy may be unnecessarily constrictive because it was devised by people unfamiliar with the industry or business to which it was applied.

The sad thing about such over-reactions or ill-formed remedies is that they could so often be easily avoided. Those who are successfully engaged in a given field of endeavor are in position to perceive needs for improvement sooner than anyone outside the field.

Professional advertising people, for example, probably spot a misleading advertisement sooner than the Federal Trade Commission. An auto manufacturer can detect a weakness in a new model car before Ralph Nader. Wall Streeters are likely to know about derelictions in certain brokerage houses before the faults force themselves upon the attention of the Securities and Exchange Commission. Labor leaders are no doubt aware of undesirable union practices before they grow to a stage that can sully the whole labor movement. Auditors can discern accounting practices that flout the profession's standards before a company falls into disaster.

All these groups -- the advertising industry, the auto makers, the Wall Streeters, the labor leaders, the CPAs -- want to have as much freedom as possible to run their own affairs and to set the standards for their work. And it is right that they should, for they are the people who are most knowledgeable about how to conduct the work intelligently and efficiently. They also know how to conduct it decently and with full regard for the public interest, whether they do so or not. The way to keep such activities in the private sector, and not to have more and more of them gravitate into an all-pervasive, cumbrous political bureaucracy, is to take alert, timely, and responsive action.

In the accounting profession, if we are to preserve the right to run our own affairs, we must make better use of the fact that we know more about accounting problems than anyone else. In all the comments in the public press these days, have you seen much written about accountancy that you didn't hear some thoughtful accountant enunciate five or ten years ago? What criticism has there been that wasn't made first within the profession?

Peter Drucker, the economist and author, has pointed out that whenever a group has been the first to suggest the need for controlling its activities, it has invariably been granted a large hand in whatever legislation had to be written. Corporate financial executives and the public accounting profession have had a hand in developing accounting standards. But they have not acted soon enough to ward off a virtual avalanche of new rules that have descended upon us from several directions.

As a result, American business today is highly regulated in the way it must report financial information to investors, government agencies, and others. This regulation is imposed upon business by several rule-making bodies, which have begun to issue conflicting rules.

No one can deny that great progress has been made in corporate financial reporting in the first three-quarters of the twentieth century. Yet, today we continue to be faced with criticism of financial reporting because of our failures to arrive at fundamental goals, together with an orderly set of guidelines for implementing the goals, and a suitable organizational structure for issuing and enforcing the guidelines.

In 1926 William Z. Ripley, a professor of economics at Harvard, caused a stir with a bristling attack in *The Atlantic Monthly* on the inadequacy of corporate financial reporting of that era. To illustrate the attitude of some managements, Ripley cited a paragraph from the annual report of a company he did not identify:

> The settled plan of the directors has been to withhold information from the stockholders and others that is not called for by the stockholders in a body. So far no request for information has been made in the manner prescribed by the directors. Distribution of stock has not meant distribution of control.

After describing deficiencies in other annual reports, resulting presumably from the same sort of thinking, Ripley wrote: "Stockholders are entitled to adequate information and the State and the general public have a right to the same privilege."

That was fifty years ago, and there were virtually no rules for accounting and financial reporting. Since then the American Institute of Certified Public Accountants has mounted several concerted efforts to define, clarify, standardize, and expand generally accepted accounting principles. Still, these efforts were not timely enough to forestall a host of legislative regulatory actions.

The Securities Acts of 1933 and 1934 brought into the picture a federal agency, the Securities and Exchange Commission, with the mission of requiring companies to make full disclosure of business and financial affairs. Their disclosure requirements have grown extensive over the years.

According to an old saying, there are two ways to deceive the public: one is to tell them nothing and the other is to tell them everything. In the 1926 case cited by Ripley, the company told stockholders nothing. Now, fifty years later, the SEC seems determined to force companies to tell stockholders everything. We are happy to comply with full disclosure, but there are times when we wonder if disclosure of massive financial details may be confusing to some stockholders.

Since 1973, the responsibility for establishing accounting standards has been assumed by the Financial Accounting Standards Board, a private sector body supported by the accounting profession and business. This Board is the latest in a series of private sector bodies which have undertaken a huge responsibility to carry out a regulatory function without having the authority to do so. Although this certainly is a commendable effort on the part of those who are regulated to have a hand in shaping that regulation, so much governmental regulation has already been undertaken that the psychological moment for maximum private sector impact has passed. And this has happened in spite of a desperate yearning on the part of the accounting profession and business to keep the rule-making function in the private sector.

The SEC is the primary agency of general scope in this field. It has worked closely with the FASB and has shown a willingness to accept FASB positions in many cases. The SEC has also flexed its muscles on occasion and overruled the FASB. This seems to be happening now in the attempts of both bodies to deal with disclosure of the effects of inflation on financial statements. The FASB came out with a proposal to require companies to present supplemental financial statements adjusted to units of general purchasing power. In contrast, the SEC last week issued new rules calling for disclosure of current replacement cost information in notes to financial statements. As a result of this conceptual conflict, the FASB proposal will probably be dropped.

Recently Congress recognized the relationship between the SEC and FASB. The energy pricing bill calls for the SEC to set accounting standards for the petroleum industry, but specifically authorizes the SEC to recognize accounting practices developed by the FASB.

Many other bodies are involved in accounting and financial reporting rule-making. Treasury Department rules have the effect of law; and, where conformity of tax and financial reporting is the price to be paid for tax saving, these rules are authoritative. Tax saving produces cash flow, and is usually more important to a company than defense of a specific principle of accounting.

Some industries are affected by still more rule-making bodies, such as the Federal Power Commission, Interstate Commerce Commission, and Civil Aeronautics Board. And there are other agencies which make rules for special purpose reporting, like the Federal Trade Commission and Cost Accounting Standards Board. These agencies may have an effect on public financial reporting in the future.

Even Congress has ruled on specific accounting principles in connection with Lifo inventories and accounting for the investment tax credit. This complex environment of accounting regulation leaves the private sector body in a precarious position.

While there remains room for the FASB to perform a constructive role in the accounting rule-making function, we should recognize its limitations. We should be aware that the FASB has been legally foreclosed from dealing with some subjects, and that its pronouncements are limited in scope and subject to approval of others. Setting accounting standards is a political process carried out in a political environment. The FASB is not writing on a clean slate -- it must deal with rules that exist in the environment that exists.

As rules proliferate, the role of the independent accounting firm is changing from advocate of preferable accounting methods selected from among several available, to advisor as to the specific accounting method which is applicable in compliance with the rules. Further progress may be made in establishing the objectives of financial reporting. But progress to the most strident voices often calls for a complete change from the historical cost-basis of accounting. For example, it is fashionable to talk in terms of introducing "economic reality" into financial reporting. The trouble is that few can agree on what constitutes economic reality and how it should be measured.

Presumably, economic reality requires reporting in terms of current values or fair values. But this would lead accounting information farther away from the commercial enterprise goal of using cash to make a profit and generate more cash to return to its owners. Nevertheless, debate on issues like this is healthy and ultimately leads to changing basic objectives of corporate financial accounting.

Meanwhile, further progress will be made in accounting rule-making, and somehow industry will survive the plethora of rules. Management will find a way to run its business under any accounting regulations imposed on it.

Even with our peculiar overlapping rule-making structures, I see hope for cooperation among rule-makers in moving toward a more coherent conceptual basis for accounting. But to expect a neat set of basic objectives, broad standards, and detailed rules -- all totally consistent with each other -- is expecting too much of a practical art. If that could be accomplished to the general satisfaction of all concerned, it would have been done long ago. Accounting progress will continue to be accomplished in a practical, political way through debates and confrontations, which are lively, spirited, controversial, and sometimes painful.

We should accept these conditions and be happy with them. History has shown that too many economic considerations are at stake for too many interested groups to permit progress in financial reporting to be simple and harmonious.

CLIENT-AUDITOR RELATIONSHIP:
IS MORE INDEPENDENCE NEEDED?
Before the Cleveland Chapter of the Ohio Society of CPAs
Cleveland, Ohio
April 24, 1972

When I agreed to speak on the subject "Client-Auditor Relationship: Is More Independence Needed?" I was intrigued by the opportunity the title offers to make the shortest speech ever heard in your organization. I would simply say "yes" -- and sit down. On reflection, however, I decided there are several things I would like to say on the subject.

Our profession's Code of Ethics notes that independence is an inward quality, an expression of the integrity of an individual. As such, it is difficult to specify precisely, but is essential to the profession. The Code goes on to emphasize the importance of both the fact of independence and the appearance of independence. It proscribes particular financial relationships with a client which might cause a reasonable observer, who had knowledge of all the facts, to doubt an auditor's independence.

These proscriptions are well-founded and sensible. But I believe that most people, when they refer to the independence of an auditor, are actually thinking about a degree of that quality which goes well beyond financial relationships. There is ample evidence to support this conclusion. Recent articles in the press reveal a more than slight opinion that the auditor should be more independent of his client than he is now.

One of the most telling pieces of evidence of the need for more independence appeared in the March 25th issue of *Business Week*. Its "Washington Outlook" column quoted an internal staff memorandum to the Securities and Exchange Commission, noting that Commissioner James Needham told an accountants' committee that the SEC has found instances of problems relating to "elementary disclosure, succumbing to obvious pressure by clients, faulty judgments and decisions at the partnership level of the certifying accounting firms, and questions of independence bordering on commercial fraud."

These are strong words, and they came from an official in a position to do something about the matter. A little research revealed that his comments were made in November, 1970. Since then the

101

Commission has, indeed, done a great deal about the matter, including the filing of several complaints against accounting firms seeking to enjoin them from violating the anti-fraud Rule 10b-5 under the SEC Act of 1934.

Litigation Revealing Attitudes

Besides press comments of this kind, a number of lawsuits, of which you are all aware, evidence the need for more integrity and objectivity on the part of independent auditors. These cases show that judges and juries expect auditors to be alert to suspicious circumstances and blow the whistle on dishonest managements. Some lawsuits against auditors reveal an effort to express a clean opinion on a set of financial statements, even though company officers had engaged in highly unusual investments and intercompany transactions and had withheld information requested by the auditors.

A few years ago, a widely publicized lawsuit demonstrated a belief by the SEC that, when an auditor knows the public is receiving misleading financial statements, the auditor should make that information public. This position, which had not before been put forward so plainly and authoritatively, obviously bore a relation to the profession's rule of ethics on client confidentiality. The profession reacted with a carefully worded Statement on Auditing Procedure, which calls for an auditor to make disclosure to a regulatory body having surveillance over the company, if management will not.

At almost the same time the Institute's SAP was issued, a merger transaction took place which, the SEC recently alleged, was based on unaudited financial statements that contained inaccurate or misleading items, which the auditors called to the attention of management, but not the shareholders. Once again, a defense has been asserted that client confidentiality prohibited the auditors from revealing the information to anyone other than corporate officers and directors.

On the other hand, all of you can probably think of instances where the auditors blew the whistle on a company. And in some of these cases the auditors were sued nonetheless. In cases like that, the auditor performing with distinction and independence still runs the risk of litigation and adverse publicity.

Not being a lawyer, I can give no legal opinion on the risks of making disclosure of something a client wants to conceal. But I submit for your consideration that risks of an alleged breach of confidentiality might well be preferable to the risks of an SEC injunction and a class action by stockholders claiming damages for failure to disclose. The public is likely to find it hard to understand why an auditor would feel an obligation to a management that was trying to avoid disclosure of information highly significant to investors.

The cases I have referred to are conspicuous and have caused considerable anguish to the accountants involved and, to some extent, to the entire profession. But there are, in addition, less prominent instances of accountants' attitudes which are also troublesome.

Client Management Advocacy

If, for example, a CPA attends all meetings of the directors of a client company, refers constantly to "our company" and "our plants," and gives the general impression that he is part of the management, are reasonable observers likely to believe he has the independence, objectivity and integrity required of an auditor?

Do you not yourselves know of cases where accountants accompany clients to regulatory agencies and argue positions which favor the client company, but are contrary to professional standards? What can observers think of the independence of accountants who do not defend professional standards when a client finds those standards hampering? Occasionally, this same kind of attitude reveals itself when members of standard-setting bodies of the Institute advocate positions that are obviously favorable to, say, an oil company-client, insurance company-client, automobile company-client, or conglomerate-client.

Even more deeply rooted seems to be the idea of an identity not with a particular client, but with business in general. Accountants like to say, for example, that "accounting is the language of business." And some accountants refer to their professional practice as a business. Some who specialize as consultants refer to "my end of the business." Others who specialize in a particular industry seem to be more at home in the industry and its trade associations than in professional accounting societies.

"Built-in" Anti-Independence Factors

In their book, *The Philosophy of Auditing*, Mautz and Sharaf note that auditing does not have any "built-in" characteristics which assure skeptics of its integrity and independence, but that it suffers instead from what they call "built-in anti-independence factors." They group these anti-independence factors as, first, those arising from the nature of the relationship between an auditor and his clients; and, second, those arising from the organization of the profession.

The factors arising from the client-relationship are the profession's apparent financial dependence on fees paid by companies, its rule of confidentiality, and its rendering of a variety of services in addition to auditing. Yet, with respect to auditor's fees, it is obvious that *someone* must pay to have audits performed, and I have heard no feasible alternative to having the client do it.

As for confidentiality, it is an important feature of the accounting profession, just as it is of the legal or medical professions. Much of the information which an auditor receives could be detrimental to a business and its shareholders if transmitted to others. So a management that could not converse with its auditors in confidence would have strong reason to withhold information necessary for the auditors to do a proper job. Nevertheless, confidentiality should not be used as an excuse for an auditor to withhold from stockholders information they ought to have.

Counseling of clients is most conspicuous in management advisory services, but is just as prevalent in tax services, and is nearly always present along with auditing. Nearly all auditors believe that it is not enough to do just an audit. Their professional competence, indeed their professional duty, requires them to give constructive advice where opportunities arise during the course of the audit. This can be immensely helpful and need not impair audit objectivity. Yet, it will always be difficult to convince the public that an advisory attitude and an independent audit attitude can coexist within the same auditor or even within the same accounting firm.

The anti-independence factors noted by Mautz and Sharaf in the organization of the profession include the emergence of a limited number of large firms, lack of professional solidarity, and a tendency toward promotional salesmanship. Eleven years after publication of their book, competitive salesmanship seems, if anything, to have intensified. Of course, the prospect of widening opportunities is important in attracting able young people into a firm -- and new clients are needed to sustain growth. This fact may be conducive, however, to laxity in maintaining professional standards when strict observance of them seems to threaten retention of an old client or obtaining a new one.

Manufactured Safeguards of Independence

Since independence is so essential to our profession, we need to create specific safeguards to counteract the anti-independence factors cited. Some of our colleagues tend to minimize these factors by saying that auditors conduct themselves with independence and objectivity because, if for no other reason, the only thing they have to sell is their reputation, and they cannot afford to let it be tarnished. Also, it is said, auditors are so keenly conscious of their legal liabilities that they lean over backward to avoid the risk of a lawsuit.

These points are certainly valid. Yet, the fact remains that the credibility of the profession has eroded. Therefore, in my judgment, new, positive actions are needed.

Proposed Restatement of the Code of Professional Ethics

One such action would be to adopt the proposed restatement of the Code of Professional Ethics. The importance of protecting and strengthening independence has been recognized by the restatement committee. Its proposal goes beyond the present rule by adding a new one on integrity and objectivity which reads: "A member shall not knowingly misrepresent facts, and when engaged in the practice of public accounting, including the rendering of tax and management advisory services, shall not subordinate his judgment to others."

In addition to this enforceable rule of conduct, the restated Code contains an essay elaborating on the proposition that "a certified public accountant should maintain his integrity and objectivity and, when engaged in the practice of public accounting, be independent of those he serves."

These additions to the Code significantly advance the profession's recognition of the basic attitude which runs to the heart of the attest function. It officially and explicitly underscores that, without the fact and the appearance of independence, an auditor cannot perform adequately his function of adding credibility to financial statements.

Who Is the Client?

In my opinion, a further major strengthening of auditor independence could be made by re-defining the word "client." Too often auditors act as if the client were a company's management, rather than its owners.

To the credit of our committee on Code restatement, the proposed rules of conduct do include a definition of "client" which reads: "The person or entity which retains a member or his firm, engaged in the practice of public accounting, for the performance of professional services." I applaud the committee for its attempt -- yet, I believe that the definition is not free of ambiguity. For example, under this definition the client could be the corporation as a whole or the person within management who retained the public accounting firm. Use of the word "client" throughout the restated Code, it seems to me, shows vestiges of the use commonly prevailing today -- namely, that the client is the president, or financial vice president, or other corporate officer who has negotiated the engagement.

A definition of "client" geared to 1972 might say that a client is a person or entity which engages a public accountant or accounting firm to perform services -- and then go on to state that, in the case of a corporation, the investors constitute the entity. Under this kind of definition an auditor could not cite the client confidentiality rule as justification for reporting to the officers and board of directors, but not the stockholders -- for it would be the latter who really constituted the client. As already provided in SAP No. 41, where it was impractical for an auditor to give notification to the stockholders at large, notification to a regulatory agency such as the SEC could be stipulated as sufficient disclosure.

Change in Auditor

An encouraging recent development affecting independence is the new SEC requirement for reporting a change in auditor. The Institute worked closely with the SEC in developing this requirement in the

Commission's Form 8-K.

In a dialogue continuing over several months, the SEC and the Institute became increasingly concerned about "shopping for accounting principles." This concern stemmed not only from the relatively few instances where a change in auditor appeared to involve a dispute with a client over accounting principles, but from the pressure that might be exerted on an auditor through the mere threat of change.

The amendment to Form 8-K on this matter, among others, was adopted in September of last year. Now, if a new auditor has been engaged, the 8-K Form filed with the Commission must report the date of engagement, and the registrant must furnish the Commission a separate letter stating whether in the preceding 18 months there were any disagreements with the former auditor about accounting principles which, if not resolved to the satisfaction of the former auditor, would have caused him to refer in his opinion to the subject matter of the disagreement. Furthermore, the registrant has to furnish the Commission a letter from the former auditor stating whether he agrees with the statements in the registrant's letter.

When the proposed new rule was circulated for comment, the Institute suggested that the letters concerning the reasons for the change of auditor be non-public, but in the final release the SEC wisely decided against this restriction. Already the *Wall Street Journal* has published a revealing article based on an 8-K report, and I hope there will be more. The bright light of publicity should go far in strengthening the hand of an auditor in dealing with a client who wants to cut corners, and also in deterring a firm from lowering standards to obtain a client.

Standing Audit Committees of Outside Directors

Another way of buttressing auditor independence is for corporations to create audit committees composed of outside directors. Such committees nominate the independent auditors of their companies' financial statements, and keep in contact with the auditors concerning their work.

Five years ago the American Institute of CPAs urged appointment of audit committees, and last month the Securities and Exchange Commission endorsed establishment of such committees in all publicly-held companies. In doing so, the SEC noted that it had recommended such committees in 1940 following the McKesson & Robbins investigation. The movement for audit committees also received strong support in a 1970 research study by Robert K. Mautz and Fred L. Neumann.

With this kind of backing, audit committees should soon become standard features of corporate organization. They provide an opportunity for auditors to discuss problems when there is a disagreement between the auditors and company management, and they can contribute significantly toward easing management pressures against auditors.

Public Sector or Private Sector

The primary role of the independent auditor is to add credibility to financial representations made by others. The audit function is thus essential to the public interest. In the performance of this function it is imperative that the public have confidence in the independence and objectivity of those doing the work. If the public loses faith in those now performing it, there will be a drastic change in the way the audit function is carried out.

I have cited four specific steps which should help strengthen auditor independence:

o   The restated Code of Professional Ethics;

o   A redefinition of "client" to mean the owners
        and investors in a business;

o   Reporting reasons for a change in auditor; and

o   Standing audit committees composed of outside directors.

The third point (reporting changes in auditors) is already an SEC rule. If improvements in auditor independence are not soon perceptible to concerned regulatory agencies, sophisticated segments of the public, and legislators, more rules and regulations are inevitable. And if more regulation fails, the entire concept of an independent audit function in the private sector will be brought into question. If auditors are not regarded as independent, what use is their function? If in this circumstance the function is considered essential, what alternative is there to having it carried out by a government agency or by the profession under strict government regulation?

Forty years ago when Congress was considering securities legislation, some congressmen suggested that the auditing function belonged in a federal agency. Leading accountants persuaded the Congress that the function could be best carried out in the private sector by the public accounting profession.

I believe that the record proves this to be so -- that the performance of the auditing function by the profession has been outstanding. But in these past forty years not only has the level of audit performance risen, so have public expectations, and even faster. If the profession cannot remain at least one step ahead of these expectations, government auditing of private business looms as a possibility.

Some CPAs shrug off this possibility, citing a presumed inability of the government to create a staff large enough to handle the job. It would obviously take some time for a federal agency to be created which could audit all publicly-held corporations. But consider that probably fewer than 50,000 accountants in the private sector are now engaged in auditing these corporations -- while probably a number nearly that large are already engaged in auditing for the federal government in capacities ranging from internal revenue agent to defense contract auditor to General Accounting Office auditor. In light of this, I believe that a large enough staff could be established within government.

On the other hand, if a federal auditing agency is not considered feasible, there is the danger that the accounting profession could be brought under government control through legislation providing for a federal CPA certificate and federally determined standards. To some, federal regulation may appear to be a golden opportunity to bring uniformity to the diverse state requirements. But it is inevitable that making the accounting profession subject to federal regulation would result in loss of professional autonomy.

Instead of CPAs determining their professional requirements and standards, a federal agency would do so. It is easy to imagine this federal agency setting education and experience requirements, determining the content of the CPA examination, laying down rules of professional conduct, and imposing accounting and auditing standards.

In order to obviate developments of this sort (which I'm certain would be unwanted by most businessmen and government officials alike), the public accounting profession must re-dedicate itself to independence and objectivity.   An editorial on the client-auditor relationship in the April 22, 1972, issue of *Business Week* concludes, "But the final decision about the future of accounting must be made by the accountants themselves. To preserve their credibility, they must first of all preserve their independence."

Basically, it comes down to a matter of attitude. Accountants must decide whether they are engaged in a commercial activity with a few professional overtones, or in a profession which, like all professions, inevitably entails some elements of business, but without allowing these elements to become dominant.

As for myself, I see but one rational and right position: accountancy is clearly a *profession*. But independent and objective conduct by the overwhelming preponderance of practitioners is required to demonstrate this to those outside the profession.

THE PROFESSIONAL GOALS OF THE INSTITUTE
Before the Annual Partners Meeting
Touche, Ross, Bailey & Smart
Phoenix, Arizona
November 18, 1968

In a throwback to another era, Richard Nixon, in his successful presidential election campaign, made a whistle-stop tour through Ohio, speaking from the rear platform of a train in each community along the railroad line. At one small village, he was impressed by a sign carried by a young girl in the crowd. The sign read, "Bring us together." Much has been made of that sign and President-Elect Nixon has pledged his intention to devote great energy to bringing together a nation that is badly divided and a world that is badly divided. This simple plea, "Bring us together" may well become a rallying slogan for the new administration.

And in a different sense, it is an appropriate capsule summary of the professional goals of the American Institute of CPAs. For a major objective of the Institute is to bring together a profession that is badly divided in many ways, and to bring together broader segments of the public which are badly divided on the matter of corporate financial reporting standards. I no longer feel constrained to speak on subjects suggested by titles appearing on programs. But on this occasion, I am more than pleased to speak about the professional goals of the Institute. The most significant goal is to bring us together in our efforts to improve accounting and reporting standards.

Recent accomplishments of the Institute have been great, but they have been achieved in a manner that is often painful and that has not always pleased many segments of the membership. The profession has become strong because of its emphasis on high technical and ethical standards. Yet, as the profession gains more stature and more visibility, there are divisive forces evidenced from within which, unless checked and reconciled, could lead to a decline in the profession's status.

Bear in mind that I am speaking of a potential decline in *status -- not in prosperity.* For the public demand for accounting services seems to be growing steadily. A good living from accounting services is probably assured for most aggressive, well-run accounting firms. But members of the Institute must decide whether public accounting is to

111

become a highly competitive service *business* or a highly principled service *profession.* I believe that we cannot have it both ways.

One schism dividing the profession is the broad gulf between small firms and large firms. Perhaps such divisiveness is inevitable in fields of endeavor which permit the side-by-side conduct of a function by both large and small organizations. But a gulf so broad that it breeds distrust on one side and disdain on the other may well lead to dismay on the part of those trying to unite the two. I will spend no time developing this point as I am sure there are men in this room who have been on both sides of the issue and who understand it far better than I.

It is not healthy for a substantial segment of the profession to be envious and distrustful of another segment. Often members in small firms believe that large firms compete unfairly with them and violate professional ethics with impunity. On the other hand, some members of large firms have the impression that those in smaller firms do not adhere to technical standards and are frequently lacking in independence of mental attitude.

Whether there is justification in either of these views I am not prepared to say. But there is official concern about the unhealthiness of the division between large and small firms. The new president of the Institute is meeting in two weeks with a few Institute leaders to discuss causes and possible corrective measures. Free and frank discussions of differences will lead to a better understanding throughout the profession. And understanding is essential to bringing together opposing groups.

Competition is a pervasive source of divisiveness, well beyond the small firm-large firm differences; and this is not all bad. Competition is a highly regarded feature of our private enterprise system. It is healthy in commercial endeavors. In a way, it is healthy in professional activities, too. For pride in quality of performance (and quality of professional firm) is bound to be good for the profession and the public it serves.

But competition to obtain a client for the lowest fee or to obtain or retain a client at the expense of technical standards is debilitating. It will weaken and, if unchecked, destroy the profession. Competition for a client based on accounting principles must be stopped. It is not difficult to get evidence that this kind of competition exists. At last spring's Council meeting, I cited four real cases of questionable accounting and reporting, and competitive reasons can be proved in two of them. If firms could agree to stick together for the highest reporting standard when a client is shopping, the profession would be greatly strengthened. I think this can be done.

Some cynics have told me that competition based on accounting principles cannot be eliminated until the principles are uniform and comprehensive. And they go on to say that principles cannot be made sufficiently uniform and comprehensive to prevent client pressures from creating competitive situations.

I do not share this dismal view. But I am concerned over the continuing need to extend the pronouncements of the Accounting Principles Board to cover more situations. Much progress has been made, but much more progress is needed. The Board is working together more harmoniously now than it has before. Yet, there are deep-seated philosophical differences among members, which sometimes make progress slow and difficult.

In mentioning these differences, I am not questioning the motives or the dedication of any individual or group. I am pointing out how hard it is to get a two-thirds vote on controversial issues; and all issues facing the Board today are controversial. It is almost impossible to get a unanimous vote on any issue. But the Board is working together.

Last month, the Board met down the road a piece at Mountain Shadows. One evening in a spontaneous burst of camaraderie, Board members held a birthday party for Donald Bevis. He was presented with a warm, black wig and other appropriate gifts; and finally the Board wished him a happy birthday -- and that was by a vote of 12 to 6!

I will say no more about the Accounting Principles Board as Ken Axelsen will report on its activities. The Board is the major effort in the Institute in bringing us together. It is not the only one. Auditing procedures are moving into the limelight. Many observers believe that elevation of auditing standards is just as important as raising accounting principles. The Committee on Auditing Procedure has not had as much staff assistance as the APB. Consequently, its progress has been too slow; and its production must be increased. The Executive Committee has been discussing ways of doing this.

The need for greater productivity of auditing standards arises from the widening legal responsibilities of accountants. Each lawsuit involving accountants focuses on an area of practice where standards should be set or raised. It is not flattering to a profession to have these obvious needs pointed out by a judge, or a jury, or the financial press. The Institute's legal council has advised that we should move rapidly to set standards where court decisions are reached. If the Institute disagrees with a requirement that appears in a court decision, the Institute's own pronouncement may overcome the effect of the court decision in a similar case in the future.

The Committee on Auditing Procedure has subcommittees working on problems which arose in the cases of Yale Express, Bar Chris, and Continental Vending. A potential obstacle to quick and appropriate action on these cases is the fact that they involve matters of disclosure as well as matters of inquiry. We are determined, however, that jurisdictional issues between the APB and the Committee on Auditing Procedure will not be permitted to impede progress. A very real obstacle to progress in dealing with these cases is that they are not settled finally.

The Institute will undoubtedly enter another *amicus curiae* brief in the Continental Vending Co. case at the appellate level. But it is just a bit saddening to think that this Committee, which was created 30 years ago in response to the McKesson & Robbins case, still has as a major part of its workload *post mortems* on other major scandals.

OMBUDSMANSHIP AND THE NEED FOR
HARD-NOSED AUDITING
Before 25th Southern States Conference of CPAs
Oklahoma City, Okla.
June 9, 1969

In Sweden they have a public office which is known as the Ombudsman. It has existed for more than 150 years. The Ombudsman is appointed by Parliament. He is independent of the government, and his job is to protect the rights of the citizens against abuse of power by government officials. Citizens take their complaints to him and he acts in their behalf in redressing the wrong when the complaints are found to warrant it.

An official Swedish description of this office says that it serves as a "safety valve in society, with a general soothing effect as a result." The official Swedish description goes on to say that such a body, with independence and special attention to the rule of law, strengthens the confidence of the citizens. It is a natural cog in the machinery of democracy. Other countries around the world have adopted this Swedish method of protecting the public.

In the financial world of our own country, we have a very special type of Ombudsman in the form of the independent auditor. Instead of serving as an independent office between the citizens and the government, he assumes this position between investors and business management. As such, as the Swedes would say, he is a natural cog in the machinery of business. But as the Americans know, the auditor is more than a cog -- he is a big wheel in the machinery of business.

No analogy is ever exact, but the interesting relationship between the third-party position of the Ombudsman and the similar position of the auditor is worthy of note. Swedish literature points out that the Ombudsman's criticism of incorrect procedure serves as a guideline to others and thus contributes to better practice.

The auditor's unique responsibility is to express an independent opinion on the fairness of financial statements. The existence of the free economy today depends on public confidence in the reliability of financial statements. In providing this confidence, the accounting profession functions as an essential wheel in the business apparatus.

A good example of a "soothing effect" in the relationship of the auditor's position between the investing public and business

115

management is the use of the audit committee of the board of directors. This practice was suggested some two years ago by the Executive Committee of the American Institute. A good number of companies have adopted it, and their auditors report that a more productive relationship results.

The intent of the Institute's recommendation was to suggest that publicly owned corporations name committees of outside directors, who are not officers or employees, to nominate the independent auditors and work closely with them in the course of their engagement. This provides the auditor with direct contact with impartial members of the board of directors who, in turn, are directly responsible to the stockholders.

The statement also recommended that when a company changes auditors, the replaced firm be given an opportunity to appear at the next annual meeting of the company's stockholders to comment on the reasons for its replacement. The public has the right to know whether differences over financial communication were involved in making the change.

Our role as auditors today is assuming staggering dimensions. It involves our legal liability to fulfill our responsibilities as public accountants on one hand and the pressing need for us to continually improve our theories and practice of accounting and auditing on the other.

These dual aspects of the auditor's role present us with the most urgent problems facing the profession. As I say this, I note that the Institute's Committee on Auditing Procedures is doing something about these problems. The Committee is meeting here in Oklahoma City, in this hotel, concurrently with the Southern States Conference. Joe Roth, its chairman, will speak to you tomorrow afternoon and he will be followed by other members of the Committee discussing with you some of the problems they are working on.

Since it was established about 30 years ago, the Committee has issued 40 Statements on Auditing Procedure. It is one of the senior technical committees of the Institute and has as its members some of the best minds in the profession. Although it has an enviable record, this Committee has not been supported by staff help to the extent of the Accounting Principles Board. This has caused some concern in view of the complexity and urgency of the problems that need to be addressed.

As a result, the Executive Committee has directed the Institute staff to devote more resources to aid in the work of the Committee on Auditing Procedures. The first tangible step in this direction was the creation of a new position in the Technical Services Division, a manager of auditing research. The position has been filled by Douglas Carmichael. He started in his new assignment on June 2nd, immediately after completion of the spring semester at the University of Texas, where he has been on the accounting faculty. Mr. Carmichael is here at the Committee meeting to consult with Committee members and get guidance on research project priorities.

Regrettably, much of the backlog of auditing research projects awaiting his attention stems from lawsuits -- lawsuits which might well have been prevented had their been a greater application of what I call "hard-nosed" auditing. I don't mean to add to the discomfort of members of the profession who have suffered through lawsuits by use of hindsight to second guess their performance. I merely wish to stress the need for all of us to learn from the experiences of others. The auditor may have opportunities in the future to avoid imposition of liability in sticky situations through hard-nosed auditing.

Often the auditor is in a position to "blow the whistle" when things go wrong, to sound a warning to investors and the public as soon as danger signals appear. This kind of action is expected of an Ombudsman, and the public is beginning to expect it of the auditor. Every auditor should be aware of these public expectations and be particularly alert for situations where he may need to take extra-precautionary auditing steps and to consider special reporting beyond the use of the standard unqualified short-form opinion. For a company teetering on the brink of financial disaster, I wonder if the standard opinion constitutes fair reporting, regardless of how complete disclosures may be in the financial statements and the footnotes.

Some say that the auditor's liability is being extended with each court decision and that auditing standards are being set by the courts. While this is a debatable proposition, legal counsel for the Institute tells us that the profession still has the opportunity to set its own standards in its own way, even on points where a court has decided differently. Courts may decide on auditing and reporting matters in a particular case, but leave the future application of the decision vague and uncertain. The profession has the opportunity to clarify application of decisions like this, and may in fact wish to set standards contrary to some of these decisions. Thus, the Committee on Auditing Procedures and our new manager of auditing research will be devoting much attention to auditing and reporting matters arising from lawsuits.

But the concern of some members of the profession over legal liability poses a serious obstacle to the work of the Committee on Auditing Procedures. These members believe that the issuance of further Statements on Auditing Procedure will increase the liability of auditors in some way.

This can hardly draw an argument. To the extent that new standards impose additional obligations, liability may well be increased. But the very existence of standards may serve to limit liability in those cases where auditors adhere to the new standards.

Just last Friday, the Committee on Auditing Procedures issued an exposure draft of a Statement on Auditing Procedure entitled "Subsequent Discovery of Facts Existing Prior to the Auditor's Report." I think you will recognize the lawsuit which gave rise to this Statement. It is a Statement on steps an auditor might take when he becomes aware of facts that existed prior to the time when he issued his report and, had he known these facts, he might have issued a different report. This Statement asserts that, in these circumstances, the auditor does have an obligation to see that appropriate disclosure is made to those likely to be relying on the financial statements and the related report. Doubtless the Committee itself will be telling you about this Statement tomorrow. Publication is expected in the fall. This Statement on subsequent discovery of pre-existing facts will be another step in efforts to strengthen the auditor's position in fulfilling his public service role. Here, again, we see application of the Ombudsman concept.

The Committee on Auditing Procedures is taking a new look at the auditor's short-form opinion. One of their concerns is that the language of the existing form of report might be interpreted in such a way that unintended legal liability results. Also, they are concerned that users of financial statements may not fully comprehend the meaning of the auditor's report and the extent to which he assumes responsibility for a company's financial statements.

While I cannot predict when a draft will be approved for exposure to the membership, I can assure you that the subject is of serious concern to the Institute, and the Committee is pursuing it diligently. To accomplish the stated purpose of the revision will inevitably call for the Committee to expand the short-form opinion into a lengthier presentation.

The Committee, incidentally, will receive shortly some interesting and contrary views from the international sector. *Study No. 2* of the Accountants International Study Group, dealing with "The Independent Auditor's Reporting Standards in Three Nations," has just been published. One of the elements brought out is the feeling among some auditors in this country in favor of a short-short form opinion, sort of a mini-opinion, as is done in the United Kingdom. This suggests use of no more than the words "in our opinion," an identification of the financial statements being reported on, and a concise evaluation of the financial statements, such as that they are "fair and reasonable."

I might point out that the Accountants International Study Group, which was established in 1966, is turning out to be another useful research body. Its studies are not authoritative; and views expressed are those of the members of the Study Group, not necessarily those of the participating bodies. The Group is made up of representatives of the American Institute of Certified Public Accountants, the Canadian Institute of Chartered Accountants, and the three Institutes of Chartered Accountants in Great Britain and Ireland. The Study Group's objectives are to provide an impetus for greater cooperation in facing mutual challenges and a stimulus for improvement of practice standards among memberships of the participating Institutes and, perhaps, internationally.

The first Study by the Group was published in January, 1968, entitled "Accounting and Auditing Approaches to Inventories in Three Nations." It dealt with a wide range of problems involved in auditing inventories, including physical inspection and valuation..

This *Study No. 2*, which has just been published, was prepared by the U.S. delegation of the international group with assistance from the Canadian and British delegations. It contains some other conclusions that are of more than passing interest. It suggests, for example, that the auditor's appointment should be made or ratified by shareholders, that he should be permitted or required to attend meetings of shareholders, and should have the right to appear before the shareholders if his replacement is proposed. The Study urges the profession in all nations to inform the investing public of the extent and limitations of the auditor's responsibilities. It says that financial statements reported on should include (at a minimum) the balance sheet, statements of income and retained earnings, and a statement of sources and application of funds.

It touches upon other aspects of financial reports that are of general interest and consistent with current U.S. practice -- for example, a recommended disclaimer of opinion on unaudited statements and avoidance of negative assurances as far as possible. Publication of this Study is timely. It is bound to create interest and it may be helpful in our efforts to make improvement in practice.

The profession is providing CPAs with the auditing tools to do a better job and, thus, contributing to needed improvements in financial reporting. Aiding in the overall technical coordination, of course, is the Accounting Principles Board. In addition to its primary function of establishing accounting principles, it works with the Committee on Auditing Procedures to ensure consistency in accounting concepts.

Incidentally, the Board is moving with greater speed than ever before. It is working with other groups concerned with bringing about improvements in corporate financial reporting, including the Financial Executives Institute, the Financial Analysts Federation, and the Robert Morris Associates. Groups such as these confer with the Board in the early stages of Opinion formulation. We are hopeful that this type of cooperation will help to speed the output of new Opinions that will be practical and lasting. Many of you are being called upon to join in this effort through your comments on exposure drafts of new Opinions, and we invite your continued, constructive collaboration.

In addition to the work of the Committee on Auditing Procedures and the Accounting Principles Board, the preparation of audit guides for specialized activities makes another contribution to the improvement of practice. These guides deal with matters which often include problems in both areas -- auditing procedures and accounting principles. As a result, their publication is approved by the chairman of the Committee on Auditing Procedures and the chairman of the Accounting Principles Board. In an effort to clarify their weight of authority, the disclaimer published in the front of each new guide has been revised to include the following language: "... it contains the best thought of the profession as to the best practices in this area of financial reporting. Members should be aware that they may be called upon to justify departures from the Committee's recommendations." Audit guides on Medicare, stockbrokers and dealers, savings and loan associations, and finance companies are well on their way to publication, either as a new guide or a revision of a previous one. Audit guides in earlier stages of preparation include those for hospitals; defense contracts; life insurance companies; health, welfare and pension funds; governmental agencies; and colleges and universities.

Guides previously issued have had important impact in their respective areas. One which has received considerable publicity deals with banks. Issued in 1968, it contained an income statement format which required provision for loan losses and gains and losses on securities transactions to be included in net income. This was a drastic departure from the income statement form traditionally used by banks and approved by the federal regulatory agencies.

The details for implementing the recommendations of the audit guide for banks are still being worked out. We have had a series of meetings with representatives of the American Bankers Association and the federal regulatory agencies, but have not reached complete accord to date.

In fulfilling his responsibility as guardian of the public interest, the independent CPA has a special duty to himself and to his profession -- that is to *know* his client. I think this need is one of increasing concern to many of us.

A doctor has the duty to heal a patient no matter who he is or what his reputation might be. A lawyer can defend a client accused of a crime, regardless of his guilt. But the CPA should be circumspect about his clients.

The doctor is dealing with a man's life, the lawyer with his freedom. But the CPA is dealing with communication between various interest groups. He acts in a judicial sense to ensure objectivity and fairness in the financial data which becomes the basis for evaluating alternative investments, as well as evaluating management's discharge of responsibilities. In this role, the CPA does not represent one individual exclusively -- rather, he represents a third party public composed of various groups and individuals.

It is the practice of some firms to investigate the background and reputation of a prospective client before agreeing to handle his affairs, and I think this is a good practice. Too often a firm is engaged, and then later discovers that his client has questionable associations.

In one case, a firm turned down a prospective client after learning that one of its directors had been subject to an SEC complaint and one of its officers had a court action against him. The partners of the firm took comfort in their wisdom a short-time later when the company came into serious difficulty with the SEC, resulting in wide public exposure.

It does great harm to the profession when a member is associated with a business scandal. Avoiding clients with questionable background and associations is in the best interests of the accounting profession. It is befitting to our type of Ombudsmanship.

Some may claim that the public must have the protection afforded by a CPA firm of repute even if a principal officer and stockholder has an unsavory reputation. They may state that denial of an ethical firm to provide services in such a situation will drive the company into the hands of an incompetent or corrupt CPA -- or possibly force the company into receivership for want of an audit report. But so far as I know, a disreputable businessman has no inherent right to be served by a reputable independent certified public accountant. If audit services are not available to a company because of its management's reputation, the public is clearly on notice that serious problems exist and special efforts are needed to deal with the situation.

In his first address to Congress, President Nixon sounded a warning about the prevalence of organized crime. He cited the role played in organized crime by lawyers and accountants, and noted that funds gained from illegal gambling are often invested in legitimate businesses. There is no indication that he was referring to practicing CPAs in this connection, but the reference to legitimate businesses certainly reveals the possibility of the Mafia moving into companies which are served by respectable CPA firms.

A CPA should be watchful of changes in ownership and management of his clients. If he finds a once solid company taken over or influenced by unsavory elements, he may have to make a difficult decision. He may decide to withdraw from the engagement or he may feel obligated to remain on the scene to protect innocent investors and creditors. If he does remain, he had better carry out the most hard-nosed auditing he knows how to do.

But organized crime is not the only pitfall facing the auditor which calls for hard-nosed auditing. Financial adversity, management incompetence, or a high degree of speculation in a company's stock are all situations calling for hard-nosed auditing -- or Ombudsmanship, if you will. In cases like this, there is a possibility that investors will suffer. And, a suffering investor may seek solace by suing the CPA.

Where a company's fortunes are falling, there may be a temptation on the part of management to hide the real situation to the extent possible. Here is where a hard-nosed auditor must take an even harder look at the company. If business is bad, maybe it is really worse than it seems. More questions must be asked, more evidence seen. If access to information is denied, then that is the very information that absolutely must be examined. When a business scandal occurs, often the charge is made that the auditors were too willing to accept explanations of management and too lax in obtaining corroborating evidence.

Some companies may present outwardly a glowing picture of health, but may be less than sound internally. Often speculative stock issues and the most liberal accounting methods go hand-in-hand. A hard-nosed auditor will examine critically the propriety of the transactions. Any evidence of sharpness in business practices, or looseness in accounting and reporting, should serve fair warning that other questionable practices may exist just waiting to be uncovered. The hard-nosed auditor will uncover them.

The Swedes established their office of the Ombudsman early in the 19th century, long before auditors became an effective force in this country. The Swedes are proud of their creation. They say the Ombudsman is a healthy, preventive influence in their country upon those who tend to be "high-handed, arrogant, negligent, or forgetful of the limits of their power."

Here in our country, we are practicing Ombudsmanship in the private sector by providing the financial consuming public with the protection it needs and demands. We, too, can be proud of our role.

SECTION III:
ACCOUNTING STANDARD-SETTING ISSUES

ACCENTUATING ACCOUNTABILITY
Before the Hawaii Society of CPAs
Honolulu, Hawaii
May 21, 1971

Ladies and gentlemen, I bring you greetings from the islands --
Manhattan, Long Island, Staten Island ....

When your invitation to this annual meeting came to my desk back
in New York, it led me to reflect for a moment on how long, and how
romantically, every American in the forty-eight contiguous states has
been aware of Hawaii. As far back as I can remember, songs like
"Aloha Oe" and "On the Beach at Waikiki" have been part of the
popular music on the mainland. There was a period when the ukulele
was as ubiquitous among the young as the guitar has become more
recently. One of the best known recording personalities in the days of
the hand-wound Victrola was known simply as Ukulele Ike. And there
probably wasn't anyone over the age of fifteen, from Bangor, Maine,
to San Diego, who was not familiar with the undulations of the hula
hula. In short, the cultural impact of this group of islands, despite their
relative remoteness in the days before air travel, was far greater than
that of many regions of the United States as the country was then comprised.

This is my first visit to Hawaii, and although I've been here for
only a few hours, I can understand why this has been so. I am enjoying
the experience immensely, and I am grateful for your having asked me
to be with you.

As the theme of my remarks, I have selected "accountability." As
you all know, various periods of time come to be labeled according to
some development that attracts widespread attention and interest. The
late Sixties were frequently referred to as the Era of Mergers. Some
time earlier, editorialists and commentators spoke often of the Air Age,
the Electronic Age, and the Computer Age. In my opinion, it's likely
that we are now entering into the "Accountability Age." Many signs
point in this direction.

The so-called consumer movement, for example, consists largely of
a demand that manufacturers be more accountable for the quality of
their products and the claims made for them on labels and in
advertising. Parents are asking that educators and school administrators
give better accountings than they have been accustomed to do as to the

127

effectiveness of their programs. People are pressing companies for fuller and more objective reports as to the effects of their operations on the environment.

Since accountability is (in the jargon of today's young people) the "thing" of certified public accountants, an age of accountability obviously affects us more than casually. One result of this fact is that Opinions and drafts of Opinions have recently been emerging from the Accounting Principles Board at a faster rate than ever before. Yet, changes in business and financial activities are occurring so rapidly that we are hard pressed to keep pace by formulating appropriate accounting standards.

The APB has a heavy agenda for 1971. Some of the subjects on which action has already been taken or which will receive early attention include the following: During the past two months the APB has issued two final Opinions -- *Number 18* on "The Equity Method of Accounting for Investments in Common Stock," and *Number 19* on "Reporting Changes in Financial Position."

The first of these deals with long-term investments in common stock. In this pronouncement the Board extends use of the equity method of accounting (which, heretofore, was required just for unconsolidated domestic subsidiaries) to all unconsolidated subsidiaries. It also requires use of equity accounting for corporate joint ventures, fifty-percent-owned companies, and investments in voting common stock which give the investor the ability to exercise "significant influence" over operating and financial policies of the investee.

The Opinion stipulates that an investment of 20 percent or more of the voting stock of a company will be considered as indicating ability to exercise significant influence, in the absence of evidence to the contrary. Conversely, an investment of less than 20 percent of the voting stock will be regarded as showing that no such influence exists, unless it can be demonstrated. Equity accounting is required under this Opinion, not only in consolidated financial statements, but in parent company-only financials issued as primary statements to stockholders.

Opinion No. 19 requires that a presentation of changes in financial position (funds statement) be included as a basic financial statement whenever a balance sheet and a statement of income and retained earnings are presented. It was the view of the Board that information concerning the financing and investing activities of a business enterprise, and a summary of changes in its financial position, are essential for owners and creditors in making economic decisions.

As you know, presentation of a funds statement has been recommended, though not required, by the accounting profession for a long time. It has been recommended also by the stock exchanges. Quite recently, the SEC declared that a funds statement will henceforth be a required item in registration statements and reports filed with the Commission.

The need for a funds statement as a required, rather than merely optional, item of information was highlighted in the past year or so when a number of companies experienced financial difficulty. At such a time, the attention of knowledgeable investors focuses on liquidity, and they want information that is not easily obtained from the balance sheet or statement of income alone. The statement of changes in financial position contributes materially to answers to such questions, and its required presentation should be welcomed by financial statement users. Thus, the new Opinion is quite timely.

In addition to these two final pronouncements, the Board in recent months has exposed for comment two draft Opinions. One would require imputing interest on long-term receivables and payables. It would require that a long-term receivable or payable be discounted at an appropriate rate when it is either non-interest bearing or bears an interest rate clearly below a reasonable rate at the time of a transaction.

Imputing interest looks to the substance of a transaction, rather than its form. The application of this method would result in more realistic reporting of the principal amount of the long-term receivable or payable and the related interest income or expense. For example, a company selling land or a building and receiving a non-interest bearing note as part of the proceeds would report a lower profit on the sale than indicated in the stated terms of sale and would report interest income over the life of the note; conversely, the buyer would report interest expense over the life of the note. The exposure period on this draft Opinion ended May 1, and it is expected a definitive pronouncement will be agreed upon in July.

You may recall that a draft on changes in accounting methods was originally exposed a year ago last February. Further action was then deferred, however, in order to give the APB time to explore alternative proposals. The Board's reconsideration of this subject led to a second exposure draft this past January.

Under the current proposal, accounting changes would be restricted to situations where it can be demonstrated that the new method will result in more useful financial information than the former method. When a change is made, its effect would be reported in the income statement for the year of change. This adjustment would appear after "income before extraordinary items" and before "net income." Supplementary disclosure of the effect of the change on net income and earnings per share for the current period (and all prior periods presented) would also be required. Comments on the exposure draft were due by May 15. It is expected that a final Opinion will be issued following the Board's June meeting.

The Board's agenda is literally loaded with items approaching the exposure stage. Although time does not permit a full review of each of these, I will briefly discuss a few of the more important subjects.

Discussion of the equity method of accounting led the APB to a separate consideration of accounting for equity securities when significant influence over operating and financial policies does not exist. The Board is reexamining present practice in this area, and is considering a proposal that investments in equity securities be measured at current market value, net of income tax effect, in balance sheets.

It is also considering alternative methods of accounting for changes in market value in the statement of income. One method being discussed would require that unrealized gains and losses, net of taxes, be included in income as they occur. Another would recognize both realized and unrealized gains and losses in the income statement on a long-term yield-basis. Other proposals would have these gains and losses reported outside the income statement.

Despite the obvious obstacles to market value accounting, I believe there is growing sentiment and authoritative support for its use by all companies in accounting for marketable equity securities. This possibility, of course, concerns the financial community generally, and is of particular interest to insurance companies, brokerage firms, and other heavy investors in these securities. Because of this, public hearings on the subject have been scheduled for May 24-25. The hearings will be the first the APB has ever held on an open-basis, as contrasted with an invitational-basis; and I think the turn-out will be large, and participation in the discussions by interested parties will be active.

The Board is studying the question of transfers of assets which do not involve cash. This includes distribution of appreciated non-cash assets from an enterprise to its owners, and exchanges of non-cash assets with non-owners. The principal question involved is whether an increase in the value of the assets should be accounted for at the time of the transfer.

Another subject the Board is considering is accounting for the purchase and retirement of debt. This is an important problem today, because many of the securities being reacquired are convertibles which are selling at a deep discount.

Inasmuch as a convertible security has some elements of equity, as well as of debt, the question arose as to whether some portion of the discount should be an addition to capital, or whether it is all income. The question is far from decided, but the trend of the Board's thinking seems to favor accounting for the discount as if the security were solely debt. This would be consistent with an earlier Opinion of the Board, which held that no amount of the proceeds should be allocated to the convertible feature of a convertible security at the time it is issued.

Notwithstanding this trend of thinking, study of the problem has led the Board to broaden its consideration to cover purchase and retirement of all debt -- whether convertible or not, and whether at a discount or at a premium. Some have questioned whether a discount on the purchase and retirement of any debt should be included in income.

More and more annual reports contain a description of the accounting policies adopted in preparing financial statements. Many favorable comments have been made on this kind of disclosure, and the APB is thinking about giving it further impetus by issuing a Statement recommending that companies describe major accounting policies in one place.

The Board has a few items of unfinished business from prior Opinions. Its pronouncements on accounting for income taxes left for further study the application of deferred tax accounting in five special problem areas: namely, undistributed earnings of subsidiaries, amounts designated "policyholders' surplus" by stock life insurance companies, "general reserves" of stock savings and loan associations, deposits in statutory reserve funds by United States steamship companies, and intangible development costs in the oil and gas industry. This last area will be considered in a proposed Opinion on accounting problems in the extractive industries, which is beginning to receive active consideration following publication of *Accounting Research Study No. 11.*

The other four problems will receive attention in 1971. Current thinking seems to favor tax allocation on deposits in statutory reserve funds by United States steamship companies, because these deposits seem to create timing differences which call for tax allocation under APB *Opinion No. 11*. The three other areas seem to result in book-tax differences which are neither timing differences nor permanent differences as defined in *Opinion No. 11*. A tentative recommendation would be to provide taxes on the differences only to the extent that planned operations can reasonably be expected to result in reversals of the differences, thus causing payment of taxes.

The Board has noted that the Administration and the Congress are considering tax incentives of various kinds to achieve social and economic goals, such as encouraging capital spending to stimulate the economy and reduce unemployment, providing job training opportunities for the disadvantaged, and curbing pollution of the environment. The Board plans to study accounting ramifications of these proposals as action on bills becomes imminent, so that appropriate accounting for specific tax incentives will be developed on a timely basis.

Because of the complex and changing nature of American business and the way in which accounting principles are applied in practice, the APB must constantly review the applicability and effectiveness of previous pronouncements. One such matter relates to accounting for leases. An earlier Opinion noted an apparent inconsistency between accounting methods recommended for lessors and lessees. In reconsidering this problem, the Board is reviewing some basic problems of both lessors and lessees.

Opinion No. 7 described the operating and financing methods of accounting for lease revenues by lessors, and described conditions under which each method is appropriate. That Opinion also specified that a manufacturer could record a "manufacturing profit" upon entering into a financing lease, provided certain conditions were met. Practice under this Opinion has raised questions as to the adequacy of criteria for this purpose. Some lessors have recorded manufacturing profit upon entering into a lease for as short a period as one year. The Board intends to tighten up in this area.

As to lessees, the Board has tentatively agreed that leases which are financing leases should be capitalized. Study is being given as to whether still more leases should be capitalized. Also under study is appropriate income statement treatment of capitalized leases. A typical lease with equal annual payments ordinarily would result in rent expense of the same equal annual amounts. Questions are being raised as to whether the combination of depreciation and interest expense that would arise through capitalization should also be made to result in equal annual amounts. Purchase of the same asset would ordinarily result in depreciation in equal annual amounts, and interest expense in declining amounts, thus resulting in a combined expense that is higher in earlier years of the asset's life and declining over time.

The Board has taken note of the proliferation of new types of stock options and other stock compensation plans, including tandem and phantom plans. It intends to develop guidelines for recognizing the compensation expense involved.

In 1970, a huge number of extraordinary items appeared in corporate income statements. This has led the Board to reconsider whether more specific criteria than those provided in *Opinion No. 9* are needed for identifying an extraordinary item.

Opinion No. 15 created the concept of a "common stock equivalent" for use in computing primary earnings per share. Yet, the Opinion stated that the concept should not be introduced into the financial statements and particularly not into net income. This is a conceptual inconsistency that has been highlighted by issuance of *Opinion No. 18* on equity accounting. The Board will consider reconciling this difference.

A Statement issued by the APB in 1967 encouraged disclosure of information by line of business when a company operates in more than one industry. Many companies have since been reporting information by line of business in annual reports, and recently such disclosures have been required in filings with the SEC. For the most part, these presentations have not been subject to independent audit. The APB, however, has on its agenda the development of an Opinion which would require disclosure of such information, and provide standards for presenting it.

Often auditors are called upon to report on financial statements of a subsidiary company, a division, or a branch of a corporation. As guidelines for reporting on a component of a business are inadequate, the APB is studying the subject with the intent of issuing an Opinion.

Quarterly financial statements are becoming more common. Stock exchanges require them, and now the SEC is doing so, too. Therefore, the APB is working on an Opinion which would set standards for interim period reporting.

Last year the Institute's Accounting Research Division published a Research Study on Accounting for Extractive Industries. Now that comments on the Study have been received from interested parties, the subject has been moved up on the APB's agenda.

Many other projects are in the research stage, including intercorporate investments, stockholders' equity, foreign investments, depreciation, inventory valuation, and industrial research and development. As each study is completed, the subject then comes to the APB for consideration of an Opinion.

The Institute's program for improving accounting principles also includes a series of audit guides for specific industries. These guides are prepared by committees of Institute-members who are specialists in the particular industry, thus expanding the capability of the Institute for setting standards beyond that represented on the APB. To assure consistency of accounting principles, however, an audit guide is released only after being reviewed by the chairman of the APB for overall conformity with the more pervasive pronouncements of the APB. Audit guides, like APB Opinions, are exposed in draft form for comment prior to final issuance.

The Institute has exposed a draft of an audit guide for life insurance companies. The industry is subject to regulations which have been designed primarily to assure protection of policyholders; and, while this is commendable, the regulatory form of financial reports is not necessarily a fair presentation for investors.

Insurance regulatory requirements are such that a vigorous company, which is acquiring new business, could be reporting meager income or possibly a loss. At the same time, a company which is suffering a decline in its volume of business may be showing high profits. This is a paradoxical situation which calls for attention, particularly since insurance companies are increasingly turning to CPA firms to add credibility to their financial statements.

To correct the deficiencies in reporting to insurance company investors, an American Institute committee is working with insurance industry associations to develop improved rules for matching costs with revenues. Good progress has been made, and new rules could be in force by the end of the year. Many financial analysts now make adjustments to reports of publicly-held stock life insurance companies for greater comparability with reports of other industries. This would no longer be necessary under the uniform guidelines proposed.

Much of the draft is concerned with how the liability for policyholder benefits should be determined. It endorses the so-called "natural reserve" method. Under this method, more realistic assumptions would be made as to acquisition costs, future interest rates, assumed mortality rates, withdrawals, and policyholder dividends. Also, costs of acquiring new business would be spread over the periods in which income is recognized. Present practice is to write-off these costs as incurred.

The Institute's Committee on Insurance Accounting and Auditing, after considering comments which were due by May 15, is expected to publish the guidelines in final form. I have already mentioned that the Accounting Principles Board is considering provisions for deferred taxes on policyholders' surplus in a stock company and the manner in which gains and losses on investments in marketable equity securities should be recognized. It is expected that the final guide will contain recommendations on these matters, as well as specify the extent to which the guide will apply to mutual companies.

Audit guides are also well along toward completion for stock brokerage firms, savings and loan associations, and hospitals. Guides are being prepared for health and welfare funds, governmental accounting, finance companies, colleges and universities, defense contracts, pension funds, fire and casualty insurance companies, land development companies, and investment companies.

A mere listing of all these efforts is sufficient to indicate the seriousness of the profession's resolve to improve financial reporting standards. And in view of the importance of APB Opinions and Institute audit guides to industry and the investing public, the Institute has just formed two high-level study groups to consider whether these efforts are sufficiently prompt and productive.

One group will study whether present procedures for establishing accounting principles can be improved; and the other will seek to refine the objectives of financial statements. Both groups will consult with interested organizations and individuals, hold hearings, and maintain a public record. The study on establishment of accounting principles is expected to be completed within six months and the study on objectives within 18 months.

Each group includes representatives of business and professional life outside public accounting. In fact, a majority of those on each study group is from outside public practice.

The group studying the establishment of accounting principles is chaired by Francis M. Wheat, a recent member of the Securities and Exchange Commission. Serving with him are a university professor, a financial analyst, a financial vice president of one of the nation's largest industrial corporations, and three CPAs engaged in public accounting practice.

The group studying the objectives of financial statements is chaired by Robert M. Trueblood, a practicing CPA and past president of the American Institute. Serving with him are a financial analyst, an economist, an industrial executive, two professors, and two CPAs from public practice.

I hope these remarks have demonstrated the concern of the Institute for seeing that the public is served by the highest attainable standards of financial reporting. The Institute expects to continue to provide leadership and assume responsibility for this function. But, we cannot reach this goal without the cooperation of the business and financial community. If we have this cooperation, I don't see how we can fail to give the public the reliable information it deserves.

So far, I have talked only about accounting issues which are presently before the Accounting Principles Board for deliberation and decision. These are pressing issues affecting business, which the profession is expected to deal with promptly.

But in this age of accountability, there are many broader issues which should be considered by the accounting profession if we wish to take advantage of the current emphasis being placed on accountability. Needs for accountability are arising in both the private and public sectors which are well beyond the traditional services provided by public accounting -- including audited interim financial statements, assurance as to adequacy of internal controls, audits of forecasts and budgets, compliance with federal programs, management audits, program performance reviews, and social accounting. Exciting opportunities exist if the profession takes the initiative in setting standards which provide professional guidelines for performing these services.

Although the accounting profession is expected to provide leadership in accountability, the public cannot be expected to wait for us to get around to these broad needs for accountability. Other disciplines may well supply the needed services if we are dilatory in responding.

Time does not permit a further discussion of this subject, but I would not feel comfortable in talking about "Accentuating Accountability" without at least calling your serious attention to these broader professional opportunities. I am convinced that the accounting profession can (and will) devote the resources necessary for it to become a dominant force in the Accountability Age.

A TIME FOR SELF-RENEWAL
IN THE ACCOUNTING PROFESSION
Before the 56th Annual Meeting of the Texas Society of CPAs
Austin, Texas
June 21, 1971

During our lifetimes, the accounting profession has experienced a remarkable rate of growth and has produced a notable record of accomplishment. Not the least notable have been the profession's contributions to the commercial and industrial development of our country -- contributions stemming from the attest function and the establishment of accounting principles.

A primary factor in our progress has been the youth and boldness of the profession. During its developmental years it was open to new experiences, receptive, not inhibited by fixed attitudes.

As a result of our ability to recognize and deal with problems, and of our willingness to respond to the needs of the times, the accounting profession has reached a considerable degree of maturity and visibility. It is precisely this maturity, however, which may pose a challenge to our continued well-being. John Gardner, in his classic work *Self-Renewal*, describes the growth and decay process in this way:

> When organizations ... are young, they are flexible, fluid, not yet paralyzed by rigid specialization and willing to try anything once. As [an organization] ages, vitality diminishes, flexibility gives way to rigidity, creativity fades and there is a loss of capacity to meet challenges from unexpected directions.

If we desire continued growth and health for our profession, we must be aware of, and vigorously defend against, the causes of stagnation which Gardner describes.

We must not become complacent because of past accomplishments, nor rigid in our thinking because of present success. For changes in our environment will continue -- changes so profound and far-reaching that it is difficult to comprehend all their implications. The rise or fall of the profession will be measured by our responsiveness to these changes.

Take, for example, the Institute's role in establishing standards of financial reporting. As you know, some critics contend that

139

pronouncements of the APB are too rigid. Others complain that Opinions are not tight enough. Some suggest that the APB does not move quickly enough, while others counter that it acts precipitately.

A number of actions have already been initiated in response to these challenges. The APB recently introduced a new procedure into its deliberative process -- the use of public hearings on the more important and controversial matters under consideration. The first of these open hearings was held last month on accounting for marketable securities -- a question of general concern to the financial community and of particular interest to groups such as the insurance industry and stock brokerage firms. The meeting proved to be a valuable source of input to the APB. Over 45 individuals and organizations submitted written briefs, while more than 20 requested time to speak at the hearing.

Opinion No. 16 on business combinations and *No. 17* on intangible assets consumed much of the APB's time in 1970. Since then, the Board's tempo of productivity has increased significantly. Two new Opinions, *No. 18* on equity accounting for long-term common stock investments and *No. 19* on changes in financial position, have been issued within the past two months. Two proposed Opinions dealing with accounting changes and imputing interest on long-term receivables and payables have been circulated for comment. And the Board's agenda is literally loaded with items approaching the exposure stage.

Another important step was taken early this year when Marshall Armstrong, President of the AICPA, formed two high-level study groups to consider whether our efforts to improve financial reporting standards are sufficiently prompt and productive. One group will study whether present procedures for establishing accounting principles can be improved; the other will seek to refine the objectives of financial statements. Both groups will consult with interested organizations and individuals, hold hearings, and maintain a public record. Each group includes representatives of business and professional life outside public accounting. In fact, a majority of those on each study group is from outside public practice.

The group studying the establishment of accounting principles is chaired by Francis M. Wheat, a recent member of the Securities and Exchange Commission. Serving with him are a university professor, a financial analyst, a financial vice president of one of the nation's largest industrial corporations, and three CPAs in public practice.

The group studying the objectives of financial statements is chaired by Robert M. Trueblood, a practicing CPA and past president of the American Institute. Serving with him are a financial analyst, an economist, an industrial executive, two professors, and two CPAs from public practice. The study on establishment of accounting principles is expected to be completed next fall and the study on objectives next year.

A current source of pressure upon accounting principles is the Treasury Department. It has recently been following a policy of permitting for tax purposes, in certain instances, use of an accounting method only if it is not at variance with the method used by the taxpayer for reports to shareholders.

Such conformity does not, at first glance, have an undesirable appearance. However, if the Treasury's policy of conformity is broadened, accounting methods used for income tax purposes are likely to control eventually the methods for financial accounting, Naturally, taxpayers would use the accounting methods which produced the lowest tax; and these would then have to be used for financial reporting, regardless of whether they were sound and proper methods for reporting to owners and creditors. One result would be to make it exceedingly difficult for the Accounting Principles Board to eliminate undesirable methods. The Institute's Board of Directors has recently appointed an *ad hoc* committee to review the matter in depth and to recommend a course of action.

The profession's role in establishing accounting principles is not the only area of our activities requiring a "self-renewal" effort. The attest function also requires fresh scrutiny.

Problems regarding the auditing function are multi-faceted. Practitioners voice concern over the quantity and the quality of Statements issued by the Committee on Auditing Procedure. Many believe the Committee has not gone far enough in modifying generally accepted auditing standards, or in issuing guidelines on acceptable audit techniques. They believe that too much of the Committee's attention has been devoted to reacting to specific events, and not enough to more forward-looking proposals. A small number of practitioners have an opposing view; they believe that so many Statements have been issued that the CPA is put in an auditing straitjacket.

Many of the concerns of the Committee arise from the flurry of lawsuits which have plagued the profession during the past few years. Much litigation arises, no doubt, because auditing standards and guidelines do not exist in a specific area, or are not precisely defined. However, much also arises because of substandard field work and reporting practices.

Some say that the auditor's liability is being extended with each court decision and that auditing standards are being set by the courts. This is debatable -- and legal counsel for the Institute assures us that the profession still has the opportunity to set its own standards, even on points where a court has decided differently.

Some members of the profession believe that further Statements on Auditing Procedure will only tend to increase auditors' liability. To the extent that new standards impose additional obligations, this may be true. On the other hand, the very existence of standards may tend to limit liability in all cases where auditors adhere to them.

The organized profession through the American Institute has recognized the problem and has initiated steps to overcome it. When Tom Holton, one of your fellow-Texans, took over as chairman of the Committee on Auditing Procedure late in 1969, he in effect doubled the number of days it meets in order to better attend to the volume of items on the agenda.

Although the full results of this effort cannot be expected immediately, significant advances are already visible. Three Statements have been issued since January, 1970, two more should be approved for publication this month, and a Statement about subsequent events will almost assuredly be issued before the end of 1971.

Statement No. 42 on reporting when a certified public accountant is not independent and *Statement No. 43* on confirmation of receivables and observation of inventories were issued in 1970. Last April the Committee, as a result of *APB Opinion 16*, issued *Statement No. 44* on reports following a pooling of interests. The two Statements on which the Committee on Auditing Procedure is currently balloting deal with piece-meal opinions and using the work and report of another auditor.

The Committee's agenda, like that of the Accounting Principles Board, is full of items under active consideration. Most notable is the expanded scope of projects on its agenda. Subjects such as qualitative aspects of inventory taking, report qualification criteria, and reliance on non-accounting experts are sure to make valuable contributions to the auditing literature.

The Institute's effort in the auditing area is being enhanced in other ways. First, the amount of resources (manpower as well as monetary) applied to this function is being studied, and it is likely an increased commitment will result. The addition two years ago of a full-time auditing research consultant has given the Committee research support in preparing position papers and background information on a more timely and thorough basis. An additional research associate will be joining him this summer.

The Practice Review mechanism, which has been operative since 1962, and the newly created Quality Review program are, in my judgment, effective ways of combating substandard auditing and reporting performances which result from lack of knowledge of the standards. The number of cases processed by the Practice Review Committee has more than doubled during the past two years, and the number of noted departures from generally accepted auditing standards has increased commensurately. In each case of a noted departure, a letter of comment, instructional in nature, is sent to the CPA.

In an effort to meet the increased work load, it is contemplated that the Practice Review Committee will be expanded and divided into two panels. This should facilitate the review of cases and preparation of letters of comment.

The Quality Review Committee, formed last year, will embark on its pilot program this summer. Generally, the Committee will function in this way: At the request of a CPA firm, a team of practitioners will review the audit working papers and reports related to a number of the firm's engagements, and will discuss the team's findings with the firm. The team will give constructive criticism and recommend ways in which auditing and reporting may be improved. CPA firms will be charged a nominal fee for this service.

I believe this to be an important self-renewal effort, offering the smaller firms the advantage of a review program similar to those which have been used effectively for many years by the large and medium-sized firms. I would urge the Texas Society to support this project and to encourage CPAs here to avail themselves of the quality review program.

Auditing today is under pressure in other ways. The factors of judgment, estimation, and materiality in financial reporting occasionally strain the credibility of auditing in the eyes of the public. This situation is made more difficult by the continued existence of alternative accounting principles. As long as choices exist among principles (and judgment is a factor in determining operating results), the public will be skeptical. Also, in a few instances, companies will shop for a more compliant auditor. The possibilities of completely eradicating this practice are slim, but it can be restricted.

One effective deterrent is about to emerge as a result of the continuing dialogue between the American Institute and the Securities and Exchange Commission. Amendments recently proposed by the SEC to the 1934 Act would require that companies file an 8-K report whenever there is a change in auditors. The proposed amendment would require a letter from the displaced firm, setting forth the firm's understanding of the reasons for the change, and indicating any problems encountered if the current year's audit has been started. The Institute has suggested that the amendment be modified to focus the reporting requirement more clearly on disagreements between auditor and client as to accounting principles or practices, financial statement disclosures, or auditing procedures. The proposed amendment would also require that Form 8-K be filed to report unusual charges or credits of a material amount, and to report changes in accounting principles or practices having a material effect on financial statements.

So far, I have talked primarily about problems that already exist and ways in which the profession is working to combat them. But the most significant part of our self-renewal is clear-sighted appraisal of what lies ahead. If the profession desires sustained growth and progress, it must look to the future. We must search for ways in which the auditor's role can be expanded to better serve the public interest, and ways in which the accounting discipline can be more fully applied.

The auditor's role, for example, might be extended to cover interim financial statements. This would require greatly improved techniques that would enable the auditor to assume that added responsibility without incurring excessive legal liability and uneconomical additional work.

For publicly-traded companies, there is a great deal of interest in quarterly reports. Stock exchanges require them, and now the SEC is doing so, too. Instances occur all too frequently in which interim financial statements present a picture that is considerably different from what appears in the year-end reports. Yet, the interim statements are often reported to the public as widely as the audited annual reports.

Another possibility for expanding the auditor's usefulness is to require a specific report on the internal controls of a company. This is already done to some extent. It is required for regulatory purposes for a few industries, such as stock brokerage firms; and occasionally it is done in response to specific requests from bankers and others.

Suggestions have been made that the auditor express an opinion on management performance. Often investors would like to know from an independent source that management has performed in adequate fashion, including its achievement of non-profit-oriented objectives. This is a most difficult assignment and one in which standards would have to be drawn very carefully before an auditor would be able to express any opinion. But it is an area to watch and, if the demand increases, I believe the accounting profession will find a way to meet it.

Profit forecasting is still another interesting possibility. Most well-run organizations of any size prepare budgets to guide the conduct of the business. Investors, too, would like to see budgeted plans. They are more interested in a company's *future* than in its *past* results, which are all that historical financial statements provide.

Association with forecasts presents many problems. Today's professional standards prohibit auditors from involvement in a profit forecast carrying the implication that they vouch for its accuracy. Yet, auditors concern themselves with forecasts for various purposes, although seldom with those intended for the public. Clearly, standards are needed before auditors can add credibility to profit forecasts.

One of the most interesting fields of potential growth for the profession is federally-stimulated audits. We already participate extensively in these programs -- more than 50,000 such audits are performed each year and the growth rate is high. Occasionally, however, obstacles are encountered to the use of independent accountants. I submit that this fact raises questions about some basic assumptions of the profession and should cause us to reappraise our policies. Let me cite just three problem areas.

First, the profession seems often to take the attitude that our staple product is the standard short-form audit report, even though government may have a need for something different. The department or agency involved may want a report on internal control, or on compliance with a particular law, or on performance evaluation of a program. These are new and intriguing areas of auditing which provide interesting challenges. Performance evaluation would in many cases require participation with people from other disciplines.

Second, some federal agencies which use independent CPAs want information on the cost of an auditing service before engaging a firm. This has caused problems in states where Boards of Accountancy and CPA Societies hold that giving any indication of estimated cost is a violation of the competitive bidding rules.

A third area where the profession encounters problems with federal administrators is in client-auditor relations. When an audit of a business or non-profit organization is called for under a federal program, who is the client -- the entity audited or the government? If the profession maintains that the entity being audited is the principal client, is it any wonder that a government administrator may question the auditor's independence for purposes of the administrator's own accountability? Even though federal agencies want to use independent accountants, the continued existence of such obstacles may force the building of large staffs of government auditors to perform needed work.

These problems cannot be solved by individual CPAs or their firms, but only by the organized profession. And if the profession does not take the initiative, the issues will probably be resolved unilaterally by government agencies, one at a time, and perhaps to our detriment.

In the three cited problem areas, I suggest that the Institute take these specific actions:

1.   Intensify efforts to establish professional standards for examining and reporting on internal control, compliance with laws, and performance under federal programs. Some good work has been done in these areas, but much more remains to be done.

2.   Assume leadership in recommending a policy to State Boards and State Societies which will help them avoid confrontation with federal antitrust laws, and which will give independent auditors reasonable opportunity to submit fee estimates in response to requests from governments, which *is* in the public interest, and still guard against unscrupulous competitive bidding, which is *not* in the

public interest.

3. Clarify client-auditor relations to assure that audit reports to federal agencies and to owners and other interested parties are equal in independence and objectivity.

These three recommendations are not solutions, but actions, which, with a lot of hard work, should lead to solutions.

All of these federal matters affect the practice of public accounting directly. But a citizen should view government also from the standpoint of its objectives in meeting the needs of the people. A citizen who is also a professional has a special obligation to consider how this knowledge could help the government in the accomplishment of its objectives. To do this in an organized way means that the Institute should take the lead in areas where it has competence. There are federal issues of broad concern on which the Institute has taken a position, many more where it should take a position, and still others where it has an opportunity to take a position if it wishes to broaden its horizons and become known as a profession concerned with the great issues of the day.

One such issue, for example, is the proposal for reorganization of the executive branch of government. These proposals were recommended by the President's Advisory Council on Executive Reorganization and outlined by the President in his State of the Union message last January. Inasmuch as professional accountants have particular interest in and knowledge about concepts of organization, it is only fitting that the Institute take a position on this subject.

Another example is revenue-sharing. When the President proposed general revenue-sharing, accountability became the most controversial feature. Critics contend the plan is devoid of accountability for the billions of dollars which would be handed over to state and local governments, and proponents claim accountability would be enhanced. Professional accountants are highly qualified to speak out on this type of accountability.

If the Institute wants to have a voice in national affairs, it must have the courage to speak up on specific proposed measures. I am pleased to say that the Board of Directors has recently expressed support for the idea that the Institute develop additional capability to study the big issues of government, to determine appropriate Institute policies concerning them, and to make the positions known to the government and public. Therefore, we can look forward to an increasing effort by the accounting profession in federal matters.

No discussion of the profession's future would be complete without relating our hope for advancement to the educational requirements this imposes. If our level of knowledge does not expand proportionately with the expansion of our activities, our striving for renewed vitality will be in vain. But again, definite action has been taken.

At its May meeting the Institute's Council adopted a landmark resolution calling for a program of continuing education within the profession. The resolution urges states to adopt a requirement that a CPA must demonstrate continuing professional education in order to remain in practice. It also urges State Boards of Accountancy to support the proposal by adopting the guidelines set forth in the report of the Committee on Continuing Education.

This, along with the other positive actions of the Institute, should indicate the profession's dedication to a program of self-renewal and our willingness and capability to respond to emerging situations. These efforts will be successful only if each certified public accountant makes the same dedication of purpose and vigorously undertakes a personal program of self-renewal. Are *you* ready to make this commitment?

ACCOUNTABILITY OF THE ACCOUNTING PROFESSION
Distinguished Lecture in Accounting
Oklahoma State University
October 28, 1971

No doubt most of you have observed, as I have, a growing emphasis in contemporary society on accountability. The public is demanding that our organizations, institutions, and individual leaders be held accountable for their actions to a greater degree than has been customary. For example:

o The idea is growing among the public that educators should render account, not only of the *financial* aspects of programs but, of the *quality* of education provided.

o Accountability is one of the most controversial aspects of federal/state revenue sharing, with great concern expressed by proponents and opponents alike as to where the responsibility lies for allocation and control of outlays.

o Demand for accountability for social and environmental effects of business activities has required corporations to reappraise their objectives and priorities.

o Penologists are increasingly concerned over the accountability of the nation's correctional institutions for the rehabilitation of inmates.

o In growing degree, the entire world seems to be holding nations accountable for the death and destruction inflicted by war.

In this atmosphere, it is not surprising that increased attention is focusing on the one profession whose very *raison d'etre* is accountability. All of you are aware, I am sure, that the accounting profession is drawing mixed reviews on its performance; and I would like to examine why this is so, to point out some substantial progress which is not yet fully recognized, and to suggest some further

149

opportunities which seem to be particularly available to the accounting profession.

While the roots of accountancy can be traced back 5,000 years to the invention of writing itself, accounting did not begin to emerge as a profession until the 19th century. In that period, English investors in American business engaged chartered accountants to examine and report on the financial condition of various enterprises. The arrangement was clearly understood: the owner in England was the client, and the accountant's report was considered as being of use to the owner alone.

But in the following decades, ownership of American business spread from the few to the many. Capital was provided by millions of investors; and, by 1932, Berle and Means could note in their book, *The Modern Corporation and Private Property*, that the owners of business did not manage it, and the managers did not own it.

Somewhere in this evolutionary change, the independent accountant's notion of who is the "client" underwent subtle transformation. While a company's management engaged the independent accountants and had extensive contact with them, the rank-and-file of investors, unseen and largely unheard, had somehow to be considered. Even so, however, management interests undoubtedly continued to weigh heavily with independent auditors. Today, we have returned to the original position that owners (now comprised of millions of stockholders, instead of individual proprietors) are the clients, and, more significantly, that auditors' reports must serve third parties and the public-at-large.

During the 1920s, the American Institute of CPAs approached the New York Stock Exchange with a proposal that listed companies give more comprehensive financial reports than many of them had been giving. Nothing came of the suggestion then, but after the speculative excesses of the period were followed by the stock market collapse of 1929, serious discussions were begun. These resulted in several key recommendations, the most important being that annual financial statements be independently audited. That recommendation was adopted by the Exchange and subsequently incorporated into the Securities Act of 1933.

The Securities and Exchange Commission was created the following year to administer the Act and was empowered by Congress to specify accounting methods. The SEC delegated the function to the profession, reserving for itself the role of watchdog. From the outset, the SEC was greatly concerned with the independence and objectivity of the auditor. And, during nearly four decades of surveillance, the watchdog has had very few occasions to growl.

During this period, the growing complexity of business and the great increase in the number of investors have challenged the profession's capacity in at least two ways. First, they have made business operations more difficult to analyze and interpret; and, second, they have made these operations more difficult to communicate to an investing public comprised of people having all degrees of financial sophistication.

The broadened base of CPAs' responsibilities has led to continuing reassessments of accounting principles, auditing standards, professional ethics, and the qualifications of professional accountants in public practice. The accelerated development of accounting principles that has taken place in the past several years clearly reflects the profession's response to a changing world.

For example, before the recent popularity of stock warrants, convertible securities, and common stock equivalents, there was no pressing need for a probing review of computations of earnings per share. That need arose in the late 1960s, and the profession acted to meet it.

Before the appearance of conglomerates with the highly imaginative methods of acquiring other companies (or for merging one company with another), there was little need for accounting principles covering such developments. When that need arose, the profession acted to meet it.

Innovations in the use of sale-and-leaseback arrangements, convertible debt, low-interest or no-interest credit, and pension funds brought new needs. And the profession acted.

I suspect that if we could resurrect a CPA who practiced early in this century and could outline for him the subject matter of recent Opinions of the Accounting Principles Board, he would not know, in many cases, what we were talking about. These Opinions were responses to conditions that did not previously exist and that earlier CPAs had not even dreamed of.

While each new APB Opinion resolves certain problems, it often also brings to attention other problems in need of solution. A new Opinion may, for example, cause business to devise operating and financing methods which are not covered by the Opinion, thus opening new areas for study by the APB.

Few questions have caused the accounting profession more trouble than that of accounting for the "investment tax credit." Although the issue seemed to have become moot with the Tax Reform Act of 1969, it is about to revive with the "job development credit," which will be part of the tax law to be enacted next month.

Once again, therefore, the Accounting Principles Board has to determine the proper accounting method to be followed. And once more, the APB seems to favor deferral of the credit and amortization of it over the life of the property as a reduction of cost. Yet, there is an understandable reluctance on the part of the APB to issue an Opinion, unless there is some assurance that the Securities and Exchange Commission will support it in practice.

We are now seeking that assurance, but we must recognize that the SEC is under no obligation to provide it, even if it should share the Board's preference for the deferral method. The subject has been explored with appropriate people in the SEC and the Treasury Department, and I am optimistic that the APB will get the support it needs. Nevertheless, I must confess that some others are not optimistic.

Ideally, the APB should issue its Opinion on the sole ground of sound accounting principles that will result in the fair measurement of income, regardless of anticipated support or lack of it. And the profession should present a united front in following that Opinion in practice. If, in such circumstances, others acted in a way that thwarted the effect of the Opinion, they would then be clearly responsible for any consequences, and the accounting profession will have performed responsibly. But, I must confess again that others do not share my view on this matter.

A current source of pressure upon accounting principles is the Treasury Department. It has recently followed a policy of permitting, under certain circumstances, use of an accounting method for tax purposes only if it is not at variance with the method used by the taxpayer for reports to shareholders.

At first glance, such conformity may seem desirable. However, if this policy were broadened, accounting methods for income tax purposes might well come to control financial accounting. Naturally, taxpayers would use the accounting methods which produced the lowest tax, and these would then have to be used for financial reporting, regardless of whether they were sound and proper methods for reporting to owners and creditors.

The Institute's Board of Directors has recently adopted a statement which favors conformity of tax accounting to financial accounting, but opposes a "booking requirement." While recognizing the different objectives of tax and financial accounting and that some deviations in reporting income for these purposes are necessary, the statement concludes as follows:

> The policy of the AICPA is to advocate conformance of tax accounting to generally accepted accounting principles, with certain exceptions which need to be continuously defined in a logical and cohesive manner by the appropriate body within the AICPA.

> A requirement that external reports for creditors, stockholders, etc., conform to income tax accounting as a prerequisite for the use of certain income tax methods has been applied by the Treasury Department and further applications are under consideration.

> This "booking requirement" may be applied inequitably among taxpayers, and also may serve as a deterrent to changes in accounting principles considered desirable by the accounting profession. Hence, the AICPA opposes imposition of booking requirements by the Treasury Department, or by Congress.

An encouraging event in the continuing development of accounting is a new SEC requirement for reporting a change in auditors. In a dialogue extending over several months, the SEC and the Institute became increasingly concerned over "shopping" for accounting principles. The concern went beyond the relatively few instances where a change in auditors appeared to involve a dispute between auditor and client over accounting principles; it went to the pressure that might be applied merely by the *threat* of a change in auditor.

Last May, the SEC issued proposed amendments to Form 8-K on this and other matters, and the final amendments were adopted on September 27. Now, if new auditors have been engaged, the registrant must report the date of engagement and furnish the Commission a separate letter stating whether, in the preceding 18 months, there were any disagreements with the former auditors about accounting principles which, if not resolved to the satisfaction of the former auditors, would have caused them to refer in their opinion to the subject matter of the disagreement. Furthermore, the Commission must be furnished a letter from the former auditors stating whether they agree with the statements in the registrant's letter.

This goes a long way toward strengthening the hand of the auditor in dealing with a client. And the public will benefit from improved accounting principles.

In my judgment, the attainments of the Accounting Principles Board in improving financial reporting standards have been substantial and have served the public interest well. Nevertheless, in an age of accountability, nearly everyone is a critic. Some say the APB has been too slow in issuing pronouncements to correct reporting abuses, while others say it has acted too fast. Some say APB pronouncements are too permissive, while others say they are too rigid and restrictive.

Because many of the complaints about APB performance come from responsible sources, the Institute has formed two high-level study groups to consider whether our efforts to improve financial reporting standards are sufficiently prompt and productive. One group, chaired by Francis M. Wheat, is studying whether present procedures for establishing accounting principles can be improved. The other group, chaired by Robert M. Trueblood, is seeking to refine the objectives of financial statements. Each group includes representatives of business and professional life outside public accounting. In fact, a majority of those on each study group is from outside public practice.

Both of these groups are plowing virgin ground, as well as re-sifting soil that has been gone over before. They have been interviewing in depth those known to have ideas on the subjects under study -- probing the past, examining the experience of other professions, and exploring what has been done in other countries. The first public hearings will be held by the Wheat group in New York on November 3 and 4.

When the "listening" phase of their work is completed, the study groups will deliberate among themselves and hammer out reports that, I feel, are sure to be landmarks in the history of accounting. According to progress reports by Mr. Trueblood and Mr. Wheat at the Institute's meeting in Detroit, neither group has yet begun to reach conclusions. However, it is apparent that the reports when finally submitted will probably call for searching new looks at some long-established traditions.

At the same time that the Institute is seeking an objective examination of accounting principles, it is also devoting increased attention to auditing standards. The Committee on Auditing Procedure is hard at work issuing Statements which provide guidance for auditors in performing their function.

A public attuned to accountability in nearly every phase of human endeavor expects auditors to adhere to high professional standards. Recent court cases seem to indicate that such standards must not only be technically supportable, but must meet the test of serving the public interest.

The computer has challenged auditors to develop new techniques of auditing and, at the same time, has provided them with a powerful auditing tool. Auditors have had to learn new approaches to reviews of internal control and the use of statistical sampling. Beyond that, auditors must continually adapt to change in a dynamic business environment simply to discharge their traditional audit function.

In response to the demands for accountability, there has been a great expansion of the surveillance required of auditors over the financial statements on which they express opinions. Already, a statement of source and application of funds has become a basic financial statement covered by the auditor's report. There is a distinct possibility that two-year income statements will be supplanted by five-year income statements -- again, covered by the auditor's report. It has been proposed that the auditor express an opinion on the highlights section of the annual report in order to assure conformity of the condensed information with the more complete audited financial statements that appear elsewhere in the report.

Looking further ahead, we may see the auditor's surveillance covering such areas as interim financial statements, budget and profit forecasts, and the quality of management performance. At one time, not too long ago, any suggestion that auditors be associated with a company's budget or forecast would have triggered a reflex reaction of disapproval. It is still the view of many that nothing so subject to indeterminable influences as a future projection should be attested to.

But investors and security analysts, more interested in the *future* than in the *past*, want profit forecasts and they want them to have at least some degree of credibility. I do not see this coming until forecasting methods have been designed that will offer greater precision than those used now. But if there is a genuine need, I am sure a system could be worked out permitting CPAs to audit, within certain parameters, the facts and figures on which the forecasts are based.

Never before has there been such a craving for credibility of information given to the public. The accounting profession is deeply involved in providing such credibility to business information. So far, it has been concerned primarily with traditional financial reporting, but a whole new area is opening up in the measurement and reporting of businesses' social responsibility.

Interest has been expressed in reports on the quality of management performance, including the achievement of non-profit-oriented objectives. If measurements are needed to permit comparison of the work of one company's managers with that of other companies in similar businesses, they will undoubtedly be forthcoming; and we will be expressing opinions as to their fairness.

If it is possible to devise accurate bases of comparison for management's performance, it follows that one could measure the value to the company of each member of management -- and, perhaps the value of all other employees. That is called "human resources accounting," and it is already being tried by at least one company. The thrust of this experiment is to produce a dollar value for the investments the company has made in people -- the costs of hiring, training, motivating, and retaining its employees. Efforts are made to establish realistic depreciation schedules, and year-by-year comparisons are made of the value of the company's human assets.

Human resources accounting is just one aspect of the broader, developing field of "social accounting" -- the evaluation of costs and benefits of programs intended to improve the human condition; or, alternatively, the determination of the consequences of *failing* to implement such programs. At the American Institute's recent annual meeting, a panel discussion on this subject was titled, "Measuring the Unmeasurable." I think that this catchy title could have been more accurate, albeit less catchy, if it had been phrased, "Measuring *what has until now been considered* Unmeasurable."

Social accounting, while still posing great unanswered questions, is no longer just being talked about. Demand for this new type of measurement has arisen, and the accounting profession is exploring ways it can work with other disciplines to help meet it.

Some accounting firms already are carrying out innovative engagements in this new field. One helped measure traffic patterns in the densely populated northeast section of the nation as part of a government study to determine where and how federal transportation funds could be spent most effectively, not only in terms of speeding trade and transportation, but also of assuring a good environment for residents of the area. As another example, the Bank of America has asked its outside accountants to devise means for determining the relative costs and benefits of various community service programs the bank has under consideration. Another accounting firm was engaged to help determine the optimum use of welfare funds in Detroit. Other CPA assignments have included a study of public use of state parks in California, of wildlife in Texas game preserves, of water pollution in Pennsylvania, and of air pollution in Missouri. On such engagements, members of CPA firms are working with experts in other disciplines, while providing their own special expertise: *measurement* and *evaluation*.

You may be interested to know, incidentally, that the Institute plans to hold an interdisciplinary roundtable on social measurement next year. The idea is to sponsor an informal meeting in which representatives of accountancy, economics, sociology, social psychology, and political science can exchange current information and thinking on the subject. We hope that the meeting will lay the foundation for future cooperation among the several professions on ways to attain advancement in the gauging of social programs.

This new type of measurement is, in my view, a logical, indeed inevitable, extension of management advisory services. (Similarly, reporting on social measurements is a logical, indeed inevitable, extension of auditing.) In its present form, the profession's advisory services embrace a wide spectrum of activities, ranging from informal suggestions for improving a company's information systems, finance practices, or operating procedures to highly structured consulting engagements using the skills of many disciplines.

Because of accountants' familiarity with the internal workings of client companies, it is natural that clients should turn to them for objective advice in many areas. So frequently have CPAs been called upon to perform the advisory role over the years that it has become an intrinsic part of practice, offered by firms ranging from the very largest to the quite small.

In this field also, the profession continues to improve the standards of performance. In 1969, the Institute began issuing a series of "Statements" for the guidance of members performing consulting work. This was a major step toward the development of technical standards for this function.

Another growing demand for CPA services comes from government. In the past, programs have been instituted at all levels of government, and large sums of money appropriated, with only cursory examination as to whether the money was being used in a way that would best achieve the results intended. This is less and less the case today. Increasingly, internal controls are now set up at the start, and there are subsequent performance audits and cost/benefit analyses.

The widened call upon the profession to help meet the accounting needs of federal agencies is only one aspect of a growing involvement with government. It is a trend I believe will continue, for there are many other such areas in which the background and experience of CPAs can help achieve sound decisions. The Institute's Board of Directors intends to study broad issues of government where the profession can possibly be helpful, and I suspect that our profile in Washington is going to be much higher than it has been in the past.

As we change our positions on accounting principles, auditing standards, our posture toward government, and other aspects of the profession to keep them in step with changing times, there is another element in need of updating. That is our professional Code of Ethics. The restatement of the Code to keep it relevant to today's world will be submitted to a vote of the Institute's membership next year. I hope we move forward here, with a minimum of quibbling and with a clear consciousness of our broad responsibilities.

The increased responsibility laid upon the accounting profession has led to a dramatic upgrading of the academic requirements for admission to (and continued practice in) it. Each year, the Uniform CPA Examination becomes a little tougher -- probing at greater depth and extending outward into new areas. We are moving toward a requirement of five years of college or its equivalent for admission to the profession and toward a requirement of continuing education to remain in practice. These are not capricious or arbitrary decisions. Rather, they are simply realistic actions to qualify us to meet the demands made of us.

Accountants are not the only persons deeply involved with accountability today. Accountants cannot possibly possess all of the skills needed to meet the demands of the public for accountability throughout the broad range of mankind's activities. Yet, no other calling is in a position to provide as much credibility to reports on economic and social functions. Accountancy is the only profession which has a base of independence and competence; and having technical, reporting, and educational standards -- all directed toward the purpose of adding credibility to information reports of others.

The opportunity exits now for the profession to expand its horizons, embrace other disciplines, and apply measurement and reporting standards wherever a demand arises which can properly be met. Prompt action is needed, however, for if the accounting profession does not rise to the occasion, other disciplines and institutions will. My personal belief is that the accounting profession will fulfill the opportunity to lead in the field of accountability.

WHAT'S IN THE HOPPER OF THE APB?
Before the Financial Executives Institute
Los Angeles Chapter
January 20, 1972

The formulation of accounting principles for business enterprises is a matter of great importance to our economic system and to the more than 30 million investors who support it. This function is being carried out by the American Institute of Certified Public Accountants' Accounting Principles Board, whose formal Opinions provide the standards on which financial statements are based.

The APB has a hopper full of subjects which will receive early attention. But before discussing them, I would like to describe briefly four Opinions which were issued in 1971 and which will affect 1971 financial statements in a variety of ways. They are *Number 18* on "The Equity Method of Accounting for Investments in Common Stock"; *Number 19* on "Reporting Changes in Financial Position"; *Number 20* on "Accounting Changes"; and *Number 21* on "Interest on Receivables and Payables."

The Equity Method of Accounting for Investments in Common Stock

The first of these deals with long-term investments in common stock. In this pronouncement the Board extends use of the equity method of accounting (which, heretofore, was required just for unconsolidated domestic subsidiaries) to all unconsolidated subsidiaries. It also requires use of equity accounting for corporate joint ventures, fifty-percent-owned companies, and investments in voting common stock which give the investor the ability to exercise "significant influence" over operating and financial policies of the investee.

The Opinion stipulates that an investment of 20 percent or more of the voting stock of a company will be considered as indicating ability to exercise significant influence, in the absence of evidence to the contrary. Conversely, an investment of less than 20 percent of the voting stock will be regarded as showing that no such influence exists, unless it can be demonstrated.

Equity accounting is required under this Opinion, not only in consolidated financial statements, but in parent company-only financials issued as primary statements to stockholders. The Opinion is effective for all fiscal periods beginning after December 31, 1971; however, the Board encourages earlier application of its provisions.

Reporting Changes in Financial Position

Opinion No. 19 requires that a presentation of changes in financial position (funds statement) be included as a basic financial statement whenever a balance sheet and a statement of income and retained earnings are presented. It was the view of the Board that information concerning the financing and investing activities of a business enterprise, and a summary of changes in its financial position, are essential for owners and creditors in making economic decisions.

Presentation of a funds statement has been recommended, though not required, by the accounting profession for a long time. It has been recommended also by the stock exchanges. Recently, the SEC declared that a funds statement will henceforth be a required item in registration statements and reports filed with the Commission.

The need for a funds statement as a required, rather than merely optional, item of information was highlighted in the past two years or so when a number of companies experienced financial difficulty. At such a time, the attention of knowledgeable investors focuses on liquidity, and they want information that is not easily obtained from the balance sheet or statement of income alone. The statement of changes in financial position contributes materially to answers to such questions, and its required presentation should be welcomed by financial statement users. Thus, the new Opinion is quite timely. It is effective for periods ending after September 30, 1971.

Accounting Changes

Opinion No. 20 defines various types of accounting changes and specifies the manner of reporting each type. It restricts accounting changes to situations in which it can be demonstrated that the alternative accounting principle is preferable.

The cumulative effect of the difference between the former accounting method and the retroactive application of the new method will be reported as a separate item appearing just above net income for the year. Financial statements of prior years will not be restated, but the effect of the change on reported income and earnings per share of those years is to be disclosed as supplemental information.

This method is called for in the treatment of changes in accounting principle, except for three situations that are to be treated retroactively. These are: a change from LIFO to another method of inventory valuation; accounting for long-term construction-type contracts; and a change to or from the "full cost" method of accounting used in the extractive industries. Changes in reporting entity and correction of errors are also treated retroactively. The provisions of *Opinion No. 20* are effective for fiscal years beginning after July 31, 1971.

Interest on Receivables and Payables

Opinion No. 21 requires a long-term receivable or payable to be discounted at an appropriate rate when it is either non-interest bearing or bears an interest rate clearly below a reasonable rate at the time of a transaction. Imputing interest looks to the *substance* of a transaction, rather than its *form*.

The application of this method would result in more realistic reporting of the principal amount of the long-term receivable or payable and the related interest income or expense. For example, a company selling land or a building and receiving a non-interest bearing note as part of the proceeds would report a lower profit on the sale than indicated in the *stated* terms of sale, and would report interest income over the life of the note; conversely, the buyer would report interest expense over the life of the note.

The proposed Opinion, however, would not apply to the following: trade receivables and payables due in customary trade terms, ordinarily not exceeding one year; amounts which do not require repayment in the future, but are applied to the purchase price (deposits, progress payments, etc.); security deposits and retainers on contracts; customary cash lending activities and demand or savings deposit activities of lending institutions; transactions in which interest rates are affected by the tax attributes or legal restrictions of government; and transactions between affiliated companies. *Opinion No. 21* applies to transactions occurring after September 30, 1971.

Exposure Drafts

The Board's hopper has recently disgorged exposure drafts of three proposed Opinions. They are destined to return for further consideration and approval. Final issuance is expected within the next two months. The subjects are: "Translating Foreign Operations," "Disclosure of Accounting Policies," and "Accounting for Income Taxes - Special Areas."

Translating Foreign Operations

Many U.S. companies with substantial foreign operations would defer certain effects of exchange revaluations in their consolidated financial statements under an exposure draft dated December 20, 1971. In it the Board deals principally with accounting procedures arising from the application of the monetary/nonmonetary approach to translation of foreign currency assets and liabilities. It proposes that certain adjustments be deferred, while others should be carried in the income statement.

Companies have used one of two concepts for translating foreign operations. Under the current/non-current approach, current assets and current liabilities are generally translated at the exchange-rate prevailing at the balance sheet date. Non-current assets and non-current liabilities are translated at the rate prevailing when the asset was acquired, the liability incurred, or capital stock issued. More frequently used is the monetary/nonmonetary approach under which all monetary assets and liabilities are translated at current-rates and nonmonetary items at historical-rates.

In general, the Board's proposal would call for deferral of the net translation adjustment, aggregated on a world-wide basis, in cases where monetary liabilities exceed monetary assets and there are long-term monetary liabilities. The amount deferred would be limited to the translation adjustment on the long-term liabilities, and would be amortized over the remaining term of those liabilities by the interest method.

However, if there are no long-term monetary liabilities, or if monetary assets exceed monetary liabilities, all of the translation adjustment "gain" or "loss" would be taken into income currently. Such adjustments arising from currency revaluations and devaluations would be extraordinary items. By aggregating the net translation adjustments for each entity included in the consolidated statements on a world-wide basis, companies would not be able to carry a credit adjustment for one foreign subsidiary to income, while deferring a debit adjustment for another.

Public comments were due by January 19, and final action is expected at the Board meeting on January 24-26. If approved, the provisions would be effective for fiscal periods beginning after December 31, 1971, with earlier compliance encouraged. Board Opinions are not retroactive, but in this case, earlier compliance is essential if the Opinion is to fulfill its purpose of providing guidance in accounting for adjustments arising in 1971 from floating currencies and revaluations. We anticipate that earlier compliance will prevail because of the general receptivity of the proposed Opinion throughout industry and by the Securities and Exchange Commission.

Disclosure of Accounting Policies

The second proposed APB Opinion in the exposure draft stage, dated December 27, 1971, is entitled "Disclosure of Accounting Policies." In recent years, an increasing number of annual reports have contained a description of the accounting policies adopted in preparing financial statements. Many favorable comments have been made on this kind of disclosure, including a supportive statement by the Financial Executives Institute. The APB is now about to conclude that information on accounting policies used by a company is essential for financial statement users in making economic decisions.

While there could be flexibility in the disclosure format, the Board would strongly recommend that disclosure be made under a separate "Summary of Accounting Policies" immediately preceding the notes to financial statements. Disclosure would be made of major accounting principles used and methods of applying them. In particular, disclosure would include principles and methods that involve a selection from existing acceptable alternatives; are peculiar to the industry in which the company operates; or are unusual or innovative applications of generally accepted accounting principles that materially affect the related financial statements.

Comments are due by February 16. The Opinion is to be effective for fiscal years beginning after December 31, 1971.

Accounting for Income Taxes - Special Areas

The third exposure draft is "Accounting for Income Taxes - Special Areas," dated January 4, 1972. The Board's *Opinion No. 11*, "Accounting for Income Taxes," left for further study the application of deferred tax accounting in five special problem areas. They are: undistributed earnings of subsidiaries, amounts designated as "policyholders' surplus" by stock life insurance companies, "general reserves" of stock savings and loan associations, deposits in statutory reserve funds by United States steamship companies, and intangible development costs in the oil and gas industry. This last area will be considered in a proposed Opinion on accounting problems in the extractive industries, which is receiving active consideration following publication of *Accounting Research Study No. 11*. The Board is further deferring consideration of tax allocation on deposits in statutory reserve funds by United States steamship companies, pending issuance of regulations interpreting the Merchant Marine Act of 1970.

As to the other three problem areas, the exposure draft notes that resulting book-tax differences may not reverse until indefinite future periods, if ever; and reversal is dependent on specific action by the taxpayer. Therefore, deferred income taxes ordinarily would not be accrued on undistributed earnings of subsidiaries, additions to the reserve for bad debts for tax purposes in excess of the book provision for doubtful accounts of savings and loan associations, and differences between taxable income and pre-tax accounting income attributable to policyholders' surplus of stock life insurance companies.

However, deferred income taxes would be accrued on undistributed earnings of a subsidiary which probably will be transferred to the parent company in the foreseeable future. Also, if circumstances indicate that a savings and loan association or a life insurance company is likely to pay income taxes, either currently or in subsequent years, because of known or expected reductions in the bad debt reserve of the association or in policyholders' surplus of the insurance company, income taxes attributable to the reduction would be accrued as a current tax expense. The conclusions with respect to undistributed earnings of a subsidiary would apply also to earnings of a Domestic International Sales Corporation (DISC).

The question of tax allocation arises in a related area under *Opinion No. 18*, which extends use of the equity method of accounting to all unconsolidated subsidiaries, corporate joint ventures, and other common stock investments of significance (usually 20% or more). The current exposure draft would treat all subsidiaries alike, whether included in consolidation or accounted for by the equity method, and would accord similar treatment to corporate joint ventures. Thus, income tax would not be accrued on undistributed earnings of corporate joint ventures and subsidiaries accounted for by the equity method, unless it were probable that earnings would be transferred to the parent company in a taxable transaction in the foreseeable future.

The exposure draft takes a different position on accruing income tax on undistributed earnings for investments in common stock other than subsidiaries and corporate joint ventures. Where the investor uses the equity method of accounting for investments in which he has the ability to exercise significant influence, but not control (usually 20% to 50% of voting stock), income tax would be provided on undistributed earnings, because of the presumption that the earnings will be realized in the form of dividends.

Comments on the draft are due by February 23, with final issuance expected in March. The Opinion would be effective for fiscal years beginning after December 31, 1971, thus coinciding with the effective date of the related *Opinion No. 18*.

Other Subjects Being Considered by the Board

In addition to the three exposure drafts, several other subjects are in-process in the Board's hopper.

Stock Compensation

The Board has taken note of the proliferation of new types of stock options and other stock compensation plans, including tandem and phantom plans, and is developing guidelines for recognizing the compensation expense involved. In March, 1971, an Accounting Interpretation was issued by the staff on stock compensation plans, which called for recognition of compensation, unless the grantee paid an amount at least equal to fair value at date of grant.

Now an Opinion has been drafted dealing with when and how compensation cost should be measured in various types of stock compensation plans. The Board's tentative conclusions are: the practice should be continued of not recognizing compensation cost under qualified stock option and qualified employee stock purchase plans. For non-qualified stock option plans and non-qualified employee stock purchase plans, compensation cost is the excess of market value of stock at date of grant over the option price (or if a formula is used, over the ultimate option price determined by the formula).

For restricted and unrestricted plans and qualified stock bonus plans, compensation cost is the excess of market value at the award date over award price, if any. For phantom stock plans, compensation cost is the excess of market value of shares issued at the date that the number of shares issuable is determined over the amount the employee pays in, if any. Because alternate stock and tandem stock option plans are a combination of more than one stock compensation plan, compensation cost should be determined for the plan most likely to be elected by the employee.

As a general rule, the tentative conclusion is that compensation cost of all plans should be allocated in a systematic and rational manner to current and future periods which are expected to benefit from operation of the plan. The proposed Opinion also states that use of treasury stock to settle plan obligations does not affect compensation costs to be recorded, and that treasury stock should not be presented as an asset.

The timetable for this Opinion calls for approval for exposure at the January 24-26, 1972, meeting with final action at the March 8-10, 1972, meeting. It would apply to all options granted and shares awarded after January 31, 1972.

Marketable Securities

Discussion of *Opinion No. 18*, on the use of the equity method of accounting for long-term investments in common stock, led the APB to separate consideration of accounting for investments in equity securities for which the equity method is inappropriate. In early deliberations the APB tentatively agreed that investments in readily marketable equity securities, including preferred stock as well as common stock, should be accounted for at market value rather than cost, with the change in value, net of taxes, included in income. As individual investors, we know we have a loss when the market declines, and a gain when it rises. So, too, does a corporate investor lose or gain as the market fluctuates; yet, these corporate investments are usually carried at cost.

The APB held public hearings on this in New York on May 25 and 26. More than 20 people spoke at the hearings and more than 40 written statements were received. The hearings have been helpful in the Board's deliberations.

More recently, the Board has tentatively agreed that investments in equity securities which are *not* readily marketable should be accounted for at fair value, rather than cost, with the change in value, net of taxes, included in income. Despite the obvious obstacles to fair value determination, there appears to be growing sentiment and authoritative support for its use by all companies in accounting for equity securities for which the equity method is inappropriate. Yet, there is an understandable reluctance by many to include changes in market values in net income on a current-basis because of the volatility of the stock market.

Special study is being given to the problems involved in insurance companies, banks, savings and loan associations, pension funds, colleges and universities, and other areas. Some people are developing a "yield theory," which minimizes current market fluctuations by spreading gains and losses, both realized and unrealized, over a period of years. Others are exploring the possibility of presenting two statements of equal prominence -- one for net income excluding changes in security values, and the other for changes in security values.

Still another proposal which will be considered at the January 24-26 meeting is that equity securities be carried at market value (or fair value) on the balance sheet with only *realized* gains and losses included in income. Net *unrealized* gains would be reported as a separate item in the equity section of the balance sheet.

The timetable for this Opinion is exposure in March and publication in July, 1972. In my view, this timetable is optimistic, given the controversial nature of the various proposals and the apparent lack of consensus as to a preferred method.

Retirement of Debt

In another area, the Board is considering the accounting for the purchase and retirement of debt. This became an important problem when many of the issues being reacquired were convertibles which were selling at a deep discount. Inasmuch as a convertible security has some elements of equity as well as debt, the question arose as to whether some portion of the discount should be an addition to capital, or whether it should all be income.

The Board tentatively favors accounting for the discount as if the security were solely a debt security. This is consistent with *Opinion No. 14*, which holds that no amount of the proceeds should be allocated to the convertible feature of a convertible security at the time it is issued.

A study of the problem led the Board to broaden its consideration to cover purchase and retirement of all debt, whether convertible or not and whether at a discount or at premium. Therefore, the proposed Opinion reconsiders all aspects of Chapter 15 of *Accounting Research Bulletin No. 43* ("Unamortized Discount, Issue Cost and Redemption Premium on Bonds Refunded").

The Board tentatively recommends the immediate recognition in income of all gains and losses and unamortized premium, discount, and issue costs of debt reacquired. This would rule out the presently accepted methods of spreading these amounts over the remaining life of the old issue or the life of a refunding issue.

Leases

Because of the complex and changing nature of American business and the way in which accounting principles are applied in practice, the APB constantly reviews the applicability and effectiveness of previous pronouncements. One such matter relates to accounting for leases. An earlier Opinion noted an apparent inconsistency between accounting methods recommended for lessors and lessees. In reconsidering this problem, the Board is reviewing some basic problems of both lessors and lessees.

Opinion No. 7 described the operating and financing methods of accounting for lease revenues by lessors, and described conditions under which each method is appropriate. That Opinion also specified that a manufacturer could record a "manufacturing profit" upon entering into a financing lease, provided certain conditions were met. Practice under this Opinion has raised questions as to the adequacy of criteria for this purpose. Some lessors have recorded manufacturing profit upon entering into a lease for as short a period as one year. The Board intends to tighten up in this area. Meanwhile, the Institute staff has issued an Accounting Interpretation which greatly restricts the recognition of lease transactions as sales.

As to lessees, the Board has tentatively agreed that leases which are financing leases should be capitalized. Study is being given as to whether still more leases should be capitalized. Also under study is the appropriate income statement treatment of capitalized leases. A typical lease with equal annual payments ordinarily would result in rent expense of equal annual amounts. Questions are being raised as to whether the combination of depreciation and interest expense that would arise through capitalization should also be made to result in equal annual amounts. Purchase of the same asset would ordinarily result in depreciation in equal annual amounts and interest expense in declining amounts, thus resulting in a combined expense that is higher in earlier years of the asset's life, and declining over time.

A public hearing on accounting for leases was held on October 14. About 165 people attended and 15 people presented oral statements. With this input to help further their deliberations, the Board is now drafting an Opinion on the subject.

Accounting for Extractive Industries

About two years ago, the Institute's Accounting Research Division published an Accounting Research Study on the extractive industries. Now that comments on the Study have been received from interested parties, the subject has been moved up on the APB's agenda.

Recent events have brought attention to the sharply different results which are reported by the full-cost and successful effort methods of accounting for exploration and development expenditures in the oil and gas industry. The Federal Power Commission has issued a rule which requires natural gas pipeline companies to use the full-cost method. The APB is proceeding with an Opinion on oil and gas industry accounting which would deal with a definition of a cost center, capitalization or expensing of exploration and development expenditures, disposition of capitalized costs, and disclosure of related information.

A public hearing on this subject was held in New York on November 22-23, 1971. The hearing did not cover allocation of federal income taxes in the oil and gas industry, or accounting and reporting matters in hard minerals industries. However, these areas remain on the APB's agenda.

Non-Cash Transactions

The Board is also studying the question of transfers of assets which do not involve cash. This includes distribution of appreciated non-cash assets from an enterprise to its owners, and exchanges of non-cash assets with non-owners. The principal question involved is whether an increase in value of the assets should be accounted for at the time of the transfer.

Interim Reporting

Quarterly financial statements are becoming more common. Stock exchanges require them, and now the SEC is doing so, too. Therefore, the APB is working on an Opinion which would set standards for interim period reporting.

Reporting on Lines of Business

A Statement issued by the APB in 1967 encouraged disclosure of information by line of business when a company operates in more than one industry. Many companies have been reporting information by line of business in annual reports, and recently such disclosures have been required in filings with the SEC. For the most part, these presentations have not been subject to independent audit. The APB, however, has on its agenda the development of an Opinion which would make disclosure of such information a requirement and provide standards for presenting it.

Reporting on Components

Often auditors are called upon to report on financial statements of a subsidiary company, a division, or a branch of a corporation. As guidelines for reporting on a component of a business are inadequate, the APB is studying the subject with the intent of issuing an Opinion.

Capitalization of Interest

The practice of capitalizing interest during construction has long been associated with accounting for public utilities. Now companies in other industries are looking with favor at the practice, not only in relation to construction, but also in other areas. Therefore, the APB is beginning to study the problems involved, with the intention of issuing an Opinion in 1973.

Extraordinary Items

In 1970, a huge number of extraordinary items appeared in corporate income statements, thus leading the Board to reconsider whether more specific criteria than those provided in *Opinion No. 9* are needed for identifying an extraordinary item.

Self-Insurance

As industry shows increasing interest in various forms of self-insurance, the APB is beginning to study this issue. Some observers see self-insurance charges as comparable to premiums paid to insurance companies, while others see them as profit-leveling devices.

Other APB Projects

Many other projects are in the research stage, including intercorporate investments, stockholders' equity, reporting foreign operations of U.S. companies in U.S. dollars, depreciation, inventory valuation, working capital, materiality, industrial research and development, and trans-national companies. As each Accounting Research Study is completed, the subject then comes to the APB for consideration of an Opinion.

Audit Guides

The Institute's program for improving accounting principles also includes a series of audit guides for specific industries. These guides are prepared by committees of Institute-members who are specialists in the particular industry, thus expanding the capability of the Institute for setting standards beyond that represented on the APB. To assure consistency of accounting principles, however, an audit guide is released only after being reviewed by the chairman of the APB for overall conformity with the more pervasive pronouncements of the APB. Audit guides, like APB Opinions, are exposed in draft form on a limited-basis for comment prior to final issuance.

Audit guides will be published in the next few weeks for savings and loan associations; hospitals; and employee health, welfare, and benefit plans. Audit guides are well along for stockbrokerage firms, life insurance companies, and colleges and universities.

What Hopper is the APB In?

I believe that the summary I have just given you answers briefly the question, "What's in the hopper of the APB?" A more significant question that might rightly be asked is, "What Hopper is the APB in?"

Recent events make that question exceedingly difficult to answer. More than a year ago, leaders of the profession acknowledged that the APB was under increasing criticism. In recognition of this, the Institute formed two high-level study groups to consider whether the APB's efforts were sufficiently prompt and productive. One group is studying whether present procedures for establishing accounting principles can be improved; and the other is seeking to refine the objectives of financial statements. Both groups are consulting with interested organizations and individuals, holding hearings, and maintaining a public record.

Each group includes representatives of business and professional life outside public accounting. In fact, a majority of those on each study group is from outside public practice. The group studying the establishment of accounting principles is chaired by Francis M. Wheat, a recent member of the Securities and Exchange Commission. Serving with him are a university professor, a financial analyst, a financial vice president of one of the nation's largest industrial corporations, and three practicing CPAs. This group held a public hearing in New York on November 3-4, 1971. The group studying the objectives of financial statements is chaired by Robert M. Trueblood, a practicing CPA and past president of the American Institute. Serving with him are a financial analyst, an economist, two industrial executives, two professors, and two CPAs from public practice.

The study on establishment of accounting principles is expected to be completed this spring and the study on objectives later in 1972. These studies were authorized by the AICPA Board of Directors, and the reports will be made to the Board. But the SEC, also, is anxiously awaiting the reports; and still others are getting into the act.

The SEC will soon hold hearings to investigate financial reporting of certain transactions of Great Southwest Corporation, a Penn Central subsidiary. Representative Wright Patman, Chairman of the House Banking and Currency Committee, has written to the SEC Chairman suggesting that the Commission examine the entire range of accounting practices and policies followed by the company -- and the extent of such practices and policies throughout industry.

Mr. Patman went on to state that it would be helpful to know the extent of the SEC's jurisdiction over accounting firms and their practices, and what additional legislative authority the SEC needs to properly monitor the accounting profession. And remember, his committee, together with its Senate counterpart, are the friendly folks who brought you the Cost Accounting Standards Board.

Speaking of this latter group, *Business Week* recently had an interesting observation about its range of influence. Reporting on the CASB's proposed new rules on costs for contractors, the magazine noted, "As the board gets into depreciation and other details of cost accounting that affect income, its rules will have an indirect impact on financial accounting, which concerns itself with balance sheets and profit-loss reports." *Business Week* then pointed out that, while the SEC has statutory responsibility for financial accounting, it has generally acquiesced to the guidelines laid down by the American Institute of CPAs and its Accounting Principles Board.

Meanwhile, Congress shot down the APB proposal calling for a single method of accounting for the investment credit, even though the proposal was supported by the SEC. The objective of the action, which was urged on Congress by industry-lobbyists and the Administration, was to provide additional stimulation to the economy, not to improve financial reporting to investors. This action devastates the APB's efforts to eliminate alternative methods. Not only does the Revenue Act of 1971 specify that no taxpayer shall be required to use any particular method of accounting for the credit, but it goes on to state that permission to change from one method to another will require the consent of the Secretary of the Treasury or his delegate.

Thus, in this area of financial reporting, the law has been made by Congress. At a second-level, interpretations have already been announced by the Treasury Department. Since the law refers to reports subject to the jurisdiction of any federal agency, presumably the SEC has authority to issue regulations at a third-level. Finally, if more interpretation is needed, the APB might possibly come in on the fourth-level to take care of remaining minuscule matters.

Treasury involvement in this matter comes at a time when the Department is well into its plan to require a closer link between financial reporting and income tax accounting through regulations on accounting methods. With increasing frequency, Treasury Department regulations make acceptability of an accounting method for income tax purposes contingent upon use of the same method in all financial reports issued to owners, investors, and creditors.

A recent proposal along this line is the revised regulation on long-term contract accounting. The Treasury Department proposes to permit the completed contract method for income tax purposes only if estimates of the cost to complete the contract are not reasonably dependable. Treasury proposes to look to the use of this method in financial reports to shareholders as evidence that the estimates are not reasonably dependable. Should this regulation become final, many contractors would be forced to forsake a preferred accounting method for financial reporting in order to retain the tax advantages of the completed contract method, or to adopt the percentage of completion method for tax purposes, thereby accelerating income tax payments and possibly requiring a new source of capital to finance the business.

Financial reporting and tax reporting should be separate because of their different objectives. Making tax accounting methods contingent upon financial reporting introduces a formidable obstacle to improvement of financial reporting standards by any body that undertakes the job.

Conflicting objectives have emerged in another government agency where a recent Federal Power Commission order requires full-cost accounting for natural gas pipeline companies. Under this method, companies improve current earnings and spread costs of unsuccessful exploration and development over the period of production from successful efforts. The avoidance of an immediate charge to income for unsuccessful efforts is regarded by many as an incentive to increase current exploration expenditures, thereby resulting in the discovery of much needed gas reserves. Although the propriety of the method is controversial in accounting circles, I believe that all would agree that finding gas reserves and reporting income fairly are not the same objectives.

And if all this is not enough to make one wonder about "what hopper the APB is in," the National Conference on Uniform State Laws is developing a uniform endowments act which would define unrealized appreciation of investments as income, and give management of non-profit organizations the discretion to include any portion of it in income for the year.

Many other potential developments could significantly affect the ability of the APB to continue setting accounting standards. For example, proposed legislation on hospitals and stockbrokerage firms calls for uniform accounting standards. Also, successful lobbying efforts in Congress on the investment credit will undoubtedly encourage further lobbying against APB proposals on other controversial accounting issues.

I believe that the Accounting Principles Board is in the middle of the legislative and regulatory hopper right now. Never before have the objectives of financial reporting to investors been so clearly subordinated to so many conflicting economic, social, and political objectives. The Trueblood study may help dramatize this conflict and suggest a way to resolve it. But resolution of it is needed now, immediately. Regardless of what organizational structure the Wheat study may recommend for carrying out the standard-setting function, whatever emerges from that hopper will be different from the APB which went into it.

Conclusion

I hope these remarks have demonstrated the concern of the Institute to have the public served by the highest attainable standards of financial reporting. The Institute expects to continue to provide leadership and assume major responsibility for this function. But we cannot reach this goal without the cooperation of the business and financial community. If we have this cooperation, I don't see how we can fail to give the public the reliable information it deserves.

FINANCIAL ACCOUNTING STANDARDS: REGULATION OR SELF-REGULATION?
Stanford Lectures in Accounting
Sponsored by Price Waterhouse Foundation
Stanford University
May 31, 1972

Professor Solomons' lecture is an eloquent plea for retaining the financial accounting standards-setting function in the private sector. Since he was also the chief draftsman of the report of the study on establishment of accounting principles, he deserves a great deal of credit for the warm reception accorded its recommendations.

All indications are that the blueprint laid out in the report will be followed in every detail, thus assuring that accounting standards will continue to be determined in the private sector for some time. The study's recommendations are artfully designed, incorporating some elements of most of the plans offered by those who presented suggestions. It is impressive that the recommendations received unanimous support of the study group's seven distinguished members of diverse backgrounds. All of the organizations designated by the study group as participants in the plan have approved the report. The Board of Trustees of the Financial Accounting Foundation will be named in June, and that Board can begin operating by July 1.

This is truly impressive speed. I join with Professor Solomons and others in wanting the new organization to be successful. But amid the euphoria that surrounds the report, we should not overlook some real dangers to its success.

We might start by examining why the APB has been replaced. Professor Solomons says he does not believe that the APB has been unsuccessful. Perhaps not. Then we must ask why he and others have recommended that the APB be abandoned, and a new organization set up separate from all existing professional bodies. This recommendation is tangential when considered as a response to the prospectus which said the main purpose of the study is to find ways for the American Institute of Certified Public Accountants to improve its function of establishing accounting principles.

Both the report of the study group and Professor Solomons' paper carefully avoid saying the APB failed; instead they offer reasons why the new FASB can do the job better. This leaves me with the uneasy feeling that there are unspoken reasons for replacement of the APB. Therefore, let it fall to me to propose that we ask ourselves here some searching questions in the hope that we may perhaps protect the new Board from some very real hazards which confronted and brought down the APB.

Can it be that the APB has been replaced, not because of structural deficiencies, but because of prevailing attitudes within the public accounting profession and attitudes of business? In calling for an investigation of the structure for establishing principles instead of the behavioral setting, was the entire study misguided? Like the investigator who wrote the Institute saying, "Please send us a list of your employees broken down by sex." I replied, "Our problem isn't sex, it's alcohol."

Is it possible that too many accountants and businessmen have been so determined to have their own way on matters of accounting principle that they preferred to bring down the structure, rather than submit to an APB Opinion that impinged on their prerogatives? Although the APB's procedures for hearing all sides of controversial issues were substantially equivalent to the procedures recommended for the new FASB, is it possible that APB watchers have not been satisfied merely by communicating with the APB? Let us look at some of the events of the last few years.

In the case of certain proposed APB Opinions, opponents have issued press releases denouncing the APB, published briefs, circulated white papers, threatened to sue the APB, petitioned the SEC, asked the FPC for a ruling, sought Treasury Department intervention, asked Congress to put financial reporting flexibility into law. Will this happen to the FASB?

The result of such pressures, in the opinion of many, was quite damaging. For example, the APB was forced to back down to a weak position on business combinations. It was legislated out of its position on the investment credit. Insurance companies have forced an impasse on accounting for marketable securities. Oil companies have brought a halt to APB consideration of full-cost accounting. And leasing companies are strangely continuing their lobbying campaign in Congress, even though the APB is obviously immobilized in its consideration of capitalizing leases.

Will not the FASB be faced with the same troublesome problems which the APB was incapable of solving? If the FASB also encounters the same attitudes, the same lack of respect for its authority, will it have a chance for success?

Professor Solomons rightly points out the strong features of the plan, which should entitle the FASB to the support it deserves. The wider base of membership, the high-salaried and full-time members, the independence of members from all other organizations, the broad-based advisory council -- all of these features should help the FASB in withstanding pressures which it will inevitably face.

Nevertheless, the attitudes of people toward the FASB will always be a concern. In addressing the spring Council meeting of the American Institute, Frank Wheat urged business statesmanship in dealing with the FASB. We can all urge statesmanship, but we must question whether this will stop an industry or a company from lobbying against an FASB proposal which would require the industry or company to report lower profits.

Professor Solomons takes issue with Charles Horngren's view of the relationship of the Accounting Principles Board with the Securities and Exchange Commission. Professor Horngren sees the SEC as "top management" and the APB as "lower management," doing most of the work, making most of the decisions, and serving as a buffer to insulate the SEC from most pressures and criticisms. From where many of us sit, Professor Horngren seems to be absolutely correct in the way he sizes up the existing public-private institutional arrangement for setting accounting principles.

We must ask ourselves once more then: Is anything altered in this relationship by substituting the FASB for the APB? Does not the SEC continue its role of top management, backed by all the legislative authority it needs in Section 19(a) of the Securities Act of 1933?

Is not the arrangement which permits the Treasury Department to exert pressure on the standards-setting Board and the SEC the same? And are not all bodies still subordinate to the Congress if they care to become involved in the process? I am not suggesting that this latter arrangement could or should be changed. But congressional involvement contributed greatly to the demise of the APB, and may loom as a threat to any successor body.

Professor Solomons deals deftly with the matter of independence, at one time stressing that the new organization will be separate from all existing organizations and at another stressing the position of primacy of the AICPA. Are these not mutually exclusive? He also says that the new Board will not be a committee of anything and that it will be answerable -- but only "in some sense" -- to the trustees of the new Financial Accounting Foundation.

I would question another aspect of Professor Solomons' excellent presentation.   Apparently, educators and lawyers can serve the government while on leave from their organizations without jeopardizing their independence; yet, he believes FASB members must sever all connections with their former firms or employers and have no agreement, formal or informal, to rejoin them upon leaving the FASB. This seems to apply gratuitously a higher standard of independence to FASB service than to government service. But this stand is weakened in Professor Solomons' comment that he would normally expect the FASB member to be welcomed back if he wished to rejoin his former firm.

However, on still a third matter of independence, Professor Solomons raises questions as to whether the FASB can be truly independent if it is financed by voluntary contributions from a few large public accounting firms.   Here I can agree completely with his statement that voluntary financial support is not a satisfactory method of financing the Foundation, except as a way of getting the new organization quickly off the ground.

In summary, while I congratulate all responsible for the impressive progress made in setting up this new Board, I have tried here to expose some old dangers which may threaten the successful implementation and operation of the new FASB -- unless there are changes in *attitudes*, as well as a change in *structure*. But I do not wish my remarks to be taken as opposition. Quite the contrary. The plan should be implemented and all concerned should do their utmost to make it succeed.

We should be grateful for the brilliant work of Professor Solomons and his associates for coming up with a sound plan for setting standards. It is an imperfect plan, but it has more appeal to more people than any other plan that has been offered.

Finally, we should wholeheartedly support it, in the hope that it can weather the storms ahead. The FASB is the only plan before us for consideration. We can see no other way to keep the accounting standard-setting function in private hands -- or as Professor Solomons says, at least to the extent that it is in private hands at the present time.

A VIEW FROM THE TOP
Before the Michigan College Accounting Educators Conference
Lansing Community College
Lansing, Michigan
March 31, 1973

Ladies and Gentlemen, I know this is on the program as "a view from the top," but it seems to me that you're the top and I'm not at the top of anything. I'm on the outside, watching what's going on these days, so perhaps my remarks should be entitled "a view from the outside."

It's nice of everyone to come out on a Saturday at a time when maybe some people like to stay in and sleep late. Sort of like the son whose mother was trying to get him up, and she said "Son, get up. You have to go to school." And he said, "Aw gee, I hate to do that. I don't want to go to school. The kids hate me. The bus driver hates me. The teachers hate me. The school board hates me. Even the janitor hates me." She says, "Son you've got to get up and go to school. You're 42 years old and you're the principal!"

I would like to talk to you today about, perhaps a little different aspect of the accounting profession which I have had occasion to observe. I think it's a great profession. There are great opportunities here. It's vigorous; it's growing. But it seems that there is constant turmoil going on in the accounting profession. There are always conflicts about the authorities and responsibilities of those practicing the profession, and I'd say conflicts about the determination of accounting standards.

And looking towards reasons for these conflicts or possible resolutions of them, I would like to look at the behavioral setting of the profession. Now I don't pretend to be a behavioral scientist. I express my views only as an accountant, but I believe that prevailing attitudes of individuals and organizations often inhibit rather than foster attainment of their stated goals. And, in addition, actions are often inconsistent with professed attitudes, which leads to an institutional setting different from that which is desired.

Now accountants often express a preference for professional standards of a broad, general nature, which permit the free exercise of professional judgment in a manner of appropriate concern. How often have we heard that? Yet, most actions, individually and collectively,

183

lead to the development of increasingly detailed rules. Accountants deplore the thought of financial accounting rules attaining the volume and complexity of, say, the Internal Revenue Code and Regulations. But rule-making bodies are moving rapidly in that direction. Accounting Principles Board Opinions are increasingly complex and detailed. They've been codified in a loose leaf service and supplemented by lengthy interpretations. Statements on Auditing Procedure are also becoming thicker and more detailed, and soon they will be codified. Securities and Exchange Commission Accounting Series Releases are being issued more frequently, and the Cost Accounting Standard Board is writing detailed cost accounting rules. One of their proposals just reached me yesterday, and it makes me ill to think of it -- methods of depreciation.

In the light of expressed preferences for broad general standards, why do detailed rules proliferate? I believe that actions of the profession and business demonstrate that broad standards are not enforceable, whereas detailed rules are enforceable; and that accountants want the protection provided by detailed rules. Let me give you an example of an unenforceable standard, APB *Opinion No. 9* (paragraph 33), issued in 1966. In one sentence, the APB introduced the principle of "residual securities" for the purpose of computing earnings per share. Under this principle an outstanding security deriving a major portion of its value from its common stock characteristics should be considered a residual security and not a senior security for purposes of computing earnings per share. This Opinion was issued at a time when imaginative new securities were being created, often for the main purpose of increasing reported earnings per share.

Attitudes of businessmen and professional accountants were not admirable in this case. Before the ink was dry on *Opinion No. 9*, a number of them gave virtuoso performances in avoiding residual securities, while still boosting earnings per share. This forced the APB into a reconsideration of earnings per share; and in May, 1969, *Opinion No. 15* was issued containing 61 pages of detailed rules on common stock equivalents and related matters on earnings per share -- much of which replaced the one sentence principle on residual and senior securities. Detailed rules are made to plug loopholes inherent in broad general standards.

In addition, detailed rules are sometimes thought to provide a safe haven for an accountant who follows them. In lawsuits against accountants, the defendant typically seeks to establish as a defense his adherence to professional standards. The accounting profession has for years been trying to establish that accountants should be held to the standards of the profession and not to some unknown lay standard of fairness developed after the fact. Each attempt to do so only serves to heighten the distinction between professional standards and fair presentation. In seeking a defense behind professional standards, the profession has broadened the possibility of being judged by unspecified lay standards of fairness.

Bob Sterling has presented ample evidence in a recent article that the responsibility of the accountant far outweighs his authority. He states that the only ways to correct this imbalance are to increase the authority or decrease the responsibility. The accounting profession seems to oppose an increase in authority and favor a decrease in responsibility. Statements on Auditing Procedure often seem to be designed to reduce responsibility by providing a rule, which if followed will free the accountant of further responsibility; and much of the same design appears to be built into the APB Opinions.

The new Code of Professional Ethics of the American Institute of CPA's begins with this statement: "A distinguishing mark for a professional is his acceptance of responsibility to the public." Accountants often express the view that broad ethical standards are needed, rather than detailed rules and regulations. And, yet, the new Code recognizes that only specific rules of conduct can be enforced. I believe that attitudes of the profession limit the effectiveness of the entire Code, and work towards substitution of detailed laws which are rarely enforceable. Great stock is placed in this Code. CPA's point with pride to the Code and enforcement of it as evidence of high standards of professional conduct. And it is a sound basis for professional practice. It is constantly being improved, a major revision having been adopted just in January, and the Code is probably as good as (or better than) those of most professional organizations. But how effective is a code of ethics in providing public protection.

Most ethics codes are designed, first, to protect members from outsiders; second, to protect members from each other; and, third, to protect the public from unethical members. The AICPA Code is enforced quite effectively in matters dealing with protection of members. The disciplinary machinery works very slowly in matters affecting the public. Enforcement of technical standards through the Code of Ethics is difficult in most circumstances and impossible in some circumstances.

The most widely publicized cases of alleged violation of technical standards involved lawsuits against individual accountants and their accounting firm, usually one of the Big Eight firms. Damage claims in millions of dollars become common place. In such a case, the Institute's disciplinary procedures are ineffective. The defendants will not provide information to the Institute's Ethics Division as long as legal actions are pending, on the ground that release of information and possible Institute action on it may jeopardize their position in the lawsuit. The Institute cannot, or at least does not, take action until the defendants last right of appeal of the courts has been exhausted. And this may take eight to ten years after the alleged violation of technical standards. Enforcement of the Code of Professional Ethics at this point is anti-climatic. The worst sanction under the Code is its expulsion from membership in the Institute, which is seldom imposed. When expulsion does occur, it usually is a mild discipline compared with that already meted out by the court. Thus, in matters of major importance, laws and courts provide the public with protection as to competence and technical standards of accountants.

Self-regulations through the Code of Professional Ethics cannot do this. This social and institutional setting makes the accounting profession appear defenseless of its members and unmindful of public protection -- quite the reverse of what the profession wants.

When an accountant is involved in a scandal, the public may view his performance in terms of carelessness, poor judgment, dereliction of duty, or fraud. But the accounting profession seems to unite and associate itself with that performance, regardless of how tarnished it may appear to the public. The profession closes ranks and seeks to protect its wounded member, instead of being indignant that a fellow member would so harm the reputation of the profession. It's no wonder that the public thinks the profession protects itself, rather than the public.

One notable issue brought together a common concern for members of the accounting profession and for the public. In 1971, the SEC issued a rule calling for registered companies to notify it of a change in accountants and to file a letter for the public record stating whether the change involved a disagreement over accounting principles. This rule was aimed at stopping the practice of "shopping" for accounting principles. It was designed to protect the public from inferior accounting principles and to protect accounting firms from unscrupulous competitors, although protection may come after the fact and merely serve to deter future actions of a similar nature.

To accomplish this the accounting profession had to ask the SEC to make a rule, because the profession lacked authority to cope with the problem. That such a rule was sought is an indication of the intensity of competition in the accounting profession. Changes in accountants reported under this rule will raise questions about the attitudes of various accountants towards accounting principles. For each accountant displaced because he took a stand an accounting principles there is a newly appointed accountant whose views on the same principles may not be revealed for some time. Until revealed, the public's suspicions may be aroused that the new accountant may be taking a more lenient position on accounting principles than his predecessor.

The function of setting accounting principles, or accounting standards, to use the currently fashionable term, presents an interesting area for the study of behavioral patterns. Let us start with the question which the Wheat Committee said overshadows all others: Should the task remain the responsibility of the private sector or should it be taken over by a governmental body?

This is the one proposition for which, surprisingly, we have nearly unanimous agreement -- accounting standards should be set through the *private* sector. Allowing this function to slip into the public sector would be detrimental to the interests of the public, business, and the accounting profession. Alleged disadvantages of transferring the standard-setting function to the public sector are that government agencies would be more susceptible to political pressures than private bodies; government agencies would be inflexible and would lack responsiveness to the needs of investors; such a development would inevitably sap the vitality of the accounting profession; and a government agency's rules might not cover all organizations and, therefore, could involve coexistence of two or more sets of accounting standards.

In the past, I, too, have embraced this conventional wisdom, and for sentimental reasons I still prefer to see accounting principles set in the private sector. But I can no longer advocate this position with great conviction. My reasons are that standards are now being determined largely in the public sector, and inevitably the function will be taken over completely by the public sector. To support that statement let me refer to recent Securities and Exchange Commission actions.

In the last year while the APB issued six Opinions and exposed four proposed Opinions, the SEC issued 15 Accounting Series Releases of general applicability and exposed four proposed Releases. The Releases are speckled with references to APB Opinions, often in a way that modifies or extends the Opinion. One Release "encourages" the AICPA committee on insurance accounting and auditing to define appropriate accounting for catastrophe reserves. Another Release "urges" the new Financial Accounting Standards Board to place high on its agenda for consideration early in 1973 the subject of accounting for leases with lessors without independent economic substance.

Still another Release (dated January 12, 1973) calls for more detailed disclosure of extraordinary items than that required by *Opinion No. 9*, and introduces for similar disclosure two new terms of art, "other material charges and credits to income of an unusual nature" and "material provisions for loss." This Release came shortly after the APB's December exposure of a proposed Opinion on reporting effects of extraordinary events and transactions, which would provide more definitive criteria in determining extraordinary items and would specify disclosure requirements for such items and for newly designated unusual or nonrecurring items. We're getting a variety of terms which are not necessarily identical. The APB Opinion when issued surely will be anticlimactic; and unless it embraces the disclosure called for by the SEC, we will be faced with coexisting standards or more accurately coexisting detailed rules.

A December, 1972, proposed amendment to regulation S-X calls for disclosure of reasons for (and amounts of) differences in income tax expense from an amount calculated by multiplying the U.S. corporate income tax rates by the income before tax.

Another December, 1972, proposed amendment to Regulation S-X, calling for disclosure of significant accounting policies, would take a quantum leap from the base provided by APB *Opinion No. 22* on the same subject. The APB Opinion was issued in April, 1972 -- but I call it the best idea of *1932*, for that was when George O. May advocated it. Now the SEC proposal would require disclosure, where significant, of the estimated dollar impact on net income of use of a principle followed as compared to alternative acceptable principles:

1. When the company uses more than one accounting principle in reporting similar kinds of transactions; or

2. When the company has changed its accounting principles in the past two years; or

3. When the principle used is not the prevailing principle used by companies in the same industry.

This has some frightful implications, and the SEC gives as examples Fifo and Lifo inventory valuation methods; straight-line and accelerated depreciation; and full-cost accounting and individual property cost accounting in the petroleum industry. Some of these exposures are difficult or even impossible to make, so I am glad to see that the SEC has withdrawn this for further consideration. I didn't think they'd give up on it, and I believe it will resurface in one form or another.

Now there are many other recent SEC proposals, but those I have cited reveal what power and direction lie for setting accounting standards. I might add, I certainly hope that professors teaching financial accounting are teaching SEC Releases as well as APB Opinions. Furthermore, the SEC has been accelerating its pace in the use of this power, both to issue its own rules and to goad the APB into action. Its rules are now being issued by a chief financial analyst, who occupies a newly created position, as well as by the chief accountant. Although the SEC is now limiting its own rules to matters of disclosure, the proposal on alternative accepted principles, if adopted, may have a practical effect of eliminating some accounting methods.

SEC spokesmen frequently state that they do not want to set accounting standards, that they want the accounting profession to do the job. For example, former SEC Chairman William Casey once said, "The accounting profession has undertaken a renewed effort to develop uniform accounting standards. The Commission, believing that accounting standards should be set in the private sector, intends to fully support the profession in achieving it."

Their actions, however, are not consistent with their stated objectives. Many of us have known that, from the beginning, the APB could not (and did not) take a position without getting SEC approval. On the other hand, the SEC can (and often does) issue a Release without consulting the APB. Communication between the APB and SEC can be a one-way street.

Now all of us may read in the daily newspapers a blow-by-blow description of what the APB wants and their likelihood of getting it past the SEC. For example, progress on the highly controversial audit guide on land development companies was reported to the press almost daily. The APB held out for (and got) SEC acquiescence for accrual accounting over the SEC's preference for installment accounting. But this should not be taken as an indication that the APB has the power of self-determination. It may be one small concession to preserve in the view of some observers the cherished notion that accounting standards are set in the private sector.

The SEC has shown a keen sense of strategy in other ways. After extolling the virtues of profit forecasts for many months, the SEC stated it would issue a release "permitting" profit forecasts to be included in prospectuses. It does not require them. Permissiveness is easier to accept than absolute requirement. Few can protest if left with a free choice. Yet, I wonder how free the choice will be if underwriters insist on exercising that free choice, as I predict they will. In these conditions, profit forecasts would become a virtual requirement in prospectuses, but unhappy managements and accountants would find it hard to criticize the SEC rule, which is only permissive.

The SEC occupies a dominant position in determining accounting standards and the APB a subordinate one. With the transition under way from the APB to the new Financial Accounting Standards Board, we should examine the organizational relationships that can be expected under the new structure.

In my view, the only change is a direct substitution of the FASB for the APB. The FASB will have the identical relationship with the SEC that the APB now has. That is, the SEC will be dominant and the FASB will be subordinate. The Securities Acts give the SEC the authority to make rules and regulations regarding financial reporting. The APB had no such legislative authority. And the FASB has no such legislative authority.

The Wheat Committee considered, but rejected, the proposal that a board be established by law as an official self-regulatory agency. Therefore, we can expect the SEC to continue to use the private sector body, now the FASB, for doing the research in detailed rule-making within parameters set by the SEC. This is a convenient arrangement for the SEC. It permits the SEC to function with a small accounting staff, while enjoying the extensive (and I might add expensive) expert services of the private sector Board. This arrangement also diverts almost all criticism and some pressures to the Board. The SEC has good reasons to want to continue the arrangement.

But there is no assurance that circumstances will always permit this arrangement, or that future commissioners will be pleased with it. With the accounting profession and business united in the desire to have accounting standards set in the private sector, why has this function moved more and more into the public sector? I believe this has resulted from behavioral patterns that are inconsistent with the stated goal. In business there seems to be a craving for simpler days when there were fewer rules and regulations -- days before a huge federal bureaucracy regulated virtually every phase of business. Yet, where problems arise which affect the public interest, regulation often isn't all the answer. Businesses had a rather consistent record of opposing most new regulatory incursions; but we have learned to live with it and, for the most part, we find it difficult now to live without it. The surprising thing is that accounting regulation has been so slow in coming.

When the APB was formed, the first efforts were directed at broad postulates and principles of accounting. Many people refused to accept the APB as a rule-making body. Also, many people, including some who were most dedicated to a private sector body, refused to accept the authority of the new APB's Opinions. Although attitudes shifted during the APB's stormy existence, the failure of business and the accounting profession to accept the authority of rules and regulations is the main reason its function has moved further into the public sector. A continuation of this attitude may cause the FASB an even stormier and shorter existence.

In a field where there are no external verities, differences of opinion will abound. In accounting there has been no bashfulness in expressing opinions which differ from those of the professional rulings. The APB has been unable to solve controversial issues. On any such issue a decision is bound to displease some, and occasionally any decision is bound to displease all. By their actions and attitudes businessmen and professional accountants seem to be saying: "We want accounting rules to be set in the private sector, only if we agree with the rules." A review of some recent rule-making attempts reveals this pattern all too clearly.

The APB was making good progress in gaining the stature of public respect in 1969 when it began to consider the subject of business combinations. This was a highly controversial and emotion-charged issue. After taking an initial unequivocal position based on principle, which would have ruled out "pooling of interests" accounting, the APB was hit by intense pressures to back away from that position. As the months went by and pressures mounted, the APB backed down step-by-step to a weak position under which poolings remain alive and well in the United States today. Industry and the accounting profession joined in fighting the APB. Some groups wrote to key congressional committees suggesting this subject should more appropriately be left to the legislative and regulatory functions of the federal government. Others threatened to sue the APB if the Opinion was issued.

Some of the APB's opponents were not satisfied with defeating the APB on business combinations. They precipitated meetings which resulted in formation of the Wheat Committee early in 1971. In doing so, their determination to bring down the structure rather than submit to a professional pronouncement was apparent. Further examples of extra-professional efforts to thwart the APB emerged in 1971.

The most widely publicized effort related to the investment credit. I will not describe that episode in detail, but I do wish to express its importance. Here was a display of raw power that should be forever a lesson to those who wish to set rules without having authority to do so. Businessmen and professional accountants went directly to congressmen with the story that the APB was trying to remove an economic incentive granted by Congress. No amount of accounting logic about matching costs and revenues could overcome this economic argument and legislative challenge. SEC support of the APB was not enough to make a difference, nor was it enough to attract blame for the debacle. The APB seemed to get all the blame.

Attitudes displayed here plainly indicate that some businessmen and professional accountants wanted to destroy the APB, if that was necessary to have their way on the investment credit. But most of the same people, removed from the emotional issue of the investment credit, would probably be strong supporters of standard-setting in the private sector. Strangely, one accountant filed a statement with the House Ways and Means Committee asking Congress to specify in the law the accounting for the investment credit; and a few weeks later his partner was lobbying Congress trying to convince them to leave accounting out of the law.

In 1971, the APB was studying accounting for investments in marketable common stocks, and Board opinion was moving toward carrying securities at market value, with changes in market value included in income currently. This would have a great effect on companies with a substantial portfolio of common stocks, such as fire and casualty insurance. Chief executives of insurance companies held meetings with each other, with an APB committee, and finally with the SEC in an effort to head off an APB Opinion. They succeeded well in this effort, with a result being that the SEC directed the APB into a narrow band of acceptable solutions which did not include carrying securities at market value. The APB dropped the subject.

Also in 1971, the APB was considering full-cost accounting versus successful effort cost accounting in the oil industry. The APB expressed a tentative preference for successful effort accounting. On the other hand, the Federal Power Commission had already issued a regulation in accordance with a petition from an accounting firm requiring full-cost accounting by natural gas pipe-line companies. The industry was divided, and opposing positions were drawn up. The full-cost method was preferred by most of the smaller independent producers, and the successful effort method was preferred by most of the large integrated companies. The antitrust issue was raised by the smaller companies, which contended that, if successful effort accounting were forced on them, they would suffer great economic loss and might even be put out of business. Once again industry, together with several accounting firms, took the issue before the SEC and forced an impasse, thus assuring the *status quo* for some time to come. This subject is not among the seven topics on the initial agenda of the FASB.

About the same time in 1971, the subject of accounting for leases was being considered. The APB had not formed a position and, in fact, had barely begun discussion on the subject. Nevertheless, knowledge of these discussions caused certain leasing companies to begin lobbying Congress to head off any possibility of an APB Opinion which would require capitalization of leases. Dozens of letters from congressmen, together with form letters from "a constituent," reached the APB. This campaign was successful, for the APB tabled the matter of leases; but the lobbying continued. Many letters continued to come in from congressmen long after it was well publicized that the APB had dropped the issue. And I know that leasing company lobbyists are ready to begin battle again any minute, like the minutemen of old.

Now these issues remain critical. The new FASB will have to give early attention to accounting for leases, marketable securities, and oil exploration costs. In addition, I believe that someone will force the subject of business combinations onto the agenda again. Some of our disgruntled friends in the accounting profession are still threatening to sue over that one. To deal effectively with these issues, the FASB will need to develop an effective way to conduct relations with Congress. Perhaps some of the posts on the new Financial Accounting Standards Board should have been given to skilled lobbyists, rather than skilled accountants.

I do not mean to be critical of the Wheat Committee, the FASB, or the organizations which banded together to implement the new Board. I think they've done a splendid job (far better than I really expected they could) in meeting the objections of most and in coming up with an accommodation of suggestions that seems to please everyone. My only concern is that perhaps they focused on the wrong subject in examining the structure, instead of examining the behavioral setting.

Will prevailing attitudes change? I doubt it. At least attitudes will not change swiftly, but perhaps may change gradually. And does this mean that turmoil within the accounting profession will continue indefinitely? Probably some dissension will always occur in an institutional structure in a democratic society. And this is not all bad. After all, the profession has grown in size, importance, and respect throughout the last few stormy decades, and I think we will have more of the same. I believe that it will continue to grow in prosperity and in stature in spite of many problems, though that growth will not be quite as much as might be obtained if some attitudes could be changed.

MAKING ACCOUNTING RULES - A POLITICAL PROCESS
Before the Michigan Association of CPAs
Michigan State University
East Lansing, Michigan
June 4, 1975

External financial reporting for decades has been developing in tumultuous and controversial surroundings. As a result, American business today is highly regulated in the way it must report financial information to investors, government agencies, and others. This regulation is imposed upon business by several rule-making bodies, which have begun to issue conflicting rules.

No one can deny that great progress has been made in corporate financial reporting in the first three-quarters of the twentieth century. Yet, today we continue to be faced with criticism of financial reporting because of our failure to arrive at fundamental goals, together with an orderly set of guidelines for implementing the goals and a suitable organizational structure for issuing and enforcing the guidelines.

Progress in financial reporting has been influenced by many groups and sectors, but it has been brought about largely by the Securities and Exchange Commission, corporate financial executives, and the public accounting profession. Financial reporting has also been influenced significantly by the United States Treasury Department, its Internal Revenue Service, and the United States Congress. I intend to demonstrate that accounting rule-making is primarily a political, rather than conceptual, process.

Early Conditions

In 1926 William Z. Ripley, a professor of economics at Harvard, caused a stir with a bristling attack in *The Atlantic Monthly* on the inadequacy of corporate financial reporting of that era. To illustrate the attitude of some managements, Ripley cited a paragraph from the annual report of a company, which he did not identify:

The settled plan of the directors has been to withhold information from the stockholders and others that is not called for by the stockholders in a body. So far no request for

195

information has been made in the manner prescribed by the
directors. Distribution of stock has not meant distribution of
control.

After describing deficiencies in other annual reports, resulting
presumably from the same sort of thinking, Ripley wrote:
"Stockholders are entitled to adequate information and the State and the
general public have a right to the same privilege." Others shared
Ripley's concern about the "limitless obfuscation" of financial reporting
in the twenties. Among them were some leading certified public
accountants, who suggested to the New York Stock Exchange that the
accounting profession and the Exchange collaborate in drawing up
reporting standards for listed companies.

The proposal brought no action at the time. But with the Great
Depression, attitudes changed and discussions between the Exchange
and the accounting profession, begun in 1932, culminated in 1934 in
publication of "Audits of Corporate Accounts."

This proved to be a seminal document. Not only did it set forth
principles to be followed in financial reporting, it also led to the first
standard form of auditor's report and to a requirement that the financial
statements of companies applying for listing with the Exchange be
independently audited.

The Securities Acts

Meanwhile, Congress passed the Securities Act of 1933 and the
Securities Exchange Act of 1934, which provided for federal regulation
of securities sales. The function was undertaken by the Federal Trade
Commission in 1933, but was soon transferred to the new Securities and
Exchange Commission set up by the 1934 Act. In line with the
arrangement being worked out by the CPAs and the Exchange,
companies subject to reporting under the Securities Acts were required
to be audited by independent public accountants.

While the Securities Acts empowered the Commission to prescribe
accounting practices for publicly-held companies, the Commission made
known that it expected the accounting profession itself to assume the
main burden of rule-setting. Yet, the SEC in 1937 began a program
through its Accounting Series Releases to publish opinions on
accounting principles for the purpose of contributing to the development

of uniform accounting standards and practices. It wasn't until two years later, in 1939, that the American Institute of Certified Public Accountants formed a Committee on Accounting Procedure, which was authorized to issue formal pronouncements on accounting principles and practices.

During the next two decades, many Releases were issued by the Commission and many Accounting Research Bulletins were issued by the AICPA Committee. Generally, the SEC was concerned primarily with disclosure, while the AICPA concentrated on accounting methods.

Growing Criticism

Despite the substantial progress that was made under these arrangements, there was a growing criticism of the state of the art and the mechanism for making improvements. Arguments arose between those who favored uniformity of accounting principles in order to provide comparability of financial statements among companies and those who favored flexibility of principles in order to accommodate the unique needs of individual companies. The words "uniformity" and "flexibility" became charged with emotion. Also at issue was whether general acceptance should be achieved by compulsion or persuasion.

Criticism was heaped on the ill-defined term "generally accepted accounting principles." In response to mounting complaints, the AICPA in 1959 formed the Accounting Principles Board (APB) to carry on the work of the former Committee on Accounting Procedure more intensively and with greater research resources.

The Accounting Principles Board

While over several decades principles of accounting had been studied, analyzed, organized, articulated, and presented by many respected scholars, there had not emerged a conceptual framework from which solutions to individual problems could be drawn in a logical and consistent manner. Therefore, the APB directed its research arm's initial effort to the search for basic postulates, from which principles would be derived, and the principles in turn would lead to rules of practice that would overcome all of the ills of financial reporting.

Although highly regarded scholars did a commendable job in finding basic postulates and broad principles of accounting, the APB promptly rejected the studies as being "too radically different from present generally accepted accounting principles for acceptance at this time." The APB then set about to issue Opinions, which primarily constituted detailed rules concerning various accounting problem areas.

Throughout the life of the APB, many business scandals occurred in which fraud and bad business judgment were involved. These scandals named management and public accounting firms as defendants, and the latter often sought as a defense their adherence to generally accepted accounting principles. This kind of situation heaped additional criticism on accounting principles and the organizational structure for determining them.

Under the APB, rule-making became more of a participatory activity, with industry and others being given an opportunity to voice their needs and concerns. Of course, I recognize that in every calling there is a wide range of ability and interest. The other day I asked a colleague what is the difference between ignorance and apathy? He replied, "I don't know and I don't care."

The APB approach to detailed rule-making brought forth a further controversy over whether companies and their accountants had to follow the Opinions or were free to depart from them if they wished. The argument brought clearly into focus a condition which had long prevailed, but suddenly had become critical: the AICPA, most recently through its APB, had assumed a regulatory responsibility which it had no authority to carry out.

Valiant efforts were made by the accounting profession to seek, through the AICPA Code of Professional Ethics, the sanctions many felt were necessary to enforce APB Opinions. Meanwhile, it was becoming more and more apparent to more and more people that the only enforcer was the SEC.

In fact, the SEC assumed a dominant position in determining accounting rules and the APB a subordinate one. The SEC used the APB for doing research and detailed rule-making within parameters set by the SEC. This was a convenient arrangement for the SEC. It permitted the SEC to function with a relatively small accounting staff while enjoying the extensive expert services of a private sector board. This arrangement diverted almost all criticism and some pressures to the APB.

The Decline of the APB

While this arrangement was fine for the SEC, it was intolerable for the APB, which faced a number of crises in 1969 and 1970 that indicated its remaining life would be short. After taking an initial unequivocal position on accounting for business combinations based on principle, which would have ruled out pooling-of-interests accounting, the APB was hit by intense pressures to modify that position. As the months went by and pressures mounted, the APB backed down step-by-step to a weak position under which poolings remain alive and well in the United States today. Industry and the accounting profession joined in fighting the APB. Some groups wrote to key congressional committees suggesting this subject should more appropriately be left to the legislative and regulatory functions of the federal government. Others threatened to sue the APB if the Opinion was issued.

Some of the APB's opponents were not satisfied with defeating the APB on business combinations. Once again the call was for a renewed search for a conceptual base for accounting and a new organizational structure. Perhaps it is of passing interest now to note that the event which, for all practical purposes, committed the AICPA to ultimate abandonment of the APB and its responsibility for accounting principles, took place on January 7 and 8, 1971, at the Watergate -- at a meeting of managing partners of twenty-one public accounting firms, clandestinely arranged, but later publicized as a major achievement in determination of accounting standards in the private sector.

Two Study Groups

From this meeting emerged studies of the objectives of financial statements and of the organizational structure for setting accounting principles. But in studying the organizational structure instead of behavioral attitudes, was the entire study misdirected?

In both studies the terminology had changed, but not the issues. The prospectus of the structure study, to become known as the Wheat Committee, called for finding "ways for the AICPA to improve its function of establishing accounting principles." The final report changed the terminology to "establishing financial accounting standards," and recommended removing the function from the AICPA and placing it in a new Financial Accounting Standards Board independent of all other groups. The charter of the objectives study (to become known as the Trueblood Committee) rejected the terms "postulates" and "principles" and stated that the purpose of the study was to refine the objectives of financial statements, which should facilitate establishment of guidelines and criteria for improving accounting and financial reporting.

Both study groups were composed of eminent men who approached their studies in a professional manner. Both final reports were quickly accepted and highly praised as representing substantial progress in improving the corporate financial reporting process.

The report on objectives is an excellent document. Who can quarrel with "The basic objective of financial statements is to provide information useful for making economic decisions"? The study does become more specific than this, and its conclusions are backed by reasoned discussion.

The difficulty, however, will come as the FASB considers the objectives study and attempts to draw guidelines from it. This process may prove to be as elusive as earlier attempts to draw practices and methods from fundamental accounting principles. Perhaps it is too much to expect guidelines to flow from objectives in an orderly fashion when we are dealing with a practical art which is already enmeshed in laws and rules emanating from several regulatory bodies.

The End of the APB

While the study to set standards was progressing in 1971, several more events transpired which had a bearing on the study group's recommendation to remove the function from the AICPA. One concerned the investment tax credit, which had embroiled the APB in controversy since the credit first appeared in 1962. This time, however, the APB had a strong majority in favor of a single method -- reducing cost over the life of the asset which gives rise to the credit. They also had the backing of the SEC.

Businessmen and professional accountants went directly to congressmen with the story that the APB was trying to remove an economic incentive granted by Congress. No amount of accounting logic about matching costs and revenues could overcome this economic argument and legislative challenge. Congress responded by writing into law that no taxpayer shall be required to use any particular method of accounting for the credit. Here was a display of raw power that should forever be a lesson to those who wish to set rules without having authority to do so. SEC support of the APB was not enough to make a difference -- nor was it enough to attract blame for the debacle. The APB seemed to get all the blame.

In 1971, the APB was moving toward a position of carrying marketable securities at market value with changes in market value included in income currently. Chief executives of several fire and casualty insurance companies opposed this position, took the issue to the SEC and effectively forced the APB to drop the project.

In 1971, the APB was also considering full-cost accounting versus successful effort cost accounting in the petroleum industry. The APB expressed a tentative preference for successful effort accounting. On the other hand, the Federal Power Commission had already issued a regulation, in accordance with a petition from an accounting firm, requiring full-cost accounting by natural gas pipeline companies. The industry was divided and opposing positions were drawn up. Once again industry, together with accounting firms, took the issue before the SEC and forced an impasse, thus assuring the *status quo* for some time to come.

Along about the same time, the APB was considering accounting for leases. Although no position had been formed, leasing companies began lobbying in Congress to head off any possibility of an APB Opinion which would require capitalization of leases. The APB tabled the matter, but the lobbying continues today. Arguments at the congressional level turn on social and economic issues, not on technical niceties of accounting principle.

These setbacks during the course of the study on establishment of standards contributed heavily to the conclusion of the study group that the function should be removed from the APB and AICPA. I cite the episodes as proof of the fundamental weakness of a private sector group attempting to carry out a regulatory function without the authority to do so.

The Financial Accounting Standards Board

The FASB is structured with that same infirmity -- it has assumed responsibility without authority. This frailty was brought to the attention of the study group, but they wished it away by pointing to good features of the FASB. Now amid evidence of increased SEC activism, even the FASB seems to be recognizing its precarious position. The FASB speaks wanly of a policy between it and the SEC of "mutual non-surprise." Apparently, this translates into a request for the SEC to get instructions out early enough for the FASB to be responsive in an acceptable manner.

The success of the FASB will depend on the willingness of the SEC to support it on controversial issues. An astronaut took a space walk, returned to the vehicle and knocked on the window. A voice inside asked, "Who's there?" When the FASB hears a knock on its window, it will know who's there.

Finally, the FASB seems to be recognizing that it is involved in a political process. It has announced that it is commencing a program to communicate with congressmen. When the FASB was being appointed, I suggested that some of the positions should be granted to skilled lobbyists, rather than skilled accountants. That suggestion was ignored.

Since its formation in early 1973, the FASB has made some progress, issuing five Statements of Financial Accounting Standards, six Interpretations, exposure drafts by filing more statements and discussion memoranda on four other topics. The completed Standards and Interpretations are relatively noncontroversial, whereas the work in-process concerns some highly controversial matters, such as price-level accounting, reporting for segments of a business, and accounting for leases. The FASB's handling of these subjects will be a real test of its ability to survive.

Meanwhile, during the short lifetime of the FASB, the SEC has issued some forty releases affecting financial accounting and reporting. And, after years of saying it does not want to dictate the content of annual reports to stockholders, the SEC in 1974 amended its proxy rules to do just that. As a result, we increased space in our annual report devoted to financial information from twelve pages in 1973 to seventeen pages in 1974.

According to an old saying, there are two ways to deceive the public: One is to tell them nothing and the other is to tell them everything. In the 1926 case cited by Ripley, the company told stockholders nothing. Now, nearly fifty years later, the SEC seems determined to force companies to tell stockholders everything. We are happy to comply with full disclosure, but there are times when we wonder if disclosure of massive financial details may be confusing to many stockholders. New rules by the FASB and SEC have greatly increased the technical accounting and reporting compliance requirements for 1974, and we are certain to encounter more rules in 1975.

The Lifo Method of Valuing Inventories

But the most significant current development in accounting stems not from new FASB and SEC rules but from the Revenue Acts of 1938 and 1939, which introduced the last-in, first-out (Lifo) method of valuing inventories. While innumerable economic events made front-page headlines in 1974, hundreds of major companies were quietly adopting the Lifo method of valuing inventories. The reasons were many: double-digit inflation, tight money, high interest rates, and a stock market which did not respond to earnings per share increases. The potential tax and related interest savings from Lifo simply loomed too large to be ignored.

Lifo inventory valuation developed during the 1930's, when it was adopted by some oil companies. The Revenue Act of 1938 authorized the use of Lifo for income tax purposes, but only for specified raw materials used by leather tanners and producers and processors of certain nonferrous metals. The Revenue Act of 1939 permitted any taxpayer to use Lifo, but restrictive Treasury Department regulations made it impractical, except for companies dealing in uniform, physical units such as oil, steel, and meat. Finally, in 1947 the dollar-value method was approved in a Tax Court case, and the use of Lifo spread to a wide variety of companies.

In pleadings with Congress for extension of the elective use of Lifo to any taxpayer, public accountants and businessmen stated that Lifo was a "generally accepted accounting principle," and therefore should be approved as a method for determining taxable income. Noting very little use of the method, a skeptical Congress decided to limit its application for tax purposes to those companies that used it in other financial reports. Consequently, since 1939 there has been a statutory requirement that, if Lifo is used for tax purposes, no other method can be used for determining income in reports to stockholders and creditors.

The legislative history indicates that the purpose of this conformity requirement was to give assurance that, with respect to a particular taxpayer, the Lifo method clearly reflects income. However, Richard B. Barker, a Washington attorney who was influential in establishing Lifo, says, "Perhaps the best answer is that the outside report requirement was put into the law as a deterrent to the use of the Lifo method of inventory valuation."

Until the 1970's, this was the only time the revenue laws were used to control private accounting. The conformity requirement has been so influential that only in recent years, after SEC intervention with the Internal Revenue Service (IRS), have companies felt comfortable in disclosing the amount of the Lifo reserve -- that is, the difference between Lifo and Fifo.

As recently as January 23, 1975, the IRS was still tinkering with the Lifo disclosures it would permit companies to make in order to comply with requirements of the APB, FASB, and SEC. An IRS release on that day allows companies adopting Lifo to adhere to APB and FASB requirements by stating the reason Lifo is preferable, and by reporting the effect of the change on income for the year of the change only.   The release also permits companies to follow the SEC requirement to disclose the excess of replacement or current cost of inventories over the stated value. Without the dispensation provided in the release, Lifo companies would have been forced to violate APB, FASB, and SEC disclosure rules.

Companies must continue to be very careful to limit the Lifo information they give in order to avoid termination of the Lifo method for tax purposes. For example, Clark Equipment Company will not disclose the Lifo effect on inventories by lines of business.

Without the requirement for financial statement conformity, most companies would probably adopt Lifo for tax purposes and use Fifo in reporting to stockholders. The conformity requirement makes a harsh choice between Lifo and Fifo: one may save taxes and report lower earnings under Lifo, or pay more taxes and report higher earnings under Fifo. This choice is like one put to a British wine expert who visited a Napa winery. A newsman asked him, "Which is more important in life -- wine or sex?" He paused, then replied, "Claret or burgundy?"

Although there are some respected accountants who argue eloquently about the conceptual superiority of Lifo for determining income, businessmen and the accounting profession seem to regard Lifo primarily as a tax-saving device. This is borne out in an AICPA survey of inventory valuation methods disclosed in 600 stockholders' reports for 1973. Only 150 of the companies used Lifo and, of those companies, only eight applied it to all inventory classes; and the trend for several years had been toward fewer companies using Lifo. Of course, this trend was dramatically reversed in 1974.

Nevertheless, most Lifo companies use Fifo for running the business and merely superimpose a Lifo reserve adjustment on Fifo results. In fact, most large manufacturing companies, whether on Lifo or Fifo, value inventories at standard costs for management control purposes.

The Lifo method is seldom used for financial reporting overseas, and is not recognized by most countries for income tax purposes. Therefore, few Lifo companies use Lifo for foreign inventories, because they receive no tax benefit.

Aside from the few permitted disclosures discussed earlier, Lifo techniques lie entirely in the domain of the IRS, and not that of any other regulatory body. In fact, the Cost Accounting Standards Board has proposed a standard that prohibits the use of Lifo in determining costs for defense contract purposes. Although Lifo is considered to be a "generally accepted accounting principle," it is primarily an instrument for tax reduction and is inconsistent with almost all other accounting theories and concepts. It is incompatible with traditional historical cost accounting principles, and also with price-level, fair value, and replacement cost concepts which receive attention in inflationary periods.

The FASB has proposed to require that companies report income in terms of units of general purchasing power of the U.S. dollar as measured by a general price index. (The SEC staff seems to favor instead a replacement cost concept.) But it seems unlikely that the FASB proposal will become final because of the Lifo financial statement conformity requirement. Unless the law is changed, the IRS is required to terminate Lifo if a company reports its income on any other basis. Given the choice of terminating Lifo or following the FASB standard, most companies would probably ignore the FASB standard.

This situation also means that the FASB is unlikely to bring about uniformity in accounting for inventories under traditional historical cost accounting. The FASB will probably not recommend Lifo as the preferred method for all companies, and the SEC requirement for disclosure of current or replacement cost of Lifo inventories implies a preference for other methods. Attempts to eliminate Lifo in financial reporting would run afoul of the conformity law. Very likely, companies enjoying the benefits of Lifo would strongly oppose efforts by the FASB, SEC, or anyone else to delete the conformity clause in the law, for fear that Congress would remove the very right to use Lifo. Furthermore, companies resisting attempts to change the law would probably successfully enlist their public accounting firms in support of their resistance.

Although statistics are not available as to the popularity of Lifo today, the many Lifo adoptions reported in 1974 probably make it the method predominantly used now by large industrial companies for valuing domestic inventories. The support of a long-established law by a majority of U.S. industrial companies would be hard to overcome. There is little reason to believe the FASB and SEC would be any more successful in an attack on the Lifo law than the APB and SEC were in their attempt to avert congressional involvement in accounting for the investment credit.

Accounting for Tax Purposes

In other respects, accounting for tax purposes has had a more significant effect on financial reporting than is frequently acknowledged. Private companies typically use accounting methods that produce the lowest income tax, and they use these methods for financial reporting purposes as well as for income tax purposes. When a private company goes public, accounting methods sometimes must be changed, but many of the methods used for tax purposes are continued. In addition, in recent years direct action by the Treasury Department is affecting financial reporting to stockholders.

Since about 1970, the Treasury Department selectively has been putting a financial statement conformity requirement in regulations on accounting for income tax purposes. The language used in the regulations is similar to the Lifo conformity language used in the Revenue Act of 1939. When two or more alternative accounting methods are available, one of which produces maximum tax benefits and the other produces better financial reports to investors, the Treasury Department has required that a method may be used for tax purposes only if it is used in financial reports to stockholders and creditors. Notable examples of this requirement are in IRS regulations on full-cost accounting for inventories and proposed, but later withdrawn, regulations on construction contract accounting. If this movement continues, it will further impinge upon the accounting rule-making function of the FASB and SEC.

A Ranking of Authorities

Where does this leave the beleaguered accounting officer in his attempts to comply with an ever-increasing welter of rules emanating from several sources? We look first at the most authoritative sources for guidance. They are in this order:

1. Congress
2. Treasury Department
3. Securities and Exchange Commission
4. Financial Accounting Standards Board

Congress has not spoken often on accounting matters, but when it has, it has become the absolute authority. Treasury Department rules have the effect of law and, where conformity in financial reporting is the price to be paid for tax saving, these rules are authoritative. Tax saving produces cash flow and this is usually more important to a company than defense of a specific principle of accounting. Third in line of authorities is the SEC; its rules also have the effect of law. Fourth in line is the FASB. Their pronouncements have been either ordered by the SEC or at least approved by the SEC, and they will be enforced by the SEC.

Some industries are affected by still more rule-making bodies, such as the Federal Power Commission, Interstate Commerce Commission, and Civil Aeronautics Board. And there are other agencies which make rules for special purpose reporting, like the Federal Trade Commission and Cost Accounting Standards Board. These agencies may have an effect on public financial reporting in the future.

The AICPA is still issuing auditing standards in which accounting matters are intricately entwined. And the AICPA has commenced issuing accounting position papers.

Several international groups are issuing statements on accounting. The Accountants International Study Group has made eleven comparative studies which lead to their conclusions and recommendations. The more recently formed International Accounting Standards Committee has issued its first standard, calling for disclosure of accounting policies by multinational companies. The Committee has proposed that the accounting bodies in each of the twenty participating countries make disclosure of non-compliance with the new standard mandatory upon their members.

In the European Common Market, the real thrust in harmonization of accounting principles is at the legislative-level in the member countries. This organization issues broad directives which must be acted upon by the legislatures to implement the directives country by country. These legislative actions are then subject to review by a special court to determine whether they comply with the directives. Harmonization of accounting rules then is clearly more of a political than conceptual process.

For the United States, an obvious answer to the problem of too many rule-making bodies is a single agency. Such an agency would be viable only if it were an independent government agency. Even this arrangement would be effective only if Congress gave the agency powers that could not be infringed on by any other agency and only if Congress itself kept hands off. An all-powerful agency does not appear to be likely in the near future; and if we had one, we might wish we were back in the hands of the overlapping rule-makers.

There remains room for the FASB to perform a constructive role in the accounting rule-making function. We should recognize its limitations. We should be aware that the FASB has been legally foreclosed from dealing with some subjects, and that its pronouncements are limited in scope and subject to approval of others. The FASB is not writing on a clean slate -- it must deal with rules that exist in the environment that exists.

As rules proliferate, the role of the independent accounting firm is changing from advocate of preferable accounting methods selected from among several available, to advisor as to the specific accounting method which is applicable in compliance with the rules.

Progress Can Still Be Made

Further progress may be made in establishing the objectives of financial reporting. But progress to the most strident voices often calls for a complete change from the historical cost-basis of accounting. For example, it is fashionable to talk in terms of introducing "economic reality" into financial reporting. The trouble is that few can agree on what constitutes economic reality and how it should be measured.

Presumably, economic reality requires reporting in terms of current values or fair values. But this would lead accounting information farther away from the commercial enterprise goal of using cash to make a profit and generate more cash to return to its owners. Nevertheless, debate on issues like this is healthy, and ultimately leads to changing basic objectives of corporate financial accounting.

Meanwhile, further progress will be made in accounting rule-making, and somehow industry will survive the plethora of rules. Management will find a way to run its business under any accounting regulations imposed on it. Even with our peculiar overlapping rule-making structure, I see hope for cooperation among rule-makers in moving toward a more coherent conceptual basis for accounting.

But to expect a neat set of basic objectives, broad standards, and detailed rules to be totally consistent with each other is expecting too much of a practical art. If that could be accomplished to the general satisfaction of all concerned, it would have been done long ago. Accounting progress will continue to be accomplished in a practical, political way through debates and confrontations, which are lively, spirited, controversial, and sometimes painful.

We should accept these conditions and be happy with them. History has shown that too many economic considerations are at stake for so many interested groups to permit progress in financial reporting to be simple and harmonious.

GENERAL PURCHASING POWER OR
SPECIFIC POLITICAL POWER?
Before Price Waterhouse & Co.'s Price-Level Accounting Seminar
Chicago, Illinois
July 30, 1975

Ladies and Gentlemen, I wish to thank Hugh Campbell and my other former partners for permitting me to share with you my views on price-level accounting. Before accepting Hugh's kind invitation, I warned him that my outlook would undoubtedly be at variance with some others on this program and probably would conflict to some extent with his firm's view. He was quite willing to accept this circumstance, and so I am pleased to be here with you today.

One thing I neglected to clear with Hugh in advance, and I would like to deal with it now: inflation has forced me, as well as Price Waterhouse, to raise standard billing rates, so that my fee is much higher today than it was when I left the firm in 1967.

Price-level accounting is an interesting phenomenon which has attracted a cult. Some devotees seem absolutely delighted at the recent high rate of inflation, for this gives them the opportunity to exclaim gleefully, "Price-level accounting is an idea whose time has come!"

I might add that the idea has been a long time in coming and its time may not have come yet. Historical cost-based accounting has had severe criticism in every inflationary period in this century. Proposed action to overcome the deficiency nearly always takes the form of adjustment of statements to recognize the change in purchasing power of the dollar.

In 1951, George O. May headed a Study Group on Concepts of Business Income. He and a distinguished group of accountants, economists, lawyers, and businessmen concluded that business income should be determined by measuring revenues and costs in units of equal purchasing power. Despite the eminent auspices, the concept never got off the ground, partly because inflation averaged less than two percent a year over the next fifteen years.

Interest in inflation accounting revived somewhat in the late 1960s as the rate of inflation increased. Then in June of 1969, the Accounting Principles Board issued its *Statement No. 3*, "Financial Statements Restated for General Price-Level Changes." When considering the

211

topic, the Board persuaded seventeen large companies to prepare price-level adjusted financial statements to test the techniques and possibly reveal problem areas that needed further attention. Having proved by these practical applications that the method worked and produced useful information, the Board urged the cooperating companies to disclose summary price-level results in their annual reports. All but one of those companies would have reported lower earnings on a price-level adjusted basis, and they chose not to disclose this.

The one company that had higher earnings on a price-level adjusted basis proudly reported this in its annual report. But a closer look is warranted. The company did not report that the improved results occurred because the company was very highly leveraged, with liabilities far in excess of monetary assets. Although the price-level earnings were high, the company was approaching financial disaster and within three years had to sell several of its businesses to avoid bankruptcy.

Typically, in periods of substantial changes in price-levels, accountants have approached the problem of determining business income from the standpoint of concepts and techniques. On the other hand, businessmen and economists seem to view the problem from the standpoint of erosion of capital through taxation and the practical politics of obtaining suitable relief.

In my opinion, these basic differences in approach have brought us to the point where the accountants' conceptual proposals will likely fail because of the partial practical relief already obtained through political processes. Meanwhile, the accountants have developed an extensive literature to support accounting recognition of price-level changes and complex techniques of implementation.

In so doing, I submit that price-level accounting's *production* department has far outstripped its *sales* department! The shelves are full of brilliant concepts and sparkling techniques which are *unassailable*, but also *unsalable* -- for the customers are not buying them. In business, when we produce more than we can sell, we build up inventories, and then suffer painfully as we are forced to reduce or halt production until we can sell those inventories. (This simile is very timely, for our industry has just over-produced in a period of weak demand.) I suggest that the accounting profession should be out selling very hard if it wants to see its products move off the shelf and into use out in the field.

Over the years, other groups have been selling their ideas and, thus, business has available to it partial recognition of the inflationary effects on its operations. Significantly, the selling has been done in Congress and the Treasury Department so that the relief obtained is in cash saved from reduced taxes. This may or may not reduce income in financial statements reported to stockholders, but it does improve cash flow.

The most important of these relief measures are the Lifo method of valuing inventories and accelerated depreciation. They represent only partial tax relief and fall short of the relief which would be obtained by recognition for tax purposes of price-level adjustments, replacement costs, or some other form of current values. Nevertheless, these measures are very important to business.

I believe most businesses will not be interested in other inflationary accounting recognition unless the new proposals provide tax relief equal to or greater than that now available. Financial reporting practices have demonstrated that businessmen are not interested in reducing reported income, even though they recognize that real income is declining in inflationary periods.

Look at the two items I have mentioned. We accountants really do not like Lifo because it has a flimsy conceptual base and it makes a mockery of the balance sheet. Back in 1939, however, they told Congress it was a generally accepted accounting principle, and therefore should be approved as a method for determining taxable income. Noting very little use of the method, a skeptical Congress wrote into law that if Lifo is used for tax purposes, no other method can be used for determining income in reports to stockholders and creditors.

We businessmen do not like Lifo either, because the conformity requirement depresses reported earnings. Consequently, even today when so much cash flow is at stake, some companies that badly need the cash have foregone the tax savings from Lifo in order to report higher earnings. Unfortunately, they are probably not getting credit for the higher earnings in the stock market, for security analysts have become quite good at deducting so-called "inventory profits" from income reported on a Fifo-basis.

Accelerated depreciation came into the tax laws in the 1940s and 1950s. As Congress did not say how it had to be reported to stockholders, a common practice is to use the fastest depreciation methods for tax purposes and less fast write-offs for financial reporting.

This circumstance gave rise to arguments lasting for decades over accounting for deferred income taxes related to the differences in the methods

Speaking of arguments and Congress brings to mind the investment tax credit. Congress specified that no one can tell taxpayers how to account for this credit in reports to stockholders. As a result, most companies report the credit in income of the year in which it reduces tax. Although it is not really an element of inflation accounting, the investment tax credit does contribute to the reduction of taxes and, therefore, helps curb the erosion of capital. I mention it also as further evidence that accountants have great difficulty in communicating with Congress.

Proponents of some form of inflation accounting often cite overseas experience as examples of what can be accomplished to adjust financial statements for changing purchasing power. A closer look, however, reveals a political environment that dominates the scene.

In Brazil, price-level accounting is practiced and it is recognized for income tax purposes. But it is only partial, and some aspects of it are required by law. Adjustments must or may be made for a variety of items, and this involves indices for fixed assets and a provision for maintenance of working capital. The entire Brazilian economy is based on indexing, the virtues of which surprisingly have been extolled by conservative economist Milton Friedman following his visit there last winter.

Replacement cost accounting is used by some Dutch companies, but the practice is not as extensive as its proponents would have you believe. Even though the theory has been developing in the Netherlands since 1917, only 39 of 200 companies in a recent study used replacement cost accounting. Significantly, it is not accepted for tax purposes.

In the United Kingdom, the Accounting Standards Steering Committee of the Institute of Chartered Accountants issued a standard calling for supplemental presentation of price-level adjusted financial statements. Of 300 large companies specifically urged to do this, only nine complied. Meanwhile, the government became disturbed about the proposal and set up the Sandilands Committee to study the broader impact of the standard. That committee came out in favor of replacement cost accounting, if anything, as opposed to the Institute's purchasing power units approach, so the issue is at a standstill.

Similarly, back in the United States, the Chief Accountant of the Securities and Exchange Commission seems to favor replacement cost accounting, rather than the Financial Accounting Standards Board's financial reporting in units of general purchasing power.   He disparagingly refers to the Board's proposal as "PuPu" accounting. In fact, we are expecting any day to see the SEC's promised proposal for required supplemental disclosure in financial statements of replacement costs of four elements: cost of goods sold, fixed assets, depreciation, and inventories -- without any disclosure of income effect.

While the FASB is sparring with the SEC, it seems to be overlooking Congress and the Treasury Department. Not long ago, I mentioned to an FASB member that those of us who use Lifo would ignore an FASB standard on price-level accounting in order to preserve tax savings from Lifo. His response was: "That problem will have to be resolved with the Internal Revenue Service." This gives me an uneasy feeling about the FASB's grasp of the situation. The conformity requirement, is not an IRS rule but a law passed by Congress. It appears to me that unless the law is changed, the IRS is required to terminate Lifo if a company reports its income on any other basis.

Very likely, companies enjoying the benefits of Lifo would strongly oppose efforts by the FASB, SEC, or anyone else to delete the conformity clause in the law, for fear that Congress would remove the right to use Lifo. Furthermore, companies resisting attempts to change the law would probably successfully enlist their public accounting firms in support of their resistance. After all, they talked us into adopting Lifo in the first place.

Price-level accounting is a simple concept, but the techniques set forth by the FASB are exceedingly complex. A great deal of work is involved in preparing financial statements in units of general purchasing power. Also the new disclosures would probably be confusing to users of financial statements. Before taking final action in trying to require this new reporting, I believe the FASB should conduct extensive cost-benefit studies to determine if it is all worthwhile.

It is fashionable today to talk in terms of introducing "economic reality" into financial reporting. The trouble is that few can agree on what constitutes economic reality and how it should be measured. Presumably, economic reality requires reporting in terms of current values, or fair values, or units of general purchasing power. But these methods lead accounting information farther away from the commercial enterprise goal of using cash to make a profit and generate more cash to return to its owners. In matters other than inflation accounting, the FASB, with full SEC blessing, seems to be strongly in favor of cash basis accounting, as demonstrated clearly in the new standards on research and development, contingencies, and development-stage companies.

Regardless of what accounting rules are imposed on business by the various rulemakers, management will find a satisfactory way to run its business. On the other hand, a rule-making body like the FASB may not be able to survive if it tries to impose an unenforceable rule.

In revealing some practical obstacles to the adoption of price-level accounting, I am not speaking slightingly of the idea of supplemental disclosure of the effects of inflation. Perhaps it is time to get price-level accounting out of the laboratory and into the real business world. In fact, the routine presentation of financial statements in terms of current purchasing power by all of business just might help influence Congress that further tax reduction is needed. But this will not be enough.

If price-level accounting is what the accountants want -- and the FASB seems to want it badly -- then they should stop talking to each other and start talking to the people with the authority to affect the economy. In short, price-level accounting's sales force should be communicating the merits of financial reporting in units of general purchasing power to the body with specific political power, the Congress of the United States.

Business requirements for capital over the next several years are immense. Obtaining that capital is essential to provide jobs and produce goods and services which lead to a healthy national economy and also a healthy world economy. A substantial amount of capital could be made available to business by providing full tax relief from the impact of inflation.

To sum up, supplementary general purchasing power information is interesting, but real nourishment would be provided to everyone if the techniques were translated into income tax reduction and resulting increased cash flow. Thank you for letting me express my views on price-level accounting.

AN OVERVIEW OF CORPORATE ACCOUNTING AND
FINANCIAL REPORTING
Before Executive Enterprises, Inc.
Eighth Corporate Accounting and Financial Reporting Institute
New Orleans, Louisiana
May 23, 1978

Corporate accounting and financial reporting have been receiving a tremendous amount of publicity recently, most of it unwelcome to public accountants and corporate executives, as well. Much of the publicity relates to the increasing rate of production of rule-making bodies; but, unfortunately, much of it also relates to criticism and perceived inadequacies of the entire accounting and reporting process. Under attack are not only reporting practices but also auditing standards, the quality of performance and the independence of auditors, and corporate behavior.

Criticism of accounting standards and the process for setting them has been around for decades. In this respect the accounting profession has displayed an enormous capacity for self-criticism, but outside criticism has also grown as the public has come to expect a higher standard of performance from a prominent and growing profession.

More recently, attention has been directed to auditing standards and practices. The reasons are many. Some major frauds were undetected by auditors. In an increasingly litigious world, auditors attracted large numbers of lawsuits and liability insurance costs soared. Also, Watergate-disclosed corporate impropriety brought about demands for higher standards of behavior.

Now committees of Congress itself are talking about possible legislation which would provide further federal regulation of the accounting profession. Critics abound, both inside and outside the accounting profession.

I will present a brief overview of the more important financial reporting matters that are pending, many of which will be discussed in detail by other speakers. Before doing that, I wish to mention what I perceive to be standard responses of the accounting profession to professional criticism of almost any nature. They are:

1.   Form a committee to study the matter, or make it a commission if it is a really big matter.

2.   The committee will recommend that we:

    a.   Change the organizational structure.

    b.   Form a "board" because it sounds more impressive.

    c.   Set forth the objectives of financial reporting and a conceptual framework of accounting; this will permit an easy resolution of all accounting problems as they arise.

3.   The board will:

    a.   Look for objectives and conceptual framework, find them, and then discover they do not help much in handling specific problems.

    b.   Then fall back on the "more is better" position and issue large numbers of standards, statements, opinions, bulletins, releases, rules, and regulations.

    c.   And, finally, form a lot more committees to implement its work.

This process seems to be automatic and regenerative and can be repeated indefinitely.

All of these approaches have been designed to keep the standards-setting function and regulation of the accounting profession in the private sector and limit federal involvement. In my opinion, these responses have resulted in financial accounting and reporting being one of the most highly regulated functions of business. What is more, the frenetic pace of institutional activity leads me to this observation about the future: "You ain't seen nothin' yet!"

Accounting Standards

Many of the standard responses I referred to have been demonstrated over the years in the search for accounting rules, variously called principles, practices, and standards. In response to criticism of accounting practices back in 1939, the American Institute of Certified Public Accountants formed the Committee on Accounting Procedure.

This Committee issued 51 Accounting Research Bulletins over a period of two decades.

In 1959, in response to criticism of the Committee on Accounting Procedure, the Committee was replaced by the Accounting Principles Board. The APB authorized studies of the basic postulates and broad principles of accounting, but rejected the resulting research reports. Later, in 1970, the APB itself issued a "Statement of Basic Concepts and Accounting Principles Underlying Financial Statements of Business Enterprises." This Statement failed to provide the basis for solving accounting problems.

In the face of mounting criticism of the APB in 1971, the AICPA, in a variation of the standard response, appointed one group to study the establishment of accounting principles and another group to study the objectives of financial statements. The results of the first study tolled the death knell of the APB and in 1973 created the new full-time Financial Accounting Standards Board independent of the AICPA. Over its 14-year span of existence the APB issued 31 Opinions and four Statements.

Although the report of the second study, by the accounting objectives group, was well received by the profession, the stated objectives still were not specific enough to permit the resolution of practical accounting problems. Therefore, one of the new FASB's first seven projects, broad qualitative standards for financial statements, was soon enlarged to encompass the entire conceptual framework of financial accounting and reporting including objectives, qualitative characteristics, and the information needs of users of financial information.

Today, the FASB has broken the conceptual framework effort into five projects:

1.   Objectives of financial reporting;
2.   Elements of financial statements;
3.   Qualitative characteristics;
4.   Measurement; and
5.   Earnings report.

The last of the five projects is not expected to be completed until 1980. The FASB should be commended for its effort in trying to cope with what has been a most difficult and controversial subject. This work has been undertaken with the implication that, once the Statements are issued, they will lead to the solution of accounting matters in a consistent and easily applied manner. In placing this kind of emphasis on the conceptual framework, the FASB may be promising more than it can deliver.

The FASB has, of course, been very active in issuing many standards and interpretations on specific accounting matters. Its current workload includes several difficult problem areas, although a recently published technical agenda reveals that most of the projects are being deferred until completion of the conceptual framework projects. In fact, only one other standard, accounting for interest costs, is expected to be issued in final form in the remainder of 1978.

Although the FASB has been in existence for only about five years, it began to attract criticism when controversial standards were issued. The response of the FASB's parent organization, the Financial Accounting Foundation, was to assign a committee to examine the structure and operations of the FASB. The structure committee has reported, and most of its recommendations have been implemented. Now the FASB meetings are open to the public under its "sunshine" rules, Board pronouncements are based on a simple majority instead of the five-of-seven rule, the AICPA right to veto election of the Financial Accounting Foundation trustees has been eliminated, a full-time independent chairman and executive director of the Financial Accounting Standards Advisory Council are in place, and other structural changes have been made. Surely the FASB has tried very hard to be responsive to the needs of its constituencies, and I believe its sincere efforts have caused it to enjoy the strong support of business and the accounting profession.

This support does not mean to imply approval of all of the FASB's controversial pronouncements. For example, hardly any financial executives approve of its Statement on accounting for the translation of foreign currency transactions and foreign currency financial statements, which the Board has steadfastly refused to reconsider. Yet, an encouraging development is the recent addition to the Board's agenda of a project on evaluation of FASB Standards. Many are hopeful that evaluation of *SFAS No. 8* will lead to a modification of it.

When the FASB was formed, the accounting standard function was transferred from the AICPA's Accounting Principles Board to the

FASB. Some thought the AICPA would be out of accounting rule-making. Not so, it turns out. In 1972, after a committee studied the matter, the AICPA formed another committee with the imposing title of "Accounting Standards Executive Committee," referred to as AcSEC. Now it is deeply involved in the accounting rule-making process, and is supported in this endeavor by several committees, subcommittees and task forces. A recent agenda listed 31 active projects. Although some of the projects relate to FASB or Securities and Exchange Commission proposals, a majority of them involve preparation of statements of position or industry accounting and audit guides. Of course, AcSEC is cooperating with the FASB through established channels. However, if the FASB does not choose to act on the subject of an AcSEC proposal, the AcSEC statement or guide is published and is applied by independent accountants as being part of generally accepted accounting principles. Recognizing its part in the rule-making process, AcSEC is now operating under sunshine rules similar to those of the FASB.

Auditing Standards

The AICPA is even more active in the area of auditing standards than accounting standards. About the same time AcSEC was formed, the auditors did not want to be outdone, so the AICPA formed the impressively titled "Auditing Standards Executive Committee," referred to as AudSEC. Today it has more than 40 projects on its agenda, assigned to nearly as many task forces, committees and subcommittees. Most of the projects will result in issuance of Statements on Auditing Standards. These Statements constitute the bedrock of generally accepted auditing standards, which auditors are expected to follow in conducting an examination of financial statements.

Much of this increase in auditing standards activity results from the increase in lawsuits against auditors over the last ten to fifteen years. Often the lawsuits have little merit, but the auditor is named as a defendant along with management and others. Lawsuits arise when companies fail or suffer substantial losses, and the auditor may be the most conveniently available party with funds to pursue. Along with increased litigation has come skyrocketing costs of professional liability insurance.

It is no wonder then that the public accounting profession has turned increasingly to defensive auditing. Often an auditor's defense is to demonstrate that he has adhered to a specific standard that is clearly set forth as part of generally accepted auditing standards. Hence, we have seen an acceleration in the issuance of standards, which is likely to continue for some time.

Public criticism of the performance of auditors has also been a strong reason for issuing more standards. A gap has developed between the performance of auditors and the expectations of users of financial statements.

Recognizing the need for a reconsideration of auditors' responsibilities in the light of changing circumstances, the AICPA in late 1974 established "The Commission on Auditors' Responsibilities" to develop conclusions and recommendations regarding the appropriate responsibilities of independent auditors. This Commission is referred to as the "Cohen Commission" for its chairman, the late Manuel F. Cohen, former SEC Commissioner. The Commission issued its final "Report, Conclusions, and Recommendations" early in 1978, but it revealed few significant changes from a "Report of Tentative Conclusions" issued in March, 1977. An AICPA committee to study the structure of AudSEC had been formed long before the final report of the Cohen Commission.

That special committee on structure has already issued its own preliminary report in which it recommends that auditing standard-setting remain with auditors and the AICPA. The structure committee rejected a major proposal of the Cohen Commission for a full-time, paid body to set auditing standards; but it recently reported that the committee majority favors a part-time board, a part-time chairman, and a full-time, paid executive director. The structure committee made a number of other recommendations for changes in AudSEC operations, including an advisory council, a staff research director, and "sunshine" rules.

In addition, the AICPA appointed several special committees to help implement the many other Cohen Commission recommendations. Meanwhile, the AICPA created a new division of firms with two sections, consisting of an SEC practice section and a private practice section.

Congressional Interest in Corporate Reporting

Much of this stepped up professional activity is designed to ward off removal of professional standard-setting from the private sector and to avoid further federal regulation of the profession. The concern is very real, for the accounting profession is receiving increasing scrutiny from Congress.

In January, 1977, the profession, business, and the SEC were shocked by a 1,760-page study on "The Accounting Establishment" issued by the staff of the late Senator Metcalf's Subcommittee on Reports, Accounting, and Management of the Committee on Governmental Affairs of the United States Senate. The report was highly critical of the manner in which the large accounting firms and the SEC were performing their responsibilities. The report contained sixteen recommendations for federal action to regulate corporate accountability, including federal establishment of accounting and auditing standards, and federal inspection of the work of independent auditors. Public hearings were held at which many references were made to the Cohen Commission's recommendations and the Financial Accounting Foundation Structure Committee's recommendations as being sufficient private sector efforts to obviate the need for regular legislation.

The final report of the Metcalf subcommittee (issued in November, 1977) cited needs for improved accounting standards, improved auditing and auditing standards, and close SEC oversight of the accounting organization and enforcement of securities laws. But the subcommittee went on to conclude that public policy goals for improving the performance of independent auditors of publicly owned corporations can best be met through partnership between the accounting profession and the SEC. The subcommittee promised to continue its oversight of accounting through additional hearings in 1978. Following Senator Metcalf's death, accounting matters were transferred to the Subcommittee on Governmental Efficiency and the District of Columbia. Subcommittee Chairman Senator Eagleton promised to continue the work begun under Senator Metcalf's direction and expand it to include various other areas of concern. He has already sent surveys to a number of organizations containing 54 questions.

In the House, Representative Moss, chairman of the Subcommittee on Oversight and Investigation of the Commerce Committee, said recently he plans to introduce legislation to regulate the accounting profession. His subcommittee has already held four series of hearings. Congressman Moss said he was "both disappointed in and dissatisfied with the self-regulatory program of the AICPA." He also said he was dissatisfied with "the SEC's unconstrained 'wait and see' attitude without any positive, well-planned alternative should the AICPA plan fail."

Throughout the congressional hearings and investigations, the SEC remained strongly supportive of professional accounting standard-setting in the private sector, even when the SEC itself was severely criticized for doing so. How did the SEC react to criticism? Quite naturally, the SEC appointed a committee to study its own disclosure requirements. That Advisory Committee on Corporate Disclosure concluded last year that SEC disclosure policies and procedures are essentially sound, but some recommendations for improvements were made. Interestingly, the Committee's recommendation for a statement of objectives as a guide to the purpose of the corporate disclosure system was not accepted by the SEC, nor was the idea that SEC rules should not be aimed at regulating corporate conduct.

SEC support of the accounting profession may soon be put to another crucial test. This time it relates to accounting for oil and gas producing companies. The Energy Policy and Conservation Act of 1975 empowers the SEC to prescribe accounting for oil and gas producing companies or to rely on accounting practices developed by the FASB if the SEC is assured that the practices will be observed to the same extent as if the SEC had prescribed them. In December, 1977, in a highly controversial decision, the FASB issued *SFAS No. 19*, which prescribes that "successful efforts" accounting is required and "full cost" accounting is prohibited. *SFAS No. 19* will be effective for fiscal years beginning after December 15, 1978.

Since then, the Department of Energy held hearings on the subject and later opposed *SFAS No. 19* at hearings held by the SEC. The DOE stated in a 58-page memorandum, that *SFAS No. 19* could cause reduction in exploration and development expenditures by five companies which quantified that figure by $150 million per year. The Department also warned that competition in the oil and gas industry may be reduced by causing small oil and gas firms to experience slower growth.

The Federal Trade Commission issued a 34-page memorandum urging the SEC not to adopt *SFAS No. 19*. The FTC said the "full cost" method is more accurate than the "successful efforts" method, and *SFAS No. 19* would cause unnecessary competitive harm to independent producers, who would be forced to change their accounting procedures in many cases. The Antitrust Division of the Justice Department also opposes this FASB Statement, because of a lack of analysis of the potential anti-competitive impact on independent oil and gas producers.

Although the agencies criticized the "successful efforts" accounting method, their strongest complaints related to perceived adverse effects on energy discovery and competition, with assumptions that smaller independent producers would reduce exploration expenditures, report lower profits, and encounter restricted access to capital. With strong opposition from three federal agencies, this issue may be the supreme test of the partnership between the SEC and the accounting profession.

If the SEC supports the FASB standard, it may well be overruled by Congress. While others were threatening congressional oversight and federal regulation, Senator Proxmire succeeded in having enacted the Foreign Corrupt Practices Act of 1977, which became effective December 19, 1977. This law applies directly to corporations rather than independent auditors. All U.S. companies and officers, directors, employees, agents, or stockholders are prohibited from bribing foreign governmental or political officials. Companies making bribes can be fined up to $1 million; individuals face a maximum $10,000 fine, imprisonment of up to five years, or both. The law requires publicly held companies to (1) devise and maintain a system of internal control sufficient, among other things, to provide reasonable assurance that transactions are properly authorized and recorded; and (2) keep records which "accurately and fairly" reflect financial activities in reasonable detail. The law amends the Securities Exchange Act of 1934, and the SEC is expected to enforce it.

Other legislation regulating business is directed at the Arab boycott of Israel. The Tax Reform Act of 1976 denies to any taxpayer that participates in, or cooperates with, such an international boycott the benefits of the foreign-tax credit deferral of unremitted earnings of controlled foreign subsidiaries, and Domestic International Sales Corporations (DISC). On June 22, 1977, the president signed a law aimed at limiting the involvement of United States corporations in the Arab boycott of Israel. This law is administered under Department of Commerce regulations.

With all the regulations pending, promised, and threatened, it seems appropriate to ask how business and the accounting profession will survive. My answer is they will survive very well indeed. While we may chafe at overkill in regulation, nearly all business executives and professional accountants want to follow sound and fair business and professional practices. We have survived very well for many years under a system that is only partially self-regulated by the private sector. We will have more regulation, and we will be able to cope with it. Whether public or private, in our democratic nation we still have the right to make our views known and to participate in the development of that regulation. As Theodore Roosevelt once said:

> It is not the critic who counts.... The credit belongs to the man who is actually in the arena, whose face is marred with sweat and dust and blood; who strives valiantly; ... who, if he wins, knows the triumph of high achievement; and who, if he fails, at least fails, while daring greatly, so that his place shall never be with those cold and timid souls who know neither victory nor defeat.

SOME VIEWS OF CURRENT ACTIVITIES OF THE SECURITIES
AND EXCHANGE COMMISSION
Before Machinery and Allied Products Institute's
Conference on New Trends in Accounting and Financial Reporting
Arlington, Virginia
June 14, 1979

Good morning, ladies and gentlemen. I am pleased to participate in this MAPI Conference on New Trends in Accounting and Financial Reporting, and to share the platform with a distinguished SEC Commissioner, John Evans.

The Securities and Exchange Commission has been in existence for some 45 years. In my opinion, it has generally done an excellent job in administering the Securities Acts and in providing full and fair disclosure of the character of securities as called for by the Acts. The SEC is a regulatory agency which operates in a political environment. Its actions are highly visible and subject to constant review and criticism by those it regulates, by the press, and by Congress. That such an agency performs well in these circumstances is remarkable.

In regulating accounting and financial reporting, which are our main concerns here today, the SEC has fairly followed due process rules called for by the Administrative Procedure Act. It can point to numerous instances where proposed rules were extensively modified or dropped in response to evidence submitted by business and the public at hearings and in statements filed with the Commission.

Although I have a lot of respect for the SEC, I did not come here to praise it. Instead, I intend to give some personal views of its current developments, point out some confusing aspects of its current posture, and suggest ways for it to clear up the confusion.

Sweeping Changes in Regulatory Direction

In the last few years, the SEC has been moving rapidly from requiring simple and limited historical financial information to be filed with the Commission in a leisurely time frame, to requiring complex and extensive current and future financial information to be disseminated widely to the public on a timely-basis. Emphasis is being switched from hard information to soft information. Some of the most significant evidence of this trend lies in recent pronouncements on

227

replacement costs, forecasts, reserve recognition accounting for oil and gas companies, and reporting on internal accounting control.

In traveling this route, which is a drastic change in direction for SEC rule-making, the SEC seems to be confused. This change started about seven years ago with a disclosure project called "quality of earnings," which has now reached massive proportions where disclosure must be made of information which is very extensive and, in my opinion, excessive. I will mention several confusing concepts the SEC seems to display, and then I will discuss them in relation to certain recent pronouncements. Here are the concepts:

1.   More is better.
2.   Tell the stockholders everything you tell us.
3.   We don't believe what you tell unless it is audited.
4.   We don't believe you when you say telling more costs more.
5.   When in doubt, estimate. You must develop a tolerance for imprecision.
6.   We believe in non-preemption of the Financial Accounting Standards Board.
7.   We believe in self-regulation of the accounting profession, as long as it does what we want to be done.
8.   We ignore reporting requirements imposed on business by other agencies.

The list omits two items that were included when I addressed this conference three years ago, but it adds a significant one. The concept of "differential disclosure" seems to have faded away, and the SEC now appears to be consistent in saying "tell the stockholders everything you tell us." Also, the SEC has dropped its "as if" proposal in matters where there are acceptable alternative accounting methods, but has threatened to reconsider it if progress is not made on a timely-basis by the FASB. The new item on the list is support of self-regulation of the accounting profession.

Support of Self-Regulation of the Accounting Profession

Business and the accounting profession greatly appreciate the SEC's support of self-regulation in the private sector. This support is absolutely essential for the function to remain in the profession, particularly so in light of investigations and criticism emanating from both houses of Congress.

The final report of the subcommittee chaired by the late Senator Metcalf, issued in November, 1977, cited needs for improved accounting standards, improved auditing and auditing standards, and close SEC oversight of the accounting organization and enforcement of securities laws. But, the subcommittee went on to conclude that public policy goals for improving the performance of independent auditors of publicly-owned corporations can best be met through partnership between the accounting profession and the SEC.

Concurrently, an investigation was underway in the House by a subcommittee chaired by Congressman Moss, who said he was "both disappointed in and dissatisfied with the self-regulatory program of the AICPA." He also said he was dissatisfied with "the SEC's unconstrained 'wait and see' attitude without any positive, well-planned alternative should the AICPA plan fail."

Throughout the congressional hearings and investigations, the SEC remained strongly supportive of professional accounting standard-setting in the private sector, even when the SEC itself was severely criticized for doing so. As a result of that criticism, the SEC appointed a committee to study its own disclosure requirements. That Advisory Committee on Corporate Disclosure concluded that SEC disclosure policies and procedures are essentially sound, but some recommendations for improvements were made.

The Commission undertook at the Metcalf hearings in June, 1977, to report periodically to the Congress on the profession's response to the challenges which Congress and others had placed before it and on the Commission's own initiatives in this area. In its first such report to Congress on July 5, 1978, the Commission stated:

> The central issue in the debate over the accounting profession's future is whether the profession should continue to be primarily and essentially self-disciplined and self-regulatory, or whether government should become more directly involved in its regulation and in the setting of the accounting and auditing standards under which the profession operates.

The Commission reviewed in detail activities of the profession and concluded that "... the progress during the past year has been sufficient to merit continued opportunity for the profession to pursue its efforts at self-regulation."

The Commission is about to report again on the accounting profession and the Commission's oversight role. We are grateful that the SEC, as just announced by Commissioner Evans, continues to find the progress of self-discipline and self-regulation sufficient to warrant keeping these functions within the profession.

Congressional pressure on the SEC and SEC pressure on the profession have created a massive bureaucracy in the profession. The AICPA created a new Division of CPA Firms and, within that Division, an SEC Practice Section, which includes a Public Oversight Board composed of distinguished individuals from outside the profession. A peer review program is required for members of the Division. The AICPA has created an Auditing Standards Board to take over the auditing standard-setting process. Although the AICPA did not follow the recommendation of the Cohen Commission and the SEC for a small full-time board, each of the fifteen members of the Board is expected to devote at least 1,000 hours per year to the Board's work. In addition to the AICPA efforts, the FASB continues to expand its work in the setting of accounting standards. Multitudinous task forces, committees, and subcommittees have been formed within each of these organizations, and extensive regulatory and technical guidance pronouncements are being developed at a rapid pace; and they seem to be expanding exponentially.

These activities are adding significant costs to accounting firms, which in turn pass them on to their clients and, ultimately, to society as a whole. I hope that expansion in regulatory costs, whether public or private, will not continue indefinitely.

While the SEC supports standard-setting in the private sector, it has on occasion overruled the profession in a manner that is most embarrassing, discouraging, and devastating. The Energy Policy and Conservation Act of 1975 empowered the SEC to prescribe accounting for oil and gas producing companies or to rely on accounting practices developed by the FASB, if the SEC is assured that the practices will be observed to the same extent as if the SEC had prescribed them. In December, 1977, in a highly controversial decision, the FASB issued

Statement No. 19 which prescribes that "successful efforts" accounting is required and "full cost" accounting is prohibited. On August 31, 1978, the SEC said it would accept either successful efforts or full cost accounting for the time being, but steps should be taken to develop "reserve recognition accounting" (RRA). Under RRA, proved oil and gas reserves would be shown as assets on the balance sheet, additions to proved reserves and changes in valuations of proved reserves would be included in the income statement, and all costs associated with finding and developing additions to proved reserves, together with all costs determined to be non-productive during the current period, would be included in the income statement. Here again, the SEC is demanding soft information.

This lack of support was a cruel and crushing blow to the FASB. Consequently, in February, 1979, the FASB issued *Statement No. 25*, suspending the effective date of *SFAS No.19* for certain provisions related to the basic method of accounting. The SEC position left the FASB with no better choice.

The SEC says it has a policy of non-preemption of the FASB, but it has preempted the FASB once in reporting the effects of inflation, and appears to be ready to do it again on the same subject. In December, 1974, the FASB issued an exposure draft which proposed to require supplementary disclosure of specified financial information, stated in units of purchasing power, in addition to financial statements in units of money. In March, 1976, the SEC issued *ASR No. 190* requiring disclosure of replacement cost information about inventories, cost of sales, productive capacity, and depreciation. The Commission announced at that time that its requirements were not competitive with the Board's proposal for general price-level adjustments, and did not prejudge the Board's conceptual framework. I do not know of anyone who agrees with the Commission on that, and the FASB deferred action on its exposure draft.

The project was resumed with the issuance on December 18, 1978, of a new exposure draft entitled "Financial Reporting and Changing Prices." This draft presents a choice between presenting supplementary information on income on a current cost-basis or on a historical cost/constant dollar-basis; however, the latter, which is essentially the units of general purchasing power method, would be acceptable only if cost of goods sold and depreciation expense are not significant. My understanding is that the SEC will probably not accept any method of reporting the effects of inflation which is not substantially consistent with its replacement cost requirements.

SEC mandated replacement cost disclosures have been made for the last three years, and the reaction to them has been largely apathetic. There is no great demand for such information on the part of users. Many issuers of statements explain in strong words the imprecision and softness of this information. Yet, there is no apparent effort on the part of the SEC to withdraw or reconsider its replacement cost reporting requirements.

Financial Forecasts

Evidence of the SEC's change in emphasis from historical to future information lies in guides which allow registrants to disclose forecasts of economic performance in their filings with the Commission. For most of its lifetime, the SEC absolutely forbade soft information like forecasts. The turnabout from its prior position of prohibiting forecasts in filings with the Commission began in 1973 and culminated with the issuance in November, 1978, of guides entitled, "Disclosure of Projections of Future Economic Performance." These guides permit, but do not require, projections in filings with the SEC. Clearly, the SEC wants the public to have access to management's predictions of a company's future sales, net income, and earnings per share.

About two weeks ago the SEC approved a "safe harbor" rule that will protect companies that make public predictions from lawsuits if the forecasts turn out to be wrong. The safe harbor rule protects a company from liability if the prediction is made with a reasonable basis and in good faith. It remains to be seen whether this protection is sufficient to encourage companies to forecast their earnings in registration statements and annual reports to shareholders.

Foreign Corrupt Practices Act

While, as I mentioned earlier, some congressmen were threatening congressional oversight and federal regulation, Senator Proxmire succeeded in having enacted the Foreign Corrupt Practices Act of 1977, which became effective December 19, 1977. This law applies directly to corporations rather than to independent auditors. All U.S. companies and officers, directors, employees, agents, or stockholders are prohibited from bribing foreign governmental or political officials. Companies making bribes can be fined up to $1 million; and individuals face a maximum $10,000 fine, imprisonment of up to five years, or both. The law requires publicly held companies to (1) devise and maintain a system of internal accounting control sufficient, among other things, to provide reasonable assurance that transactions are properly authorized and recorded; and (2) keep records which "accurately and fairly" reflect financial activities in reasonable detail. The law amends the Securities Exchange Act of 1934, and the SEC is expected to enforce it.

On February 15, 1979, the SEC tightened the screws by issuing two new rules that bolster the FCPA. One rule prohibits falsifying books or records of a corporation -- and the falsification does not have to be a "material" one to constitute a violation of this provision. The other rule prohibits officers or directors from making false or misleading statements to accountants. This prohibition includes statements to internal auditors in some circumstances, and it applies not only in connection with audits of financial statements but also in connection with the preparation of various kinds of reports. It is disturbing that the SEC insisted on these two rules when they were dropped from the proposal by Congress upon final enactment of the FCPA.

The SEC's pursuit of this subject does not end there. SEC Release 34-15772 dated April 30, 1979, proposes a report on internal accounting control in annual reports to stockholders which, if adopted, would represent a major step toward continuous auditing and reporting. The requirement would be an amendment to Regulation S-K. Management would have to state its opinion as to whether as of any date after December 15, 1979, and prior to December 16, 1980, for which an audited balance sheet is required, and for periods ending after December 15, 1980, for which audited statements of income are required, the system of internal accounting control of the registrant and its subsidiaries provided reasonable assurances that the objectives of internal control were met. These objectives are those stated in *Statements on Auditing Standards (SAS) No. 1*, Paragraph 320.28 and incorporated in the Foreign Corrupt Practices Act of 1977.

In its proposal, the SEC states that there is no materiality test for determining compliance with this particular requirement. Instead, a cost/benefit analysis would be required. Stated simply, if the amount of risk exposure exceeds the cost of a control to provide reasonable assurance, the control should be in place. This lack of a materiality standard is ill-advised and unfair.

As a further requirement for one year only (for statements as of dates after December 15, 1979, and prior to December 16, 1980), management would describe any material weaknesses in internal accounting control which have been communicated by the independent accountants that have not been corrected, and state the reasons why they have not been corrected. Although "material weakness" is a concept which independent accountants use frequently, there are no authoritative standards against which an identified weakness can be judged to determine if it is a material weakness. This may give rise to arguments between managements and auditors as to what is a material weakness, but I do not expect to see many such weaknesses reported.

For periods after December 15, 1980, the SEC proposes that the statement of management on internal accounting control be examined and reported on by an independent public accountant. The examination is to be sufficient to enable the independent accountant to express an opinion as to (1) whether the representations of management are consistent with the results of management's evaluation of the systems of internal accounting control; and (2) whether such representations of management are, in addition, reasonable with respect to transactions and assets in amounts which would be material in relation to the registrant's financial statements.

If adopted as proposed, this requirement would have a major impact on auditing and reporting. It would require management to maintain a system of self-review of controls, documentation, monitoring, and reporting throughout the organization to provide reasonable assurance that the objectives of internal accounting control were being met every day. It would require the independent accountant to extend his examination so that his opinion would apply to every day of the period. If these conditions prevail, and the independent opinions are reported, an argument can be made that the accountant should be able to express an opinion on the fairness of presentation of financial statements as of quarterly or any other interim dates.

The SEC deals with costs and benefits of its proposal in the same manner that it has consistently applied in most of its recent pronouncements. That is, the SEC has no idea of what costs of compliance will be, but it believes that the benefits of the new requirements to present and prospective investors should outweigh any additional costs. However, the SEC does acknowledge that the benefits are not subject to quantification, and it has asked for specific comments on costs and benefits.

The FCPA has already caused additional costs of compliance, which for some companies is substantial. The proposal for examination by an independent accountant will add still more cost, and this cost should be easily measurable. The technical auditing partner of one Big Eight accounting firm has estimated that the additional fee for this examination will range from 5% of the audit fee to 60%, depending on the adequacy of the accounting system. Someone has to pay for all this accountability, and it is time for all of us to consider how much cost of doing business we want our government to impose on us.

Beyond that, there are a number of conceptual and legal issues about the SEC proposal that make me dismayed, saddened, annoyed, and downright angry! What right does the SEC have to demand that a company disclose to the world its opinion as to compliance with an act of Congress? Congress did not require this kind of reporting when it passed the FCPA. What makes the SEC think it has the right to force this kind of reporting? I expect the SEC proposal to be challenged by the legal profession -- in comments on the proposal and in the courts, if necessary.

And who ever heard of a federal bureaucracy having the right to compel those regulated to make a positive public statement as to their compliance with a particular law? You may point out that the management representation refers merely to a required statement as to whether the system of internal accounting controls provides reasonable assurance that the objectives of internal accounting control are being met. Yet, those objectives are now so closely and so precisely identified with the FCPA that the SEC requirement effectively becomes a statement that the company has obeyed the FCPA. So why stop there? Why not have the SEC ask a company to state whether it has complied with all provisions of the 1934 Act, the 1933 Act, the FTC, EPA, OSHA, ERISA, the Ten Commandments, and the 55 mile per hour speed limit?!

Since the SEC requirement boils down to a compliance provision, is management the proper party to make such a representation? This becomes a legal matter -- and only a lawyer or the courts can properly express a legal opinion as to compliance with a law. How can the SEC force management to express a legal opinion?

There is no demonstration that users of financial statements will benefit from specific compliance reporting. The SEC has emphasized that the FCPA is codified as Section 13(b)(2) of the 1934 Act and, therefore, does not apply to 1933 Act filings. Yet, Form S-16 requires incorporation by reference to periodic information filed under the 1934 Act; and, thus, the 1933 Act liability would attach to that information, which would include the proposed management representations.

But what is really frightening about the SEC's artfully constructed proposal is the entrapment feature. If, at any moment of time during the year, the system of internal accounting control did not provide reasonable assurance, even though such failure was not wilful, the company must report this to the public and, therefore, it must disclose that it has been in violation of the FCPA. This is the ultimate "Catch-22." This approach looks like a page out of a totalitarian dictatorship manual, not the fair and evenhanded justice of a democracy that respects individual rights.

As a further insult, this rule is said (by some of my legal friends) to be administered under civil law proceedings which would require any company to prove it was innocent of charges a plaintiff might bring, regardless of how frivolous. In short, you are guilty unless you can prove yourself innocent; and remember there is no materiality standard. Why does the SEC pursue this grossly unfair course of action? Its zealousness in establishing an extremely adversarial attitude toward corporate America is most puzzling. Even more puzzling is its apparent condoning of the vile statement of one of its staff members who was quoted in the *New York Times* as equating corporate officials with muggers, rapists, and embezzlers. Perhaps I have missed it, but I am unaware of any public disavowal of this view by the Commission or of any reprimand by the Commission.

The FCPA refers to management's responsibilities; yet, the SEC proposal seeks the aid of independent auditors in enforcing the law. Is this within the scope of the SEC's authority? Can the SEC force an independent accountant to express his opinion on management's representation as to compliance with a law?

Strong internal controls and adherence to laws and ethical behavior have long been objectives of corporate America. I do not condone the transgressions of the few that (for whatever reasons) may not have been able to maintain the standards to meet these objectives. But, I am convinced that the SEC, in proposing its reporting requirement, appears to be on a vendetta against all of business.

I urge the SEC to withdraw its internal control reporting proposals. They are not needed, and they are not fair. After all, reporting on internal controls was an item which the Cohen Commission report included among several matters of management responsibility, which it thought should be reported on by management. The idea was warmly embraced by the Financial Executives Institute, which in June, 1978, recommended that its members voluntarily publish a report explaining management's responsibilities for financial statements and internal controls. This recommendation was made by FEI's Committee on Corporate Reporting, of which I am a wholeheartedly concurring member.

The AICPA appointed a special advisory committee on reports by management to consider this issue. I am the chairman of that committee, which is now preparing and soon will be publishing a final pronouncement recommending that management voluntarily report to shareholders on its responsibility for financial statements, and its reliance on systems of internal accounting control to discharge that responsibility. The FEI and AICPA positions call for explanation of the *process*, rather than reporting on legal compliance. I believe this approach is far superior to the pernicious efforts at ensnarement inherent in the SEC's latest proposal. The SEC should drop all further efforts at rule-making related to the FCPA.

If, however, this advice is not followed by the SEC, I recommend that the whole proposal be turned around to achieve these three recommendations:

1.   Provide a safe harbor, wherein a company will be free from liability if its representation had a reasonable basis and was made in good faith;

2.   Shift the burden of proof from the company to the plaintiff, who claims damage due to inadequacy of internal accounting control systems; and

3.   Require no statement as to compliance with the FCPA other than negative assurance -- that is management might state that, having given reasonable attention to the requirements of the law, it has no knowledge that violations thereof exist.

If you find some of these issues disturbing, as I do, I urge you to write to the SEC before the exposure period expires on July 31. The SEC has in the past considered the comments of respondents, and, in many cases, has modified or even dropped its proposals. I believe the SEC is more impressed by a large outpouring of well-reasoned individual comments than by a few responses by professional and trade associations. So please comment to the SEC on the internal control reporting proposal.

Corporate Governance

The SEC was very active in the last year in issuing new rules on corporate governance. The rules are lengthy and confusing, because aspects of related topics appear in different rules.

The rules require disclosure in proxy statements of the number and identity of directors, how often the board meets, and whether there are standing audit, nominating, and compensation committees. For each such committee, disclosure must be made of what its function is, who serves on it, and how often it meets. For the nominating committee (if there is one), disclosure must be made of whether it will consider board nominees recommended by shareholders and, if so, what procedure a shareholder must follow to recommend a nominee. For the audit committee (if there is one), disclosure must be made of whether the committee or the full board recommended or approved a change in auditors, if one took place, and whether the committee pre-approved non-audit services by the outside auditor, and whether the possible effect of such services on the independence of the auditor was considered in giving approval.

The rules also call for disclosure of a great deal of information about individual directors and board nominees, including: age; position; prior service on the board; other corporate directorships held; family relationships; company securities owned; options, warrants, or rights held to acquire company securities; indebtedness to the company; and compensation received as a director under standard and special arrangements. Some of this information had to be disclosed before 1978, but all items are specifically touched on in 1978 releases. Companies must identify any director who has missed 25 percent or more of the board and assigned committee meetings combined in the past year. They also must identify any director who has resigned as the result of a disagreement with the company and has asked that the matter be made public.

The proxy statement must describe, for each director-nominee, relationships with the company as an employee, customer, supplier, creditor, legal counsel, investment banker, or control person. For the five highest paid executives, disclosure must be made of total current remuneration, both cash and cash-equivalent, including perquisites or personal benefits, and contingent and future compensation.

This represents a lot of disclosure about boards of directors and their top managements, but it is much less disclosure than the SEC originally proposed. The final rules dropped the labeling of directors, definitions of customary functions of committees, and disclosure of certain hard-to-measure "perks" and reasons for a change of auditors.

But the SEC did not back down on its claim of authority to require the disclosures. Many critics had argued that the proposals went beyond requirements for information, and were really requirements that companies act in approved ways or structure their boards in specified ways. The Commission pointedly disagreed with this argument, and denied that any of the rules were designed primarily to influence corporate conduct. It said the rules were designed primarily to provide useful information to shareholders.

The SEC has a right to express that opinion, but in other actions it has shown a preference for certain practices where boards of directors are concerned. A predominance of independent directors and audit, nominating, and compensation committees are examples. The new rules do not require these practices; yet, they tacitly approve and recommend them. In a number of lawsuits, the SEC has imposed board organization changes, the addition of outside directors, and the formation of audit and other committees with specified makeup.

In summary, I believe the SEC has gone beyond its authority in attempting to enforce some aspects of the Securities Acts. It appears to be demanding certain actions, organizational structures, and behavior on the part of business organizations. The time has come for the SEC to retreat from its aggressive, adversarial attitude toward business, and bring its rule-making into a more reasonable framework -- in light of benefits to users of financial reports and the costs to business.

APPENDIX A:
LISTING OF LEONARD M. SAVOIE'S SPEECHES

October 29, 1959: "Address to the Fall Discussion Forum on the Accounting Function," Before the National Association of Accountants, (Fort Wayne, IN)

January 21, 1960: "Practical Problems in Public Accounting" Before DePaul University's Accounting Society, (Chicago)

[Date unknown] "Increasing Our Capabilities and Resources Through Professional Development," Before the 1961 National Contract Meeting, [location unknown]

January, 16, 1962: "Professional Development," Before Price Waterhouse's New York Managers' Meeting

May 2-4, 1962: "Motivating Staff Development," Before the Sixth Annual Conference on Personnel of the California Society of CPAs, (Palo Alto, CA)

May 14, 1962: "How Partners Can Help Make Our Professional Development Program Effective," Before Price Waterhouse Partners' Meeting, [location unknown]

June 4-7, 1962: "The Professional Development Program of the United States Firm," Before the Price Waterhouse Canadian Partners' Meeting, [location unknown]

July-August, 1962: "How Counseling Is to be Carried Out," Before the Counseling Seminars, [location unknown]

October 12, 1962: "Professional Development Progress Report," Before the Price Waterhouse National Managers' Meeting, [location unknown]

June 22, 1963: "Managers' Participation in the Counseling Program," Before the Price Waterhouse New Managers' Meeting, (New York)

November 13, 1963: "Where Do We Go From Here in Developing Accounting Principles?" Before the University of Colorado's Tenth Annual Institute on Accounting, (Boulder, CO)

April 29, 1964: "Human Relations and More Effective Work," Before the California Society of CPAs Eighth Annual Conference on Personnel, [location unknown]

June 26, 1964:   "Managers' Participation in the Professional Development Program," Before the Price Waterhouse New Managers' Meeting, (New York)

September 28, 1964: "Comparability in Financial Statements," Before the Massachusetts Society of CPAs, (Boston)

November 18, 1964: "The Management Accountants' Responsibilities for Business Ethics," Before the Rochester, NY, Chapter of the National Association of Accountants

February 15, 1965: "The Management Accountants' Responsibilities for Business Ethics," Before the Mid-Hudson Chapter of National Association of Accountants, [location unknown]

February 17, 1965: "The Accounting Principles Board: What It Is, How It works, and What Its Role in Business Is," Before the Syracuse Chapter of New York Society of CPAs

May 21-22, 1965: "Opportunities in Accounting and Auditing," Before Price Waterhouse Planning Seminar, (Westchester, NY)

June 22, 1965: "The Input Needs of the Accounting Profession," Before the Annual Meeting of the Illinois Society of CPAs, (Chicago)

[Date unknown] "An Accounting Principles Board Success Story: The Funds Statement," [audience and location unknown]

October 8, 1965: "Constructive Business Suggestions to Management Arising Out of Recurring Audits," Before the Price Waterhouse Partners' Meeting, [location unknown]

October 20, 1965: "Don't Be An Educational Drop-Out," Before the Washington, D.C., Chapter of the National Association of Accountants

October 21, 1965: "Comparability in Financial Statements," Before the Price Waterhouse Roundtable, (New York)

January 27, 1966: "International Accounting Problems," Before the American Management Association's Advanced International Management Course [location unknown]

February 19, 1966: "Trends in Financial Accounting and Reporting," Before the Council for Technological Advancement Financial Council, Machinery and Allied Products Institute, (New York)

March 12, 1966: "Trends in Financial Accounting and Reporting," Before the Accounting Council of Machinery and Allied Products Institute, [location unknown]

December 12-14, 1966: "U.S. Versus Local Accounting Principles," Before the Price Waterhouse Caribbean Firm Meeting, (Jamaica)

February 25, 1967: "Continuing Education for the Accounting Practitioner," Before the Southern California Accounting Educators' Conference, (San Fernando Valley State College)

March 20, 1967: "How Corporate Financial Reporting Can Be Made More Responsive to the Needs of the Investor," Before the New York Chapter of the National Association of Accountants

[Date unknown], "Accounting -- A Social Force," [audience and location unknown]

[Date unknown], "Responsibility for Establishing Accounting Principles," [audience and location unknown]

September 23, 1967: "Report of the Executive Vice President" Before Members of Council of the AICPA, [location unknown]

November 13, 1967: "The Role of the Accounting Principles Board in Establishing Accounting Principles," [audience and location unknown]

January 30, 1968: "Closing the Audit Gap," Before the Twentieth National Credit Conference of the American Bankers Association, (Bal Harbor, FL)

February 16, 1968: "Accounting Principles Board Activities," Before Machinery and Allied Products Institute Financial Council, (Washington, D.C.)

[Date unknown], "What to Look for in Financial Reports in 1968," Before the Tenth Annual Woman Investor's Clinic of the Federation of Women Shareholders in American Business, [location unknown]

April 4, 1968: "Raising Accounting Standards," Before the Harvard Business School Associates, (Boston, MA)

April 29, 1968: "Public Responsibilities of the Private Sector," Before Members of Council of the AICPA, (Boca Raton, FL)

May 7, 1968: "The Accounting Profession Looks Ahead," Before the New York Chapter of the American Society of Women Accountants' Annual Public Relations Dinner

May 15, 1968: "Financial Communication -- The Public's Right to Know," Before the National Industrial Conference Board, (San Francisco)

September 19, 1968: "Meeting Consumer Needs," Before a joint meeting of the Washington Society of CPAs, Financial Executives Institute, and Mortgage Bankers Association, (Seattle)

October 12, 1968: "Marketing Myopia," Before Members of Council of the AICPA, (Washington, D.C.)

November 13, 1968: "The Public Interest Aspects of the Performance of Computer Services by CPAs," Before the Fourth Semi-Annual National Conference of CPA Computer Users, (Washington, D.C.)

November 18, 1968: "The Professional Goals of the Institute," Before the Annual Partners' Meeting of Touche, Ross, Bailey & Smart, (Phoenix, AZ)

November 19, 1968: "Dilemmas of Corporate Accountability," Distinguished Morton Wollman Lecture Before The Bernard M. Baruch College, (The City University of New York)

December 11, 1968: "Current Developments of the Accounting Principles Board," Before the Boston Chapter of the Financial Executives Institute

January 28, 1969: "The Challenge to Accountancy and the Business World," St. Louis Chapter of the Financial Executives Institute

March 3, 1969: "Credibility in Tomorrow's Financial Statements," Before Los Angeles Chapter of the California Society of CPAs, Robert Morris Associates, and L.A. Bank Credit Men's Association

April 11, 1969: "Can Happiness Be Found in Business Marriages?" Before the Financial Division of the American Mining Congress, (Chandler, AZ)

May 6, 1969: "The Road to Progress in Accounting," Before Members of Council of the AICPA, [location unknown]

May 15, 1969: "Raising Accounting Standards," Before the Conference on Empirical Research, (University of Chicago)

May 16, 1969: "International Dimensions of Accounting," Seminar on International Accounting, (University of Illinois)

May 28, 1969: "Responsibilities of the Accounting Profession for Adequate Public Disclosure," Before the Conference on Corporate Public Disclosure, (Northeastern University, Boston)
June 2, 1969: "The Role of the CPA in the Space Age," Before the North Carolina Association of CPAs, (Asheville, N.C.)

June 9, 1969: "Ombudsmanship and the Need for Hard-Nosed Auditing," Before the Twenty-fifth Southern States Conference of CPAs, (Oklahoma City, OK)

September 8, 1969: "Our Profession Looks Ahead to the 1970s," Before the Fifteenth Graduate Accounting Conference, (Pennsylvania State University)

November 18, 1969: "The Business Community and the Public Interest," Before the Atlanta Chapter of Georgia CPAs, Atlanta Society of Financial Analysts, Financial Executives Institute, National Association of Accountants, and Planning Executives Institute, (Atlanta)

April 1, 1970: "Statement of the American Institute of CPAs on Uniform Cost Accounting Standards," Before the Senate Banking and Currency Committee Subcommittee on Production and Stabilization, (Washington, D.C.)

April 10, 1970: "Accounting Problems and Institutional Investors," Before Practicing Law Institute Course on the Institutional Investor, (New York)

April 20, 1970: "International Accounting and World Trade," Before the Mississippi Valley World Trade Conference, (New Orleans)

April 21, 1970: "Challenges to Accounting Principles in the 1970s," Before the National Conference of Electric and Gas Utility Accountants, (Dallas)

April 22, 1970: "Accounting Principles in the 1970s," Before the 1970 Conference of Accountants, (Tulsa, OK)

April 28, 1970: "Remarks of Leonard M. Savoie," Before the Society of Accounting Students, (University of Hartford, CT)

May 5, 1970: "Living with a High Profile," Before Members of Council of the AICPA, (Boca Raton, FL)

May 23, 1970: "The Accounting Profession in the 1970s," Before Laventhol, Krekstein, Horwath & Horwath Annual Partners' Meeting, (Lake Geneva, WI)

May 26, 1970: "Merger Accounting," Before American Management Association's Annual Financial Conference, (New York)

June 2, 1970: "The Accounting Profession in the 1970s," Before the Massachusetts Society of CPAs Fifth Annual Spring Conference, (Bermuda)

June 15, 1970: "Statement of the [AICPA] on Cost Accounting Standards," to the House Banking and Currency Committee, (Washington, D.C.)

June 15, 1970: "Statement of the [AICPA] for the Conglomerate Merger Hearings of the Antitrust Subcommittee of the House Committee on the Judiciary," (Washington, D.C.)

September 22, 1970: "The Impact of Cost-Accounting Standards," Before the AICPA's Eighty-third Annual Meeting, (New York)

October 13, 1970: "Keeping Confidence in Corporate Accounting," Before the New York City Chapter of the Financial Executives Institute

November 19, 1970: "Cost-Accounting Standards," Before the Joint Conference on Defense Contracts Accounting, (New York)

November 20, 1970: "Game Plans and Professional Standards," Before the Conference Institute, (New York)

January 11, 1971: "Current Developments in Accounting Standards," Before the New York Society of Security Analysts, (New York)

January 12, 1971: "The Role of the Auditor," Before the A-B-C Financial Communications Forum (on Current Issues in Corporate Financial Reporting), Chicago.

January 12, 1971: "The Role of the Auditor," Before the Illinois Society of CPAs, Robert Morris Associates, and Chicago-Midwest Credit Management Association, (Hillside, IL)

February 15, 1971: "Accountability and the Accounting Profession," Before the Milwaukee Chapter National Association of Accountants and the Wisconsin Society of CPAs, (Milwaukee)

April 26, 1971: "The AICPA and New Accounting Guidelines," Before the American Management Association, (New York)

May 10, 1971: "The Accounting Profession's Role in Federal Government Matters," Before Members of Council of the AICPA, (Colorado Springs)

May 19, 1971: "A Review of Some Developments in Formulation of Accounting Principles," Before the Financial Analysts Federation Twenty-fourth Annual Conference, (Cleveland)

May 21, 1971: "Accentuating Accountability," Before the Hawaii Society of CPAs, (Honolulu)

June 7, 1971: "Meeting Public Demands for Accountability," Before the West Virginia Society of CPAs, (White Sulphur Springs, WV)

June 21, 1971: "A Time for Self-Renewal in the Accounting Profession," Before the Texas Society of CPAs Fifty-sixth Annual Meeting, (Austin)

September 21, 1971: "A Review of Some Developments in Formulation of Accounting Principles," for Financial Analysts Federation tape recording session with William Norby and David Norr, (New York)

September 27, 1971: "Statement for the Subcommittee on Commerce and Finance of the House of Representatives Committee on Interstate and Foreign Commerce," (Washington, D.C.)

October 1, 1971: "The Professional School of Accountancy," Before the Professional Advisory Board, (University of Illinois)

October 5, 1971: "Meeting the Demand for Informative Annual Reports to Stockholders," Before the AICPA, [location unknown]

October 9, 1971: "Report to the Members of Council of the AICPA," (Detroit)

October 12, 1971: "The Role of Management Advisory Services in the Practice of Public Accounting," Before the AICPA's Eighty-fourth Annual Meeting, (Detroit)

October 25, 1971: "Accountability of the Accounting Profession," Before the Virginia Society of CPAs, (Virginia Polytechnic Institute and State University, Blacksburg, VA)

October 28, 1971: "Accountability of the Accounting Profession," Distinguished Lecture in Accounting, (Oklahoma State University, Stillwater, OK)

November 4, 1971: "A Review of Some Developments in Formulation of Accounting Principles," Before the Airline Finance and Accounting Conference, (Washington, D.C.)

November 10, 1971: untitled address to the State Society Planning Conference, (Atlanta)

December 16, 1971: "New Developments in Lease Financing," Before the First Annual Business Financing Conference, Co-sponsored by Business Week and Institutional Investor, (New York)

January 20, 1972: "What's in the Hopper of the APB?" Before the Los Angeles Chapter of the Financial Executives Institute

February 2, 1972: "What's in the Hopper of the APB?" Before the Southern Connecticut Chapter of the Financial Executives Institute, (Darien, CN)

April 24, 1972: "Client-Auditor Relationship: Is More Independence Needed?" Before the Cleveland Chapter of the Ohio Society of CPAs

May 1, 1972: "Taking Timely Action," Before Members of Council of the AICPA, (Boca Raton, FL)

May 23, 1972: "Recent Developments in Accounting," Before the Financial Analysts Federation's Twenty-fifth Annual Conference, (New York)

May 31, 1972: "Financial Accounting Standards: Regulation or Self-Regulation?" Stanford Lectures in Accounting, sponsored by Price Waterhouse Foundation, (Stanford University)

June 20, 1972: "A Look at the Profession in the Next Five to Ten Years," Before the Georgia Society of CPAs Annual Meeting, (Asheville, NC)

September 19, 1972: "Recent Developments in Accounting," Before the American Mining Congress' 1972 Convention, (San Francisco)

October 26, 1972: "Recent Developments in Accounting," Before the Southwestern Chapter of Michigan Association of CPAs, (Benton Harbor, MI)

November 15, 1972: "Recent Developments in Accounting," Before the Michigan Association of CPAs Central Chapter Meeting, (East Lansing)

January 16, 1973: "Recent Developments in Accounting," Before the Michiana Chapter of the National Association of Accountants, (Mishawaka, IN)

February 7, 1973: "Should You Become an Accountant?" Before the Junior & Senior Student Body of Buchanan (MI) High School

February 8, 1973: "Accounting Attitudes," Before the Financial Executives Institute, (Indianapolis)

March 31, 1973: "A View From the Top," Before the Michigan College Accounting Educators Conference, (Lansing, MI)

April 25, 1973: "Accountability of the Accounting Profession," Before the Accounting Club of Manchester College, (North Manchester, IN)

April 27, 1973: "A Corporate Perspective on the Revision of Reporting Standards," Before the Bankers Magazine Conference on Corporate Financial Reporting, (Washington, D.C.)

April 28, 1973: "Financial and Accounting Aspects in International Business," Before the International Accounting Seminar, (University of Illinois)

May 10, 1973: "Accounting Attitudes," Before the University of Kansas Accounting Colloquium III, (Lawrence, KA)

May 30, 1973: untitled address to the Clark Equipment Company's Branch Managers' Meeting, (Savannah, GA)

September 18, 1973: "Accounting Attitudes," Before the Michiana Chapter of the National Association of Accountants, (Elkhart, IN)

October 17, 1973: "A Controller's Viewpoint," Before the Tyler Management Club, (Niles, MI)

February 22, 1974: "A View of the Accounting Profession and Accounting Education From a Professional Accountant in Industry," Before the California CPAs 1974 Accounting Education Conference, (California State University at Hayward)

February 23, 1974: "A View of the Accounting Profession and Accounting Education From a Professional Accountant in Industry," (California State University at Long Beach)

April 21-23, 1974: "Planning Profit Improvement at Clark," Before the Planning Session for Clark Equipment, (Battle Creek, MI)

May 18, 1974: "A View of the Accounting Profession From a Professional Accountant in Industry," Before the Indiana Association of CPAs Annual Convention, (New Orleans)

September 24, 1974: "A View of the Accounting Profession From a Professional Accountant in Industry," Before the Calumet Chapter of the National Association of Accountants, (Harvey, IL)

October 15, 1974: "The Importance of Individual Job Performance," Before the Clark Professional Women's Club, (Buchanan, MI)

November 5, 1974: "A Discussion of 'Inventory Profits,'" Before the Society of San Francisco Security Analysts, (San Francisco)

November 5, 1974: "Remarks of Leonard M. Savoie" Before the Society of San Francisco Security Analysts, (San Francisco)

February 18, 1975: "Clark Equipment Co. -- A Corporate Report," Before the Industrial Truck Division Sales Recognition Meeting, (Pittsburgh)

March 13, 1975: "Life with LIFO," Before the Investment Analysts Society of Chicago, (Chicago)

March 19, 1975: "Current Developments in Setting Accounting Standards," Before the National Association of Accountants, (Dayton, OH)

April 2, 1975: "The Purposes of Education," Before Alpha Eta Chapter of Beta Alpha Psi, (University of Michigan)

May 1975: "Life with LIFO," [audience and location unknown]

May 19, 1975: "Current Developments in Setting Accounting Standards," Before the Executive Enterprises Second Corporate Accounting and Financial Reporting Institute," (Washington, D.C.)

May 20, 1975: "Current Developments in Setting Accounting Standards," Before the AMR International Conference Current Developments in Financial Reporting, (New York)

June 4, 1975: "Making Accounting Rules -- A Political Process," Before the Michigan Association of CPAs, (Michigan State University)

July 14, 1975: "Holding Business Accountable," Before the Summer Institute on the American Economy, (University of Miami, FL)

July 30, 1975: "General Purchasing Power or Specific Political Power?" Before the Price Waterhouse & Co. Price-Level Accounting Seminar, (Chicago)

September 18, 1975: "Making Annual Reports More Readable," Before the Center for Continuing Education, (University of Notre Dame)

October 28, 1975: "Quarterly Reporting," Before the Chicago Chapter of the National Investor Relations Institute, (Chicago)

October 31, 1975: "Making Accounting Rules -- A Political Process," Second Accounting Symposium at Grand Valley State College, (Allendale, MI)

November 6, 1975: "Making Accounting Rules -- A Political Process," Before the AMR Conference on Critical Issues in Year-End Accounting and Financial Reporting, (Washington, D.C.)

March 29, 1976: "Business Ethics and Government Regulation," Cardinal O'Hara Memorial Lecture, (University of Notre Dame)

March 29, 1976: "Inflation Accounting," College of Business Administration Faculty Seminar, (University of Notre Dame)

April 23, 1976: "Should the Practice of Public Accounting be Limited to the Graduates of Professional Schools of Accounting?" Before the Ohio Society of CPAs' Symposium on Professional Schools of Accounting, (The Ohio State University)

May 12, 1976: "Making Accounting Rules -- A Political Process," Before the AMR 1976 Midyear Accounting, Reporting, and Disclosure Conference, (Washington, D.C.)

June 28, 1976: "Some Views of Current Activities of the Securities and Exchange Commission," Machinery and Allied Products Institute Conference on New Trends in Accounting and Financial Reporting, (Arlington, VA)

March 22, 1977: "Inflation Accounting," Distinguished Speakers Series, (University of Kentucky)

March 31, 1977: "Analyst Presentation," (for Clark Equipment Co.), (Grand Rapids, MI)

April 5, 1977: "Inflation Accounting," Michigan State University's Chapter of Beta Alpha Psi, (Michigan State University)

September 27, 1977: "Wooing Wall Street: The Corporate View," Before the Financial Analysts Federation and the Investment Analysts Society of Chicago, (Chicago)

October 18, 1977: "Inflation Accounting," Before the Michiana Chapter of the National Association of Accountants, (South Bend, IN)

October 27, 1977: "Inflation Accounting," Before the Michigan Association of CPAs Annual Joint Meeting with Beta Alpha Psi of Western Michigan University, (Kalamazoo, MI)

November 22, 1977: untitled address to the Investment Analysts Society of Chicago Basic Industries & Resources Group, (Chicago)

May 23, 1978: "An Overview of Corporate Accounting and Financial Reporting," Before Executive Enterprises, Inc., Eighth Corporate Accounting and Financial Reporting Institute, (New Orleans)

September 7, 1978: untitled address to Baird & Co.'s 1978 Machinery Seminar, (Milwaukee)

September 21, 1978: "Setting Investment Objectives," The Financial Analysts Federation and the Investment Analysts Society of Chicago, (Chicago)

October 27, 1978: "Beta Alpha Psi," Before Alpha Chapter, (University of Illinois)

January 9-10, 1979: "What Business is Doing to Comply with the Foreign Corrupt Practices Act Requirements for an Adequate System of Internal Accounting Controls," Before AICPA Sixth National Conference on Current SEC Developments, (Washington, D.C.)

May 7-8, 1979: "Reports by Management," Before the Third Internal Accounting Controls Conference, (New York)

June 11-12, 1979: "Management Reports," Before the Financial Executives Institute Second Conference on Internal Accounting Controls and Management Reports, (Los Angeles)

June 14, 1979: "Some Views of Current Activities of the Securities and Exchange Commission," Before the Machinery and Allied Products Institute Conference on New Trends in Accounting and Financial Reporting, (Arlington, VA)

September 24-25, 1979: "Management Reports," Before the Financial Executives Institute Conference on Internal Accounting Controls and Management Reports, (Chicago)

October 5, 1979: "Current Corporate Reporting Practices," National Conference for CPAs in Industry and Government, (Dallas)

June 25, 1980: "Crucial Financial Issues of the 1980s," Before the CTS 1980 Accounting Conference, (Elkhart, IN)

October 23, 1980: "Crucial Financial Issues of the 1980s," Before the Michigan Association of CPAs, (Kalamazoo, MI)

January 5, 1982: "The Impact of the Federal Income Tax on Accounting Principles," Before the Accounting Forum, [location unknown]

May 24, 1982:   "Accounting for Income Taxes," Before Executive Enterprises, Inc., Sixteenth Corporate Accounting and Financial Reporting Institute, (Washington, D.C.)

June 8, 1982: "The Tradeoff Between Internal and External Auditing: Identifying Research Issues," Before the Accounting Research Center Advisory Council of the Kellogg Graduate School of Management, (Northwestern University)

November 12, 1982:   "Personal Views of Accounting Education," Before the Twenty-third Annual Illinois Accounting Educators Conference, (Northern Illinois University, DeKalb, IL)

September 22, 1983: "Current Issues in Corporate Financial Reporting," Before the Kankakee Valley Chapter of National Association of Accountants, (Kankakee, IL)

Chapters in Handbooks:

"The Objectives of Corporate Financial Reporting -- the Firm's View," Chapter 1 in *The Modern Accountant's Handbook* (J.D. Edwards and H.A. Black, editors), Dow-Jones-Irwin, Homewood, IL (1976).

"Interim Financial Statements," Chapter 5 in *Handbook of Accounting and Auditing* (J.C. Burton, R.E. Palmer, and R.S. Kay, editors), Warren, Gorham & Lamont, Boston, MA (1981).

"The External Audit," Chapter 16 in *AMA Management Handbook* (W.K. Fallon and W.H. Wagel, editors), American Management Association, New York, NY (1983).

Pamphlets:

"Corporate Reporting and Speculation Fever, Credibility in Tomorrow's Financial Statements," American Institute of CPAs, 1969.

"The Biggest Job Facing Business Today," American Institute of CPAs, 1970.

Refereed and Other Publications:

"Case of Newman, Ruggles & Handley: Continuing Professional Development," *Illinois Certified Public Accountant*, (1960) Vol. 22, No. 2, pp. 14-17.

"The Case of the Dubious Deferral," *Harvard Business Review*, (1963) Vol. 41, No. 3, pp. 162-171.

"Where Do We Go From Here in Developing Accounting Principles?" *Proceedings of the Tenth Annual Institute on Accounting*, University of Colorado, (1963) Vol. 10, pp. 53-61.

"Accounting Improvements -- How Fast, How Far?" *Harvard Business Review* (1963) Vol. 41, No. 4, pp. 144-159.

Reprinted in Spanish as: "Progreso en la Contabilidad: Que Tan Rapido, Que Tan Lejos?" *Direccion y Control*, Mexico City, Mexico, Marzo-Abril, (1964).

"Accounting Principles -- Where Do We Go From Here?" *Price Waterhouse Review*, (1964) Vol. 9, No. 1, pp. 34-40.

Book review of *Contemporary Accounting Problems* (by Leonard E. Morrissey), *The New York CPA*, (1964) Vol. 34, No. 7.

"Human Relations and More Effective Work," *Illinois CPA*, (1964) Vol. 27, No. 1, pp. 1-6.

"Including the Funds Statement in Corporate Annual Reports," *Price Waterhouse Review*, (1964) Vol. 9, No. 3, pp. 32-35.

"The Management Accountant's Responsibilities for Business Ethics," *Management Accounting*, (1965) Vol. 46, No. 8, pp. 3-9.

Reprinted in *Industrial Accountant*, (1965) Vol. 5, No. 10.

"Comparability in Financial Statements," *Massachusetts CPA Review*, (1965) Vol. 38, No. 6, pp. 221-229.

"The Accounting Principles Board," *Financial Analysts Journal*, (1965) Vol. 51, No. 3, pp. 3-7.

"The Continuing Education Drop-Out -- An Increasing Problem," *Price Waterhouse Review*, (1965) Vol. 10, No. 2, pp. 57-60.

Reprinted in *Texas CPA*, (1967) Vol. 40, No. 2; and in *Louisiana CPA*, (1967) Vol. 27, No. 2.

Book review of *The CPA Plans for the Future* (by John L. Carey), *The Quarterly Review of Economics and Business*, University of Illinois, (1965) Vol. 5, No. 4, pp. 93-94.

"The Input Needs of the Accounting Profession," *The Illinois CPA*, (1965) Vol. 28, No. 2, pp. 1-26.

"Professional Accounting in 25 Countries," *Journal of Accountancy*, (1965) Vol. 120, No. 4.

Discussion of "The Effect of Alternative Accounting Rules for Nonsubsidiary Investments" (by N. Dopuch and D. Drake), *Empirical Research in Accounting: Selected Studies* (a supplement to *Journal of Accounting Research*), University of Chicago, 1966, pp. 224-227.

"Financial Variables in International Business," *Harvard Business Review*, (1966) Vol. 44, No. 3, p. 21.

"Trends in Financial Accounting and Reporting," *Price Waterhouse Review*, (1966) Vol. 11, No. 2, pp. 26-31.

"Business Ethics," *Price Waterhouse Review*, (1967) Vol. 12, No. 1, pp. 30-36.

   Reprinted in *Georgia CPA*, (1967), Vol. 8, No. 1; and in *Price Waterhouse Review* (1977), Vol. 22, No. 3.

"Controversy Over Accounting Principles Board Opinions," *Journal of Accountancy*, (1968) Vol. 125, No. 1, pp. 37-41.

"What to Look for in Financial Reports in 1968," *Financial Analysts Journal*, (1968) Vol. 24, No. 3, pp. 37-39.

"Financial Communication -- the Public's Right to Know," *Financial Executive*, (1968) Vol. 36, No. 12, pp. 20-28.

"Raising Accounting Standards," *Empirical Research in Accounting: Selected Studies* (a supplement to *Journal of Accounting Research*), University of Chicago, 1969, pp. 55-62.

"Meeting Financial Consumer Needs," *Financial Analysts Journal*, (1969) Vol. 25, No. 2, pp. 47-51.

"What Issues Will Challenge CPAs in the 1970s?" *Ohio CPA Journal*, (1969), Vol. 28, No. 2, pp. 97-104.

"International Dimensions of Accounting," *The International Journal of Accounting Education and Research*, (1969) Vol. 5, No. 1, pp. 79-84.

"Accounting Principles in the 1970s," *University of Tulsa Conference of Accountants*, (1970) Vol. 24, pp. 15-22.

"The Accounting Profession in the 1970s," *Massachusetts CPA Review*, (1970) Vol. 44, No. 1, pp. 7-15.

"Achieving Cost Accounting Standards," *New York Certified Public Accountant*, (1971) Vol. 41, No. 5, pp. 353-356.

"Role of the Auditor," *Journal of Commercial Bank Lending*, (1971) Vol. 53 (June), pp. 2-11.

"Opportunity to Raise Standards of Professional Ethics," *CPA Journal*, (1972) Vol. 42, No. 1, pp. 14-15.

"Case of the Disclosure Debate," *Harvard Business Review*, (1972) Vol. 50, No. 1, pp. 142-158.

"A Look at the Profession in the Next Five to Ten Years," *Georgia CPA*, (1972) Vol. 14, No. 1, pp. 3-22.

"Goals of the Financial Accounting Standards Board," *CPA Journal*, (1973) Vol. 43, No. 2, pp. 95-96.

"Financial and Accounting Aspects in International Business," *The International Journal of Accounting Education and Research*, (1973) Vol. 9, No. 1, pp. 13-22.

"Accounting Attitudes," *Financial Executive*, (1973) Vol. 41, No. 10, pp. 74-84.

> Reprinted (excerpt) as "Destruction of the Accounting Principles Board" in *CPA Journal*, (1974), Vol. 44, No. 2; and in *Chartered Accountant* in Australia, (1974, March).

"A Note on the Purposes of Continuing Education," *University of Michigan Business Review*, (1976) Vol. 28, No. 1, pp. 31-32.

"Price Level Accounting, Practical Politics, and Tax Relief," *Management Accounting*, (1977) Vol. 58, No. 7, pp. 15-18.

Book review of *Financial Times World Survey of Annual Reports 1980*, *International Accounting Forum*, (1981) Vol. 12, pp. 6-7.

"Reports by Management: Voluntary or Mandatory," (with D.N. Ricchiute) *Journal of Accountancy*, (1981) Vol. 151, No. 5, pp. 84-94.

"The Impact of the Federal Income Tax on Accounting Principles," *The Accounting Forum*, (1981) Vol. 51, No. 1, pp. 44-51.

"Voluntary Management Reports," (with D.N. Ricchiute) *Journal of Accountancy*, (1981) Vol. 152, No. 4, p. 112.

"Is Expensing Depreciable Assets Now Economically Attractive? A Guide Under the New Tax Law," (with J.M. Johnson) *Journal of Accountancy*, (1982) Vol. 153, No. 1, pp. 96-98.

"Improved Accounting Methods for Foreign Currency Translation," (with N.G. Rueschhoff) *Financial Executive*, (1982) Vol. 50, No. 2, pp. 35-42.

Book review of *Controllership: The Work of the Managerial Accountant* (by J.D. Willson and J.B. Campbell), *The Accounting Review*, (1982) Vol. 57, No. 2, pp. 462-463.

"Expensing Depreciable Assets," (with J.M. Johnson) *Journal of Accountancy*, (1982) Vol. 154, No. 1, pp. 56-58.

"Corporate Liquidity: a Comparison of Two Recessions," (with J.M. Johnson and D.R. Campbell) *Financial Executive*, (1983) Vol. 51, No. 10, pp. 18-22.

"Expensing Vs. Depreciating Assets Under Section 179: a Reexamination Under TEFRA," (with J.M. Johnson) *Journal of Accountancy*, (1983) Vol. 156, No. 7, pp. 90, 92, 94, 96.

"Cash Flow, Liquidity, and Financial Flexibility," (with D.R. Campbell and J.M. Johnson) *Financial Executive*, (1984) Vol. 52, No. 8, pp. 14-17.